RETRIEVING THE TRADITION
AND RENEWING EVANGELICALISM

Retrieving the Tradition and Renewing Evangelicalism

A Primer for Suspicious Protestants

D. H. WILLIAMS

WILLIAM B. EERDMANS PUBLISHING COMPANY
GRAND RAPIDS, MICHIGAN / CAMBRIDGE, U.K.

© 1999 Wm. B. Eerdmans Publishing Co.
255 Jefferson Ave. S.E., Grand Rapids, Michigan 49503 /
P.O. Box 163, Cambridge CB3 9PU U.K.

Printed in the United States of America

04 03   7 6 5 4 3 2

Library of Congress Cataloging-in-Publication Data

Williams, Daniel H.
Retrieving the tradition and renewing evangelicalism:
a primer for suspicious Protestants / D. H. Williams
p.   cm.
Includes bibliographical references.
ISBN 0-8028-4668-8 (pbk.: alk. paper)
1. Evangelicalism.   2. Tradition (Theology)   3. Fathers of the church.
4. Free churches — Doctrines.   I. Title.
BR1640.W55   1999
230'.044 — dc21   99-32615
CIP

Dedicated to the thousands of
20th century Christian martyrs,
whose blood calls out to us
that the Tradition of the Church
is worth dying for

Contents

Acknowledgments

I am much indebted to Professor Frederick Norris (Emmanuel School of Religion), Professor Lewis Ayres (Trinity College, Dublin), Professor E. Glenn Hinson (Baptist Theological Seminary in Richmond) and my graduate assistant, Mr. Bryan Hall (Loyola University, Chicago). They have each generously read portions or whole versions of the manuscript and offered useful criticisms. My thanks also go to Professor Robert Wilken (University of Virginia) who encouraged me to pursue this task when it was still only an inchoate inspiration in my own mind.

A timely grant from Loyola University's Endowment for the Humanities enabled me to take time from teaching and pour it into a period of concentrated writing during the summer of 1997.

With special gratitude I wish to acknowledge the role my wife Cindy has played in all my work including this project. Over these last two years she has patiently and politely listened to pages of text being read in their earliest and most disjointed stages.

Finally, I offer my deepest thanksgiving to the Giver of the greatest gift of all, as Ambrose of Milan poetically rendered it,

> I did not have what was His;
> He did not have what was mine.
> He assumed what is mine,
> that I might share in what is His.

Advent 1998   D.H.W.

ix

Prologue

This is a book I have been meaning to write for a long time. From my earliest days as a graduate student, I harbored a keen interest in understanding why the early church unfolded as it did — in thought and in practice — as well as how the church of the past is connected with the faith of the present. And yet within my own Baptist context, I have found little sense that engagement with the writings of the early church or the great confessions of Christian orthodoxy were of much importance to the pursuit of faithful Christian thinking and living. In fact, I once was informed with kindly intentions by a deacon of the first church I pastored that the study of the early creeds and councils is something Catholics or Episcopalians do, but true Christians need only uphold the complete authority of the Bible and the empowering of the Holy Spirit in a personal way. However liberating this may sound, such a position has served to isolate the current Christian experience of God for many believers, disconnecting them from the rich heritage of the church in its formative years where the doctrines of Christ and the Holy Spirit were developed, where the experience of Christian martyrs were realized, and where concepts of faithful biblical interpretation were devised. There is in fact an acute problem of continuity afflicting evangelical Christianity, just as it has generally troubled Protestantism, for numerous reasons that I will try to outline in the chapters to follow.

Most of what is contained in this book is meant to address the situation of Protestant evangelicals, especially those communions within evangelicalism designated as the Free Church, or "believers' church," a term

1

that is only slightly less ambiguous than speaking of "evangelicals." The two categories are not synonymous but they do significantly overlap; the first is related to historical patterns of ecclesiology whereas the second is more cultural and ideological. It will be useful perhaps for the reader if I lay out brief working definitions at the outset of this study.

Most historians speak of the "Free church" as that nonmagisterial part of the Protestant Reformation, that is, the Anabaptist or "left wing"[1] of the sixteenth century which had no uniform beginning, eventually becoming variegated into scores of self-sustaining movements such as the Hutterites, Mennonites, and Quakers, as well as those that stem from Pietist and Puritan roots, such as Baptists, Quakers, Congregationalists, Evangelical Free, Methodists, and later, the Holiness and Restorationist movements — Nazarene, Disciples of Christ (or the Christian Church), Brethren, Pentecostal, Church of God, Adventist, and of course, Independent or Bible Churches. Quite obviously this list is not comprehensive. The epithet "Free Church" has a legacy which dates back to the sixteenth century, and originates from a self-designation (as opposed to the pejorative, "Anabaptist") of the earliest gathering of believers that saw themselves as "the Lord's free people."[2] It is based upon the conviction that the church is not an institution on account of its structure or external rites, but exists only when it is voluntarily composed of the faithful. Thus Max Weber spoke of the church as that which no longer looked upon the religious community or visible church "as a sort of trust foundation for supernatural ends," rather as a community of personal believers of the regenerate, and only these. There is little or no sacramental attribution to any place, thing or ritual, because only the believing members of the congregation are holy by reason of the indwelling of the Holy Spirit. In practice, this has

---

1. For historical description of the earliest stages and groupings of this part of the Reformation, see F. H. Littell, *The Origins of Sectarian Protestantism: A Study of the Anabaptist View of the Church* (New York: Macmillan, 1964). Since most of the descendents of the Free church phenomenon on the European continent or in England are Trinitarian, I am deliberately omitting the antinomian and anti-trinitarian elements of the sixteenth century that have been also referred to by historians as manifestations of the "Free church."

From the beginning, Anabaptist congregations were radically decentralized. Well over twenty Anabaptist groups have been enumerated, scattered primarily throughout Switzerland, Germany, and The Netherlands.

2. "The First Anabaptist Congregation: Zollikon, 1525," *Mennonite Quarterly Review* 27 (1953): 17-33. The use of the term "Free church" appears among the English Puritans, typified as such for their Nonconformist policies.

involved the rejection of any hierarchical form of church government, not only in the sense of eschewing an episcopal form of authority, and in some cases, any clergy at all, but also "free" from dictates of the state or empire which, at different times of the church's history, has given its endorsement to a particular communion within the church. The believer is free, therefore, to follow the faith in accord with his or her conscience (and if pertinent, theological guidance offered by the denomination or church leadership), having no other ultimate authorities than the Bible and the Holy Spirit. It follows, as we will see in chapter 1, that any notion of an authoritative tradition of the church is problematic and difficult for many Christians to understand in terms of cultivating spirituality or thinking theologically.

Defining twentieth-century evangelicalism is notoriously difficult because of its doctrinal and historical diversity, and the reader will find a host of studies that provide various definitions and descriptions.[3] There is no one identifying confession, and many evangelical groups which share the Free Church legacy renounce the very idea of confessionalism — "No creed but the Bible." It is therefore useful to think of evangelicalism as more "a mood and an emphasis than a theological system" as Winthrop Hudson once phrased it.[4] And for this reason, evangelicals have tended to be identified by how they act and by what they choose rather than what they believe. Of course, evangelicalism has certain shared theological qualifiers which consist of the general importance attributed to personal experience in matters of faith, a stress on biblical inerrancy or infallibility, strong commitment to missionary activity, and an outlook that sees the church against the world, which often means, among other things, opposition to liberal Protestantism or Roman Catholicism. Evangelicalism has been distinguished from fundamentalism, at least since the middle of this century, as the former has sought a greater degree of rapprochement with

3. W. McLoughlin, ed., *The American Evangelicals, 1800-1900* (New York: Harper, 1968); J. Woodbridge, M. Noll and N. Hatch, eds., *The Gospel in America: Themes in the Story of America's Evangelicals* (Grand Rapids: Zondervan, 1979); Leonard Sweet, "The Evangelical Tradition in America" in *The Evangelical Tradition in America* (Macon, Ga.: Mercer University Press, 1984); D. Dayton and R. Johnston, *The Variety of American Evangelicalism* (Downers Grove, Ill.: InterVarsity Press, 1991), and D. J. Tidball, *Who are the Evangelicals? Tracing the Roots of the Modern Movements* (London: Marshall-Pickering, 1994).

4. Winthrop Hudson, *Religion in America*, 2nd ed. (New York: Scribner's Sons, 1973), 78.

the surrounding culture as an important means for church growth.[5] The result of this rapprochement is that a renewed evangelical ethos has developed in the United States, Britain and elsewhere, which means that we have come to define evangelicalism by social and cultural factors as much as by theological or historical ones. Indeed, a strong case has been made that social and cultural factors are the predominant shapers of current evangelical activity — a point that is raising serious concerns today.

As theologians such as Jürgen Moltmann have pointed to the Free church form of ecclesiology as holding the future of Protestantism, it is an opportune time to ask questions about what *kind* of faith will shape this future. It is true that the strengths of the "believers' church" model and evangelical charismata are making themselves felt around the world, acting as vehicles of renewal alongside of institutional forms of Christianity. But it seems that form or method, rather than content, is dominating the evangelical thrust, and where the problem about the lack of content is being addressed, there is no agreement.

I come to the task of writing this book with the dual advantage of being both a practitioner and a historian, a position which religious studies jargon calls an "observer-participant." It is a useful position to have. Both Protestant pulpit and professorial occupation in a Roman Catholic university have helped to shape my understanding of doctrine and church, and of how these latter two must have a continuous relationship of interchange and interdependency for either one to remain true to the apostolic faith "once delivered to the saints." Let me say plainly that as a true son of the Protestant Reformation, my criticisms of the believers' church model and of evangelicalism should be understood as both sympathetic and constructive. The concerns I outline below are not based on the polemical tensions of Protestant evangelicals versus Roman Catholics, but are internal to the debates already going on among evangelicals themselves, that is, what conservative Protestantism has become and yet needs to become in order to speak definitively within a religiously pluralist culture.

It will also become clear to the reader that an underlying purpose of this book is to integrate the serious study of patristics (study of the "Fa-

---

5. The line between evangelicalism and fundamentalism has always been a matter of nuance, as aptly demonstrated by George Marsden's *Fundamentalism and American Culture: The Shaping of Twentieth Century Evangelicalism, 1870-1925* (Oxford: Oxford University Press, 1980).

thers," or more broadly, the life and literature of early Christianity) into current theological reflections of evangelicalism, a task that has already begun though very much in its infancy. Few who would identify themselves as evangelicals have chosen academic careers in patristics, partly because there is little or no exposure to the field in the teaching curriculum of most Protestant seminaries, and partly because the post-apostolic period has been marginalized by the very life and practice of most churches evangelicals attend. This legacy has functioned in such as way as to leave a huge gap in the historical consciousness of the Free church.

It is therefore vitally necessary that such an integration begin 1) at levels of conversation which touch upon issues of importance to evangelicals, and 2) that the patristic data would be handled in a manner that does not simply appropriate it for our own modern agenda so that the historical context and sense of doctrinal development are violated in the process. The methods of handling the ancient evidence are not all that different from a responsible treatment of Scripture. My hope is that this book will provide a positive step in drawing these criteria together for the benefit of future studies. But more importantly, I want the reader to see what I eventually came to see in the study of the early Fathers, namely, that a constant dialogue was maintained between *theology* and the *life* of the church to the enrichment of both, and that orthodox (i.e., faithful) thinking and believing came about as a result of the church's attempts to voice its experience of God in its search for truth. This is not only a crucial step for apprehending the dynamics of the early church, but it is a dialogue to which the church of today must return.

I have purposely kept the technical language to a minimum in complying with the generalist aim of this project. The word "primer" in the subtitle of this book is intentional, and I will not assume the reader's familiarity with historical texts and methods, though we will likely cover new and strange ground for many evangelicals. I also intend to approach the topic at hand on the presumption that many readers have been raised with the understanding that the very notion of a Christian "Tradition" is cause for suspicion. To say that evangelicalism is tradition-deprived is perhaps true in the formal sense for most Free Church Christians, and there are important underlying reasons for why this is the case. Believers whose (unacknowledged) "tradition" has taught them that the Bible is our only guide for the faith and that there is no reliable Christian Tradition must first sort out the background for this rejection before they can begin to incorporate the early history of the church as *their history.* I have therefore written with the anticipation that a certain amount of reorientation is in order.

Perhaps the greatest difficulty this book will face is that many potential readers upon encountering a defense for the role of the church's Tradition will assume that I am attacking the privileged status of biblical authority. Nothing could be further from my intent. One kind of usage of "tradition" has been in reference to that which is completely autonomous of Scripture, and may even propose practices which find no sanction or even the least bit of support biblically. It is with this sort of "tradition" in mind that Carl Henry sounds a warning because it threatens the comprehensive unity of divine revelation by adducing an additional independent source of revelation.[6] Whether this was the intent of the language used at Vatican I is a controversial point that we need not entertain here. However, that will not be the sense of the word represented in the pages below. On a strictly historical basis, it can be argued that whenever "tradition" took a trajectory that disengaged it from Scripture, it became the most vulnerable to corruption and to the loss of catholicity. At the same time, the other half the historical equation says that one cannot separate the history and use of the Bible apart from the Tradition. Thus, I will argue that the church's Tradition sits in indispensable relation — historically and theologically — to the Christian use of Scripture and to the development of doctrine and spirituality. This was true in the early church; it is still true today.

I shall explain in chapter 1 more thoroughly why I have chosen to capitalize the word Tradition as distinct from "tradition." It will become clear that I am indebted to the last forty years of ecumenical discussions for my own approach to the subject. For the moment, let it suffice that the Tradition indicates the core teaching and preaching of the early church which has bequeathed to us the fundamentals of what it is to think and believe Christianly. Having recently watched a junior high school production of "Fiddler on the Roof," I was struck by how fitting in this regard were Tevye's opening words: "Because of our tradition, everyone knows who he is." Augustine said something similar once about the church's faith symbolized in its creed as that by which Christians can recognize each other.[7] The Tradition of the Christian faith is that fundamental Christian identity

---

6. Carl Henry, *God, Revelation and Authority*, vol. 2 (Waco: Word Books, 1976), 77f.

7. Augustine, *Sermon* 213. 2.

for every believer no matter which of the traditions — Protestant, Roman Catholic or Orthodox — he or she may profess. The English Puritan Richard Baxter referred to what I am trying to define here as "mere Christianity," which C. S. Lewis described as

> no insipid interdenominational transparency, but something positive, self-consistent and inexhaustible. I know it, indeed to my cost. In the days when I still hated Christianity, I learned to recognize, like some all too familiar smell, that almost unvarying *something* which met me. . . .[8]

While the various traditions within Christianity have long been in conflict to our harm, each has helped in both preserving and distorting that underlying foundation of the apostolic faith which I am calling the Tradition. My interest is not in explicating the points of distortion, or defending one against another, but rather digging out that underlying foundation and proving that there can be no faithful use of Scripture or practice of the church without it.

In preparing the research for this book, I have been repeatedly encouraged by evangelical catholics, like kindred spirits only recently discovered, who have sought to confront the problem of a Christian faith which has attempted to stand tall without the deep roots of its history. Even as I write these words, there are other exciting attempts being made by evangelically sponsored or supported projects to foster an understanding of the church's Tradition through an encounter with the theological resources of the ancients. InterVarsity Press has just published the papers of a conference which dealt with evangelical-Roman Catholic-Orthodox relations in light of the "great tradition."[9] Larger undertakings include a series of volumes to be published by Wm. B. Eerdmans Publishing Company entitled The Church's Bible that will put at the fingertips of pastors and Christian leaders select extracts of patristic exegetical commentary on major passages of the Bible, all translated into English with annotation that guides the reader without smothering.[10] Thomas Oden of Drew University is

8. C. S. Lewis, "Introduction," in *St. Athanasius: On the Incarnation* (Crestwood, N.Y.: St. Vladimir's Orthodox Seminary, 1944; reprint, 1993), 6.

9. J. S. Cutsinger, ed., *Reclaiming the Great Tradition: Evangelicals, Catholics and Orthodox in Dialogue* (Downers Grove, Ill.: InterVarsity Press, 1997).

10. The general editor of the series is Robert L. Wilken. Initial commentary volumes are slated for the Gospels of Matthew and John, Romans, 1 Corinthians, Isaiah, Song of Songs and two volumes each for Genesis and Psalms. Other biblical books are expected to be treated.

spearheading a similar project.[11] All of this is in addition to the multiple editions of English translations of patristic texts that are continuing to be published, such as Fathers of the Church, Ancient Christian Writers, and Library of Christian Classics, among others. An increasing wealth of resources for the ecumenically and historically minded Protestant (and Roman Catholic) is available as never before, providing for the working pastor, educator, seminarian, and diligent laity a critical foundation for the theological renewal of contemporary evangelicalism.

11. Thomas Oden, gen. ed., The Ancient Christian Commentary on Scripture series (Downers Grove, Ill.: InterVarsity Press). Twenty-seven volumes encompassing the biblical canon, plus two more on the Apocrypha, have begun to be published.

CHAPTER 1

Rediscovering the Church's Tradition

Men grind and grind in the mill of a truism, and nothing comes out but what was put in. But the moment they desert the tradition for a spontaneous thought, then poetry, wit, hope, virtue, learning, anecdote, all flock to their aid.

Ralph Waldo Emerson

Time makes ancient good uncouth. . . .

James Russell Lowell

 Within conservative Protestant circles, particularly in evangelicalism, there is an increasing number of voices expressing concern about how little the direction of the church's future is being informed by the Christian past. If one word could sum up the current theological situation, it would be _amnesia._ The real problem with amnesia, of course, is that not only does the patient forget his loved ones and friends, but he no longer remembers who he is. Too many within church leadership today seem to have forgotten that the building of a foundational Christian identity is based upon that which the church has received, preserved, and carefully transmitted to each generation of believers. In other words, the memory of how the historic faith of the church was established and subsequently

9

molded as the pattern for informing the faith in each new age has become irrelevant for the ministry.

New trends for church growth or the establishment of "seeker sensitive" settings have replaced the church's corporate memory for directing ecclesial policies and theological education. Pragmatics in ministry threaten to swallow the necessity for theology and marginalize the craft of "reflective understanding"[1] about God which ought to have its primary place of exercise in the church. While pastors have become more efficient administrators and keepers of the institution, along with being excellent performers, they are losing their ability to act as able interpreters of the historic faith. Likewise, biblical exegesis is too often guided by no other authority than the marketplace of ideas and the social and emotional agenda of the congregation. Interpretation of the text is far more indebted to the latest trends in interpersonal dynamics, effective communication style, or popular pastoral psychology. And all the while, the issue of determining Christian identity has lost its way in the mists of emotionally charged and professionally orchestrated worship. It is not that Christians are purposely ignoring Paul's final words to Timothy, "preserve the pattern of sound teaching . . . guard the good deposit that was entrusted to you," it is that they are no longer sure what this "deposit" consists of, or where it can be found. In some cases, finding this "deposit" does not matter anymore.

In his book *After Virtue,* Alasdair MacIntyre seeks to illustrate the current shiftlessness of contemporary morality by proposing a theoretical scenario of a modern society where almost all the knowledge of the natural sciences is lost. His illustration is quite applicable to our present concerns. A series of environmental disasters are blamed by the general public on the scientists with the result that laboratories are destroyed, physicists are lynched and books and instruments are burned. In the end, an anti-intellectual movement takes power and successfully abolishes teaching science in schools and universities, ignoring or imprisoning any remaining scientists. Much time passes. Eventually there is a reaction against this destructive movement and enlightened people attempt to revive science, although they have largely forgotten what it was. All they possess now are fragments: a knowledge of past experiments detached from the context which gave them significance, parts of theories unrelated to other bits and pieces of theories, a few instruments which no one knows how to use, half

---

1. J. C. Hough Jr. and J. B. Cobb Jr., *Christian Identity and Theological Education* (Chico, Calif.: Scholars Press, 1985).

chapters from books or single pages from articles. Nonetheless, all these fragments are reconstituted in a set of practices which go under the name of science, though nobody realizes that what they are doing is not natural science in any proper sense at all. Because so much has been lost, the use of terminology and existing data are used in arbitrary ways; even the choice of their application suits purposes not related to the original scientific intentions.[2]

Like the scattered remnants of scientific knowledge, telltale signs of the patristic Tradition can still be found within evangelical churches: baptism in the name of the Trinity, Christ admitted as fully human yet worshiped as God, occasional acknowledgement of the Apostles' or Nicene Creed, and, more fundamentally, the authoritative use of a collection of documents known as the New Testament. But these vestiges of the early faith are just that, *vestigia*, i.e., footprints or tracks that speak of a doctrinal and confessional past which has been peripheral for so many evangelicals that it has ceased to guide the direction of many present-day congregations and in some cases, is forgotten. There is a shared sense that the central elements of the Christian faith must be preserved in the church, but it is not clear why or what practical purpose they serve for the present needs of everyday ministry.

As I will discuss presently, the primary reasons for this widespread condition of amnesia are, directly and indirectly, an outcome of the Free Church/evangelicalism's negative perspective of most of church history, as well as the result of European and North American Christianity's voluntary subjection to cultural faddism and trendiness. On this latter point, it does not matter whether a given congregation is growing numerically at a fantastic rate or barely hanging on; the vacuum created by the absence of theological awareness and guidance provided by the church of previous ages is being quickly filled with a hankering after new techniques and gimmicks in the exercise of ministry. Loren Mead has labeled this condition the "Tyranny of the New" in which all our energy is used up inventing the new and marketing it. He writes, "When the new way is considered the only way, there is no continuity, fads become the new Gospel and in Paul's words, the church is 'blown to and fro by every wind of doctrine.'"[3] Because we live in an era of rapid

---

2. Alasdair MacIntyre, *After Virtue: A Study in Moral Theory* (Notre Dame: University of Notre Dame Press, 1981).

3. Loren Mead, *The Once and Future Church* (New York: The Alban Institute, 1991), 77.

change occurring within the church, church leaders want very much to be "in-step" and oriented towards what is to come. Indeed, the value and importance of the future seems self-evident and is commonly employed in order to inspire congregations to act. In Star Trek–like fashion, the future is what holds the hope of the present, symbolizing the discovery of new horizons and the inexorable march of technological progress which promises to usher in limitless benefits.

Postmodern philosophy has yet to fully replace this essential plank of the Enlightenment wherein rationality and the growth of knowledge lies on one side and traditionality and ignorance on the other as antitheses. The accepted paradigm of knowledge is that the acquiring of truth excludes tradition. Thus, the acknowledged normative power of a past practice or belief has become very faint as a persuasive argument for directing decisions. In a corresponding way, the traditionality of a belief or arrangement offers little resistance to arguments which proceed on the presumption of efficiency, expediency, "up-to-dateness" or progressiveness.[4] Disturbingly, though not surprisingly, the idea of moving into the future without securing those critical points of continuity with the church of earlier ages seems not to trouble many Christian leaders, nor are they concerned about how such an orientation might provide for the church's subsequent direction and distinctiveness. Modernity has done its work only too well.

As the structures of ministry and systems of thought undergo major transitions, evangelicals of all types are beginning to recognize an acute need for the stable and the fundamental, especially in matters of faith. To live in a "post-Christian" society, as analysts are now referring to the North American religious scene,[5] means that we can no longer expect the culture to mirror Christian sentiments or moral agenda. It also means that we will have to confront a fragmentation of the Christian message. Like MacIntyre's imaginary world, pieces of the original are utilized with little or no regard for the other bits or for the context from which they proceeded. As a result, one cannot avoid the problem of how far we should accomodate the Christian message to the surrounding culture without losing Christian identity, a problem which has become a major concern and dividing point

---

4. Cf. the introduction to Edward Shil's now classic study, *Tradition* (Chicago: University of Chicago Press, 1981).

5. See Harold Bloom, *The American Religion: The Emergence of the Post-Christian Nation* (New York: Simon and Schuster, 1992).

between conservative church leaders. While there is a growing hunger for rediscovering the essentials of what it is to think and live Christianly that goes beyond the moments of high-powered "praise and worship" experiences, the formation of a distinct Christian identity in years to come will not be successful unless we deliberately reestablish the link to those resources that provide us with the defining "center" of Christian belief and practice.

There is no getting around the fact that such a process of rediscovery will entail serious reconsideration about what the church's history means for today's church. Before we can responsibly go into the future, we must go back. But I am not talking merely about a revival of interest in historical Christianity. Simply encouraging readers to develop a historicist's perspective of the church misses the point here. What I want to argue for in this book is that if the aim of contemporary evangelicalism is to be doctrinally orthodox and exegetically faithful to Scripture, it cannot be accomplished without recourse to and integration of the foundational Tradition of the early church. This is taking a more urgent line than Robert Webber's clarion call twenty years ago when he encouraged evangelicals to maturity through a recovery of their roots in the pre-Reformation.[6] Tradition is not something evangelicals can take or leave. To make any claim for orthodox Christianity means that the evangelical faith must go beyond itself to the formative eras of that faith, apostolic and patristic, which are themselves the joint anchor of responsible biblical interpretation, theological imagination, and spiritual growth.

"The Church is apostolic indeed, but the Church is also patristic,"[7] wrote George Florovsky, meaning that there is no way one can remain faithful to the gospel without learning how the Fathers defended it, without sharing in their struggles to formulate it. The foundation of both an apostolic canon of Scripture and the theological canon of apostolicity are the result of the mediating work of subsequent generations of Christians, called the "Fathers" of the church. This does mean that everything the early Fathers (or Mothers) taught is immune from ancient influences or practices which Christians would no longer endorse today. I am not proposing an idealized portrait of that period. But appealing to the Bible

6. Robert Webber, *Common Roots: A Call to Evangelical Maturity* (Grand Rapids: Zondervan, 1978).

7. George Florovsky, *Bible, Church, Tradition: An Eastern Orthodox View* (Belmont, Mass.: Nordland, 1972), 107.

alone and the personal enabling of the Holy Spirit, however central these are, do not insure orthodoxy (they never have!), since these cannot function in isolation from their reception and development within the ongoing life of the church. Dividing Scripture from the Tradition or from the church creates an artificial distinction which would have been completely alien to the earliest generations of Christians. As I will discuss more fully in chapter 3, much of our understanding of the Bible and theological orthodoxy, directly or indirectly, has come through the interpretive portals of the early church which is itself an integral part of the Protestant charter no less than it is for Roman Catholicism or Eastern Orthodoxy.

Without the church's Tradition, I will contend that Free church communions, especially independent and "community"-type churches, (1) will increasingly proliferate a sectarian approach to Christian faith, characterized by an ahistoricism and spiritual subjectivism which Philip Schaff aptly called "the great disease which has fastened itself upon the heart of Protestantism,"[8] and (2) will be more susceptible to the influences of accommodating the church to a pseudo-Christian culture such that the uniqueness of the Christian identity is quietly and unintentionally traded away in the name of effective ministry.

There is much to unpack in this thesis, and I am undertaking something of a risk by laying it out here before introducing the steps that lead to this conclusion. Most important is the stumbling-block that the concept of Tradition, as an authoritative platform for faith, poses for most conservative Protestants. But I hope to make plain that it is indispensable for articulating a uniquely Christian perspective. Even if we should claim that this Tradition is not immune from needed periodic course correction or revision, as Protestants have rightly defended — *ecclesia reformata sed semper reformanda* — the integrity of Christian orthodoxy is placed in jeopardy when the church's growth and public discourse fail to regard the way orthodoxy has been constructed through the conflicts and controversies of the church in history. At the very least, the present church will be doomed to repeating the same heretical notions in ignorance. I am reminded of G. K. Chesterton's personal confession of how he experimented with "all the idiotic ambitions" of the day trying to be in advance of his age, with the result that "I only succeeded in inventing all by myself an inferior copy of

8. Philip Schaff, *The Principle of Protestantism,* trans. from the German by John Nevin (Chambersburg, Penn.: Publication Office of the German Reformed Church, 1845), 107.

existing traditions."[9] The most strident antitraditional and anticonfessional position soon realizes that it has created its own tradition and confessions which are but crude derivations, and often deviations, of the original.

There is, however, more at stake than historical circularity. We also discover that no amount of creative packaging and marketing of the gospel will rescue church ministry if we lose the theological center which enables us to define the faith and prescribe the kinds of intellectual and practical relations it should have in the world. Given the centrifugal and atomistic forces already inherent among Free Church and evangelical forms of Christianity, the lack of an identifying center is theologically debilitating. Our unending search for a Spirit-filled and biblically refined faith has not paid off in enhanced clarity or ecclesiastical unity, but in an increased fragmentation of the church.

This is the great irony affecting much of Protestantism. On the one hand, we must acknowledge that the Reformation helped reestablish the biblical pattern in terms of understanding the gospel and the nature of salvation, which ought to be defended at all costs. When medieval Catholicism had drifted so far from the center, such that the large portions of the church no longer heard the word of God at the heart of its Tradition, the reforming movements of the fifteenth and sixteenth centuries helped to reset its course. But on the other hand, the elevation of Scripture and rejection of church authority caused Protestants "to mute the voices of that weighty preaching with which the church of antiquity had come to understand the meaning of Scripture," and eventually, "the councils, the creeds, the grand theologians, the apologists, and the philosophers — all could now be abandoned."[10] In effect, the Tradition has been lost at the cost of making the course correction, and the "center" that the Reformers were hoping to restore splintered into a multitude of conflicting versions of the faith.

In the last decade or so, Protestants of all stripes are noticing that something is seriously missing. It is time for evangelicals to reach back and affirm a truly "catholic"[11] Tradition by returning to the ancient sources themselves, to correct the former correction, as A. J. Conyers put it, and to

9. G. K. Chesterton, *Orthodoxy* (New York: Doubleday, 1936), 12.

10. A. J. Conyers, "Protestant Principle, Catholic Substance," *First Things* 67 (November 1996): 17.

11. See Appendix I.

drink again at the wells of the consensual teaching and preaching of the early church. I want to add my own puny voice to the growing chorus declaring that the path of renewal for evangelicalism must happen through an intentional recovery of its catholic roots in the church's early spirituality and theology. Herein we will find not an avenue that leads to the loss of our distinctiveness as Protestants, but, as the sixteenth-century Reformers found, to the resources necessary to preserve a Christian vision of the world and its message of redemption.

Remembering the Past

It is no accident that the writers of the Old Testament in times of faithlessness or during major transitions rehearsed how God had dealt with Israel in ages past. The "story" of Israel's calling in Abraham, deliverance from its oppressors, and establishment in the land was an essential part of the nation's covenantal relationship to God. Recounting the redemptive acts of God was for the people's edification, as well as a critical part of reconstructing their identity as a holy nation. One of the most commonly used words of Moses, the psalmist, and the prophets in their admonition to the people of God is "remember."

> Remember the days of old,
> Consider the years of all generations.
> Ask your father, and he will tell you,
> Your elders, and they will inform you. (Deut. 32:7)

Christianity, like its Jewish parent, is fundamentally a historical faith. This means much more than saying Christianity has a history which Christians ought to know. Too often church history is presented or perceived as a bewildering mass of important personalities, ideas, and dates, most of which has little if any relevance to the daily challenges that most believers face. One need only say the word "history" and you can watch the saints' eyes start to glaze over as if it were a subject of no practical consequence for Christian living. On the contrary, Christianity *is* historical in the sense that God has acted within *our* history through the revelation of Jesus Christ, and that this history is the medium through which God has done it. The history that separates us from the birth, life, death and resurrection of Christ is also the indispensable nexus which connects us to our salvation.[12] Protestants forget that the guiding inspiration of the Protestant Reformation was fueled by a need to rediscover the Christian past. The Reformers were acutely aware that everything in the Christian message is rooted in the unique event of God as Emmanuel, which means Christian history is the very process of receiving, transmitting, and renewing that original gospel of the apostles. The lesson is that renewal is inextricably related to the church of the past.

It was also from Judaism that Christianity inherited its prophetic character. Prophecy in the Old Testament was a response to a present situation, usually in trying circumstances, that declared a word from God. Its primary aim was to call God's people to faithfulness. Even when the message was one of judgment, the intention of the prophecy was for the eventual recovery of the people to the covenant that had identified them. Faithfulness, not futurism, is the primary point of the prophetic message, a point too often misunderstood by enthusiastic believers largely because the apocalyptic motif has come to dominate present-day evangelical conceptions. Within this latter sense, prophecy in the Old and New Testaments represents a kind of encoded blueprint for the future culmination of this age.[13] In fact, however, the emphasis of the biblical prophetic declaration was always tied to a reinvestment of Israel's spiritual heritage. The call to a renewed faithfulness was never detached from Israel's history. Stephen's last address before a menacing Jewish audience in Acts 7 provides an excellent example of the prophetic purpose. His brief overview of Israel's covenantal history was meant not only as a reminder of the nation's consistent rejection of the prophets, but also to demonstrate that faithfulness is connected with God's past revelation among his people. Thus, the announcement of God's "Righteous One," i.e., the Messiah, is a message which is offered in relation to an understanding of what God has been doing all along. Such an understanding lies at the very heart of the apostolic message of the gospel.

None of this is meant to insinuate that God cannot speak anew within our present situation. Nevertheless, detachment of the Christian past from applying the word of God in the present risks the predicament of having Scripture explained (or ignored) according to the whims or agenda of who-

---

12. Albert C. Outler, *The Christian Tradition and the Unity We Seek* (New York: Oxford University Press, 1957), 39.

13. For the predomination of apocalyptic interpretations in American Protestant concepts of prophecy, see Paul Boyer, *When Time Shall Be No More: Prophecy Belief in Modern American Culture* (Cambridge: Belknap Press, 1992).

ever is doing the explaining. There is nothing to prevent the free flight of self-serving proclamations (usually prefaced with the words, "God has led me") which address the hopes and fears of its target audience unless we acknowledge that faithfulness begins with a reappropriation of our unique identity through the historical legacy of Christian thought and life. For good reason has Robert Wilken argued that the Christian intellectual tradition is inescapably historical: "Without memory, our intellectual life is impoverished, barren, ephemeral, subject to the whims of the moments."[14]

Because of the character of individualization within Free Church ecclesiology, it is particularly liable to idiosyncratic forms of declarations and preaching that claim no other guidance than that of the Holy Spirit. Certainly the divine leading of the Spirit is necessary for the proclamation of the gospel, and yet whatever claims to be prophetic loses its force and anointing once it becomes loosed from the history of the covenant. Protestants must reconsider the work of the Holy Spirit in the life history of the church no less than in the life of the individual believer. For it is with the church that God's new covenant was formed, and it is the church that he gave all attending graces and gifts that it may faithfully fulfill its mission.

The Church's Tradition?

The chief difficulty within Protestant evangelicalism is not simply the problem of forgetting its past; it also has to do with a general suspicion of that which is usually called "tradition." The church's "tradition" carries little authority for most evangelicals because it is associated with the institutional and sacramental structure of the Roman Catholic Church from which Protestants supposedly broke away. In other words, "tradition" has been generally understood as (1) an artificial product of hierarchical Catholicism and therefore a corruption of the apostolic faith, and (2) antithetical to the absolute authority of the Bible. The first perspective is based on an interpretion of church history between the death of the apostles and the Protestant Reformation as "fallen" from New Testament principles, and therefore of little doctrinal relevance for normative Christianity. This is an important historical point for Free church historiography to which I shall return below and in chapter 4.

14. Robert Wilken, "Memory and the Christian Intellectual Life," in *Remembering the Christian Past* (Grand Rapids: Eerdmans Publishing Company, 1995), 179.

Related to the second point is the longstanding and prevalent conception that the scriptural principle of *sola scriptura* is compromised by any acceptance of extracanonical authority. Too often it is assumed that to embrace the church's ancient Tradition must necessarily entail a denial of the Bible's unique revelatory status. The contrast is made between the standing of Scripture as the sole word of God from that of ecclesial creeds, decrees, councils, etc. — all human foundations prone to err. That many evangelicals still do not understand the early Christian concept of tradition or how it functioned in relation to Scripture is very evident in some recent publications.[15] It is worth noting in passing the reasons for this resistance.

Long inherent within fundamentalist and evangelical Christianity is an antitraditionalism and anticredalism which has played a key role in its theological outlook and interpretation of the Bible. After all, Protestantism was born in reaction to the tyranny of ecclesiastical authority and practices exalted on account of their venerated traditions. Protestant consciousness was shaped by an awareness that the true faith had been seduced and distorted by a contrived religious system which left a lasting suspicion of religious hierarchy, elitism, and ritual. No less stamped on this consciousness were the later influences of the Enlightenment, especially its emphasis on individualism, egalitarianism, and lack of tolerance for honoring practices or beliefs in accordance with the classical principle of antiquity.

Protestant Christianity in the antebellum period of American history reaped the effects of social democratic theory based on Enlightenment ideology in its rejection of traditional authorities and in its lauding of the priority of human reason and conscience. The historian is confronted not only with the long-term effects of the Reformation in its various incarnate forms, but also with emerging species of idiosyncratic Protestantism which arose within the American context, such as Seventh Day Adventism or Disciples of Christ (Christian Church). A combination of the sovereignty of the common man and the right to private judgment was instrumental in leading to a populist kind of hermeneutic that captured the pious imagination, particularly of those in Free Church or congrega-

15. See J. Armstrong, ed., *Roman Catholicism: Evangelical Protestants Analyze What Divides and Unites Us* (Chicago: Moody, 1995). As promising as the book sounds, the room for constructive dialogue with Roman Catholicism is quite limited given that an inerrantist agenda frequently overwhelms the discussion. For the same problems, see *Sola Scriptura! The Protestant Position on the Bible*, ed. D. Kistler (Morgan, Penn.: Soli Deo Gloria, 1996). See Appendix II.

tionalist settings. Anyone with a Bible in his or her hands could hear God speaking directly, and all formal theological approaches were seen as impediments to a straightforward and ready reception of the Bible's unadulterated teaching.

In 1800, a Calvinist Baptist pastor, Elias Smith, demanded the absolute right of all persons to explain the New Testament for themselves. The central plank of Smith's message was to call for the "inalienable right" of the common person to follow the Scripture wherever it may lead: "Truth is no man's property. . . . I further protest against that unrighteous and ungodly pretense of making the writings of the fathers, the decrees of councils and synods, or the sense of the church, the rule and standard of judging the sense of Scripture, as Popish, Anti-Christian, and dangerous to the church of God."[16] Smith's views were representative, as American church historian Nathan Hatch observes, of how "democratic values and patterns of biblical interpretation were moving in the same direction, mutually reinforcing ideas of volitional allegiance, self-reliance and private judgment."[17] For Alexander Campbell, one of the founders of the Disciples of Christ, these ideals took the form of a strong anticlericalism. Like many of his generation, Campbell believed that the stripping away of theology and tradition would restore unity and vitality to the Christian church.[18] In his search for the authentic faith of the New Testament church, Campbell espoused the popular platform "no creed but Christ" while emphasizing the liberty of the believer's own judgment as led by the Holy Spirit.[19] Instead of "human creeds" the Bible alone is the norm for doctrine, morality, and

---

16. Nathan O. Hatch, "Sola scriptura and Novus ordo seculorum," in *The Bible in America: Essays in Cultural History*, ed. Nathan O. Hatch and Mark A. Noll (Oxford: Oxford University Press, 1982), 67.

17. *Ibid.*, 74. Under very different circumstances, Charles Finney reached the same hermeneutical conclusion as Smith when, after being ordained in the Presbyterian Church, he came to reject the Westminster Confession: "being unable to accept doctrine on the ground of authority. . . . I had nowhere to go except to the Bible."

18. Nathan O. Hatch, "The Right to Think for Oneself," in *The Democratization of American Christianity* (New Haven: Yale University Press, 1989), 163.

19. Exactly how hostile Campbell was toward the church's tradition is a debatable point among scholars within the Disciples of Christ (Christian Church). William Tabbernee has argued that the rallying cry "No creed but Christ" was a rhetorical device that was meant to focus attention on what Campbell and others believed was a misuse of creeds. It did not mean that all creeds were anathema. "'Unfencing the Table': Creeds, Councils, Communion and the Campbells," *Mid-Stream: The Ecumenical Movement Today* 35 (1996): 417-431.

the practice of piety. The mediation of ecclesiastical traditions or offices which had served to broker the believer's apprehension of truth was rejected as an unnecessary encumbrance to the process. Whatever good the sixteenth-century Protestant Reformation had done, it had not completely restored authentic Christianity, since it did not sufficiently recognize how wide the chasm was between God and the established church. What was needed was a divine channel of purity for the reinstitution of the primitive gospel and practice. The legacy left by this perspective, as seen through the kaleidoscope of movements which it spawned in the ensuing century, shows how the search for a simplified and unifying factor of faith resulted in a cacophony of conflicting voices, all claiming to have found the original faith of the apostles.

Built into this antitraditionalism was an anticredal conviction, since the conciliar creeds of the fourth and fifth centuries were thought to be either manifestations of a corrupted religious system or statements of ecclesiastical politics which were so culturally conditioned that they had no bearing for subsequent Christianity.[20] In those instances where, for example, Baptist constituencies have issued confessional statements,[21] the reader is expected to understand that these are meant to act as guides only for delineating the joint sentiments of that body, and not as "creeds" setting norms for the faith. To do otherwise would violate the prerogative of every believer to his or her own interpretation of the Bible, contrary to an official construal of norms for the faith.

Endemic to anticredal attitudes has been an apocalyptic or millenarian view of history — a central and abiding component of dispensationalist movements. According to this view, history, like society at large, has been in the process of degeneration since the days of the apostles, and correspondingly, there is a deep negativity toward every human institu-

20. A good example of this perspective is Mennonite writer John Toews, *Jesus Christ the Convener of the Church* (Elkhart, Ind.: Mennonite Church, 1989) who views Scripture and the fourth-century creeds as mutually exclusive on the argument that the creeds served the churches of their era only, and are too narrow and culturally specific to help us in developing a biblical Christology today.

21. See H. L. McBeth, *A Sourcebook for Baptist Heritage* (Nashville: Broadman, 1990). Baptist publications make it clear that Baptists are not a credal people, which does not mean the ancient creeds have no place in the life of the church, but that their theology or modes of expression are not binding on the church since the creeds were written to address specific situations that may not have relevance today. See William P. Tuck, *Our Baptist Tradition* (Macon: Smyth and Helwys, 1993), and Walter B. Shurden, *The Baptist Identity* (Macon: Smyth and Helwys, 1990).

tion, civil and religious. This accounts for a general skepticism toward authority, except, of course, the ultimate authority: God's revealed word. As an institution, the church is usually suspected of being aligned with the institutions of the world and thus not a reliable guide when it comes to "rightly divining the word of truth." The church's clergy are put in the same boat, as they are permitted to prompt and guide the Christian but not wield any real power. Believers are urged to eschew creeds, confessions, or councils and are told to "study the Word itself" since the truth is conveyed in simple terms known to all.

Likewise, the study of theology is denigrated by the "endtimes" mindset as an unfortunate process of participating in a fallen system. Contemporary prophecy experts often parade the lack of academic credentials or absence of ecclesiastical affiliation as a strength and basis for the trustworthiness of their message. They are, it is claimed, untainted by the epistemological corruptions affecting those who were formally trained in institutions that propagate the ideology of the fallen system. So Jack Van Impe warns that "our seminaries are filled with apostates," and we are admonished, "Quit listening to clergymen and lay people who are too lazy to study prophecy, and begin listening to God."[22] The church's history and legacy of faith as transmitted through confessional theology is perceived as an impediment to nurturing orthodoxy. It is no surprise, therefore, that Lewis Sperry Chafer, influential dispensationalist from the early part of this century and former president of Dallas Theological Seminary, perceived his lack of formal training in theology as a virtue. By not examining what others had written, he claimed, he was preserved from their errors: "The very fact that I did not study a prescribed course in theology made it possible for me to approach the subject with an unprejudiced mind and to be concerned only with what the Bible actually teaches."[23]

That God is sovereign means, among other things, that there must be grounds for confidence in the church's history unfolding as a series of acts divinely superintended. Nevertheless, we have seen how a negative view of church history is at work behind the antitraditionalism which has typified Free Church evangelicalism. This is compounded by the privatization of faith and the interpretive license of every man or woman to expound the Bible with little other guidance than the subjective operation of the Spirit

22. Boyer, *When Time Shall Be No More*, 306-8.
23. Lewis Sperry Chafer, *Systematic Theology*, vol. 8 (Dallas: Dallas Seminary Press, 1948), 5-6.

— a method which has been read into the post-Reformation teaching of *sola scriptura* and the priesthood of every believer. Any *essential* connection between the historical theology of the church and the Bible is thereby severed. It is important to note that such a perspective does not require a knowledge of the historical theology of the church in order to achieve a faithful understanding of the Bible. When overlap of the two does occur, it seems almost fortuitous, perhaps driven by a personal or denominational decision, but in any case not a movement that is indigenous to the task of biblical teaching or worship.

The "Evangelical Crisis"

The present ahistorical and atheological condition of evangelicalism is symptomatic of what some scholars have been warning us about for over a decade now. While there may be grounds for claiming that evangelicalism holds the key to the future of Western Christianity,[24] and that numerical growth is occurring among conservative churches,[25] the immediate prognosis concerning their theological health is uncertain. Finke and Stark's *The Churching of America, 1776-1990* makes it abundantly clear that evangelicalism has become the dominant force in American religious life. While the membership and resources in the mainline churches are dwindling away, evangelical congregations, some of enormous size, have become the acknowledged centers of late twentieth-century religious activity. But the reasons for the mainliners' loss are not those which have led to the evangelicals' gain. The fleeting doctrinal distinctions and theological integrity which are said to have has so crippled Episcopalianism, Methodism, or Presbyterianism[26] have not been recaptured by conservative Protestant bodies so as to

24. Alister McGrath, *Evangelicalism and the Future of Christianity* (Downers Grove, Ill., 1995), 12. "Evangelicalism is one of the powerhouses of the modern Christian church in the western world" (17).

25. See L. R. Iannaccone, "Why Strict Churches are Strong," *American Journal of Sociology* 99 (1994): 1180-1211. But see also Mark Shibley, *Resurgent Evangelicalism in the United States: Mapping Cultural Change since 1970* (Columbia, S.C.: University of South Carolina Press, 1996), who asserts that the cause of recent evangelical growth is not due to its strictness and exclusivity but because "contemporary" evangelical churches are becoming more like the culture, not less.

26. Kenneth Woodward, "Dead End for the Mainline?" *Newsweek*, 9 August 1993, 46-48.

be the reason for their current monopoly. On the contrary, evangelical church historian Mark Noll laments the present state of evangelicalism as woefully lacking "an evangelical mind" in that attention to the intellectual life of the faith has ceased to inform the religious agenda of evangelicals. "To put it most simply, the evangelical ethos is activitistic, populist, pragmatic and utilitarian. It allows little space for broader or deeper intellectual effort because it is dominated by the urgencies of the moment."[27]

A similarly ominous assessment is offered by David Wells who, with harsh and somber tones, describes how "the evangelical church has cheerfully plunged into astounding theological illiteracy."[28] The problem is not simply a lack of knowing something about theology. Too many evangelicals cannot articulate a reflective faith shaped by their own evangelical heritage and how that heritage should be integrated within the various disciplines of modern learning and the arts. For all their successes in achieving better programming, creating more dramatic worship experiences, and drawing bigger crowds, evangelicals are devoid of a distinctive message that makes an impact on the culture they inhabit. In their quest to reach the "baby-boomers," they have come to reflect the cultural preferences of their audience: anti-institutional, informal, nondogmatic, therapeutic and tolerant of other lifestyles.[29] Yes, rapid growth is occurring, but in what direction and at what cost?

Wells insists that the forces of modernity have corroded the evangelical theological identity by means of substitution. Theology is disappearing in the churches because the drive for truth, and even the significance of ideas, has been replaced by an emphasis on technique — that is, a technology of practice which is based on methods of business management and psychology, and whose goal is set on the expansion of the church assembly and the mastery of the self.

> As nostrums of the therapeutic age supplant confession, and as preaching is psychologized, the meaning of the Christian faith is privatized. At a single stroke, confession is eviscerated and reflection reduced mainly to thought about one's self.

27. Mark Noll, *The Scandal of the Evangelical Mind* (Grand Rapids: Eerdmans Publishing Company, 1994), 12.

28. David Wells, *No Place for Truth, or Whatever Happened to Evangelical Theology?* (Grand Rapids: Eerdmans Publishing Company, 1993), 4. Cf. E. T. Oakes, "Evangelical Theology in Crisis," *First Things* 36 (October 1993): 38-44.

29. Shibley, *Resurgent Evangelicalism*, 88.

Where this modern "wisdom" comes to supplant confession in defining and disciplining what practice should mean, where reflection has been reduced simply to reflection upon the self, and where the hard work of relating the truth of God's Word to the processes of modern life has been abandoned, there once again theology has died and all that is left of it is an empty shell of what that wisdom used to be.[30]

This situation, in turn, has led to a loss of coherency within the church as the very content of faith *(fides quae creditur)* no longer informs the central task of the church. Preaching easily slips into the mode of moralizing or entertaining, and eventually the flock of God can no longer stomach the diet which exposes them to or causes them to think deeply about the content of the Christian faith. Congregations are well schooled in neatly dividing the faith into practical and theoretical aspects, believing that only the former is of concern to them.

Although Wells offers no cure for the disease he has diagnosed as currently undermining evangelicalism's integrity, he suggests that it will involve reconnecting the ties which have been broken between twentieth-century evangelicalism and "historic Protestant orthodoxy." The breach between the two has been amply demonstrated. It may be rightfully asked, however, whether his tentative solution goes far enough. Admonishing the church to give heed to the "Word of God" in light of its perceived inability to address the moral and theological challenges before it still leaves the problem of where one should turn for the needed resources.[31] To point us in the direction of the origins of Protestantism is not a return to Christian roots. For the Reformers were themselves seeking to restore the church in accordance with the model of the early Fathers that they accused medieval Catholicism of having abandoned. Their initial vision entailed a unification of the church through purification which was determined by a return to the Bible and to the orthodoxy of the patristic sources. Nevertheless, Wells and others have successfully persuaded us that there will be no healthy church without a healthy interest in confessional theology, beckoning the church to set its priorities around truth and not itself.

It is not overly melodramatic to say that the very content of contemporary Protestant Christianity is up for grabs. We are in a process of radi-

---

30. Wells, *No Place for Truth*, 101.

31. Wells' latest book, *Losing Our Virtue: Why the Church Must Recover Its Moral Vision* (Grand Rapids: Eerdmans Publishing Company, 1998), is similarly stronger in its diagnosis than it is in constructing an alternative platform for theological faithfulness.

cal revision within a climate that no longer assumes the church's doctrine and history ought to inform the direction of contemporary theology or ecclesiastical practice. Ideology is taking the place of theology, and faithfulness has less to do with doctrine than with following a conservative agenda of social or political concern. Theology and biblical hermeneutics have become the domain of the "professionals" whose work need not be advised by a knowledge of and concern for the church. The question looms before evangelicals about how far they will accommodate their methods and aspirations to the present culture before they are no longer able to be distinguished from it. What kind of impact can such a Christianity have if the uniqueness of the Christian identity has become so fragmented or so secularized that its voice offers nothing different than what can be found elsewhere?

Continuity or Discontinuity?

Another great irony in Protestant evangelicalism is its intention to be biblically astute and historically sensitive. There is an implicit and essential belief that a clear link does exist between the New Testament church and our time. For preaching to have any relevance at all, it is necessary to be able to draw a line connecting the church of the apostles and our own time. It is a hallmark of evangelicalism that one can draw that line between these two points in its mandate to preach the gospel. The Bible is, besides other things, "our" story. Indeed, at the basis of most reform or renewal movements that make up Protestantism is the idea of a "return" to the New Testament as the model for the practice of orthodox Christianity. And at the heart of this view is the assumption that such a return is possible.

No less pertinent to this understanding is the prevailing perception among many within the Free Church that Christianity after the apostles soon became distorted. The rise of the episcopacy, dependency on tradition rather than the Bible, veneration of martyrs, infant baptism, and so on, all spoke of a faith which had become misaligned and detached from the pristine spirituality of the New Testament. According to some scenarios, the worst had happened by the time of the emperor Constantine in the early fourth century, when the apostolic faith was dominated by "Catholicism," which continued to dominate the Christian faith with extrabiblical teachings for the next 1500 years. Central to the above scenario is the assumption that it was not until the Protestant Reformation that the patristic and medieval veneer of corruption was finally sloughed off, making possible a return to the pure, unadulterated teaching of the New Testament. This meant that most of the ecclesiastical and theological history from the post-apostolic period to the Reformers was an unfortunate accumulation of religiosity which needed to be purged from the believing church, not embraced.

I will later discuss this influential historical pattern in more depth, but for the moment suffice it to say that the above model entails an ahistorical jump from the apostles to the sixteenth century which typifies most of the theology and biblical exegesis done by evangelicals. Like Superman, they are able to leap over the patristic and medieval developments of Christianity with a single bound. Church historian Jaroslav Pelikan has observed that "even Protestants who see no value in structural continuity — continuity of ministry and sacraments and institutions — value continuity in doctrinal principles and religious experience."[32] But what kind of continuity is this? How can any church today claim a connection with the apostolic era when it has remained ignorant of and often rejected in practice the church age which followed the apostles and which was *the* critical period for the very formation of the New Testament, for the propounding of the doctrines of Christ and the Trinity, for the confessions of redemption and eternal hope — in short, for the development of what it is to think and live as an orthodox Christian?

One might argue for a spiritual or moral continuity with the first-century communities, as many Protestant historians have tried to do;[33] nonetheless, there is no denying that one is left with a perspective of historical *discontinuity* coloring much of the way in which the church unwittingly operates. That is, the practice of one's faith and engagement with the world need not have any actual relevance to the legacy which the pre- and post-Constantinian Christians have bequeathed to us.

The irony of this situation can best be exemplified through the Nicene doctrine of *homoousios* ("same substance"). Since the end of the fourth century, Christians have always drawn on the language and theol-

---

32. Jaroslav Pelikan, *Development of Christian Doctrine* (New Haven: Yale University Press, 1969), 16.

33. J. D. Murch, *The Free Church: A Treatise on Church Polity with Special Relevance to Doctrine and Practice in Christian Churches and Churches of Christ* (Louisville: Restoration Press, 1966), 36; W. M. Patterson, *Baptist Successionism: A Critical View* (Valley Forge, Penn.: Judson Press, 1969), 15.

ogy of the Nicene Creed (A.D. 325) and its later expositions that the Son shares the same substance as the Father. The point is that Jesus Christ, the Son of God, is God the Son who possesses the very same divinity as God the Father. This is what makes the salvation offered through Mary's son a truly divine gift that can restore us to the divine image. Such a doctrine is a basic and central tenet of evangelical theology, or at the very least, functions as the essential backdrop for the evangelical understanding of the person and work of Christ. And yet, the mere existence of the Nicene Creed or its significance in having a central role in establishing the Christian identity is rarely acknowledged, if ever, as having pertinence to their faith. The silence is sometimes deafening.

But the truly ironic part is that the touchstone word of the Nicene faith, *homoousios,* is not found in the Bible. In fact, the absence of this term in the Bible caused something of a scandal among the first generation of Christians after the Council of Nicaea. Not a few bishops in the east and west opposed its usage for this very reason. Prior to Nicaea, the pattern had been that all credal language and terminology was to be drawn from the Bible. Bishops looked suspiciously and disapprovingly at any credal terminology that did not somewhere appear in Scripture. The same could be said for calling the Father, Son, and Holy Spirit "persons,"[34] an appellation no less central to later orthodox formulations, as in the so-called "Athanasian Creed" (or *Quicunque*), but nowhere found in Scripture. This also caused a great deal of confusion and mistrust because "person" used to be a term applied by the modalists to God in order to express His appearance in three modes or *personae*, sometimes as the Father, sometimes as the Son, and other times as the Spirit (i.e., no real distinctions between the three). Nevertheless, one could say that the language of Nicaea was a nominal extension from New Testament teaching about Christ, just as Athanasius argued in his *On the Definition of the Nicene Creed,* written a quarter of a century after the famous council met. The necessity of new terminology to meet the theological needs of new crises did not obviate the fact that these doctrines were no less an outcome of the church's preaching, reflection, and practice for over three centuries. And those who constructed the creed and signed it hoped to make clear what the Bible's teaching intended.

34. Indicating distinction within the Trinity using "persona" was used as early as Tertullian but generally not favored because of its modalist connotations. Not until the fifth century with the council of Chalcedon (451) and the so-called "Athanasian Creed" does the term become an accepted part of trinitarian definition.

For all the emphasis that evangelicals have placed on the Bible and the Bible alone as the only grounds for their faith, their tacit but universal acceptance of the Nicene and post-Nicene Christ is not derived from the Bible alone. We must recognize that the Bible alone has never functioned as the sole means by which Christians are informed about their faith. It was never meant to. One cannot move simply from the Bible to the chief doctrines of the Christian faith without passing through those critical stages of development that link the past and present together and which make our present interpretation of the Bible intelligible. An important lesson learned by the bitter conflicts of the "Arian controversy" of the fourth century was that for achieving doctrinal orthodoxy one cannot interpret the Bible from the Bible alone. It became recognized that there was need for a vocabulary and conceptual categories that stem from the Bible but were also outside of the Bible.

The point is that the issue of historical and doctrinal continuity has yet to be sufficiently addressed within evangelical circles. There is much at stake. The late R. P. C. Hanson was right when he said, "[Roman] Catholics are apt to harp too much perhaps on continuity, but Protestants tend to forget it altogether. It is not a subject that can be safely forgotten."[35]

Protestant liberal theology has long discounted the possibility of establishing a link with the thought-world of early Christianity on account of the cultural and ideological gap that exists between the present and the past. The patristic scholar Francis Young has argued for the problematic nature of achieving orthodoxy because all doctrinal development is environmentally conditioned and determined by such factors as politics, philosophical presuppositions, and the chances of history.[36] Maurice Wiles has similarly suggested that no norm of Christian doctrine is available for the reason that the evolution of Christianity is like a stream which wanders where it will and has no discernible control.[37] While the categories of "orthodoxy" and "heresy" do present historical problems for patristic scholars — and conservatives have been rightly

35. R. P. C. Hanson, *The Continuity of Christian Doctrine* (New York: Seabury Press, 1981), 64.

36. Francis Young, "A Cloud of Witnesses," in *The Myth of God Incarnate*, ed. John Hick (Philadelphia: Westminster Press, 1977), 23. Hick himself asserts that "orthodoxy" is no more than a myth that inhibits the creative freedom of modern scholarship.

37. Maurice Wiles, *The Remaking of Christian Doctrine* (London: SCM Press, 1974).

accused of too often simplifying the complexity of issues involved — these problems do not annul the possibility of determining a mainline catholicism as distinct from other parties who also claimed to possess the Christian teaching. Diversity in the earliest period of Christianity is not antithetical to positing a central axis of faithful self-awareness that functioned within the historical processes, the latter unfolding through the sacramental activities and intellectual exchange of living communities. The very existence of an orthodox faith has been found to be far more durable and tenacious than modern scholarship once depicted.[38] And yet, as much as conservative Free Church thinkers may criticize the conclusions of their liberal contemporaries, their methods are strikingly alike when it comes to church history. Both find the patristic era intrinsically interesting and draw theological lessons from its conflicts and discoveries. But both tend to devalue the role of "classical Christianity" as an integral part of contemporary Christian faith on the basis that patristic contributions came about as the result of problems and issues that have only a distant relevance to our own times. One cannot simply draw a line from there to here. The difference is that conservatives make a special exception for the biblical documents which are purported to speak beyond the confines of their original contextual boundaries because they are inspired by the Holy Spirit.

Revival of the Tradition and Evangelicalism

Evangelical historian Mark Noll declared in a recent interview, "What I would appeal for now is the development of an ability to let ancient Christian traditions provide norms for the more recent tradition — fundamentalist, Pentecostal, Holiness movements. We need to have a dialogue across the centuries."[39] He is not alone in this conviction. Over the course of the last decade, a growing number of Protestant evangelicals are no longer content to live with this isolation, relatively cut off from a spiritually rich and theologically fruitful heritage. Many of these have left their Free

38. See Robert Wilken, "The Durability of Orthodoxy," *Word and World* 8 (1988): 124-32, and P. Henry, "Why Is Contemporary Scholarship so Enamored of Ancient Heretics?" *Studia Patristica* 17 (1982): 123-26.
39. "Scandal? A Forum on the Evangelical Mind," interview with Mark Noll, Alister McGrath, Darrell Bock, and Richard Mouw, *Christianity Today,* 14 August 1995, 22.

Church settings for more "high church" oriented communions where orthodoxy is celebrated in historically sensitive settings. Through a series of steps leading from Campus Crusade for Christ to the Antiochian Orthodox church, Peter Gillquist with two hundred others were received as priests, deacons and laity in 1987. This was a process that Gillquist described as "a journey to the ancient Christian faith" by which he said they were returning to the original church.[40] Franky Schaeffer has likewise converted to Eastern Orthodoxy, having more radically repudiated the theology of "born-again" evangelicalism.[41] The same kind of yearning for the voices of ancient orthodox teaching and worship which has led some to the Orthodox Church brought Thomas Howard first to Anglicanism and then to Roman Catholicism, for which he was forced to resign his post at Gordon College.[42] A widespread movement in Wheaton College in the late 1970s and early 1980s, inspired by the conviction that evangelicalism needed to recognize its continuity with the church in history, caused a number of professors and students to follow the "Canterbury Trail."[43] Many of these formed or joined Episcopalian churches without eschewing their evangelicalism. Out of this movement came the "Chicago Call: An Appeal to Evangelicals," a gathering of forty-five evangelical intellectuals led by Robert Webber of Wheaton College. The group met in May 1977 and produced a document that urged fellow evangelicals to claim the fullness of the church through a recovery of the historic continuity with the great creeds, worship, views of creation and redemption, and spirituality of the ancient church.[44]

One ought not to have to leave the Free Church in order to embrace the norms of the ancient Christian Tradition. But the fact that so many

40. Gillquist chronicles the "journey" in *Becoming Orthodox*, rev. ed. (Ben Lomand, Calif.: Conciliar Press, 1992). An excellent summary and interpretation of evangelical Protestants turning to Greek Orthodoxy is provided by Timothy Weber, "Looking for Home: Evangelical Orthodoxy and the Search for the Original Church," in *New Perspectives on Historical Theology: Essays in Memory of John Meyendorff*, ed. B. Nassif (Grand Rapids: Eerdmans Publishing Company, 1996), 95-121.

41. Frank Schaeffer, *Dancing Alone: The Quest for Orthodox Faith in the Age of False Religion* (Brookline, Mass.: Holy Cross Orthodox Press, 1994).

42. See Howard's first-person account of his pilgrimage in *Evangelical Is Not Enough* (Nashville: Nelson, 1984).

43. Robert Webber, *Evangelicals on the Canterbury Trail: Why Evangelicals Are Attracted to the Liturgical Church* (Waco: Word Books, 1985).

44. R. Webber and D. Bloesch, eds., *The Orthodox Evangelicals: Who They Are and What They Are Saying* (Nashville: Nelson, 1978).

have left is indicative of the lack of hospitality which typically exists in Free Church communions toward the acknowledgement of such norms. Given the concerns for doctrinal fidelity and passion for fulfilling the "Great Commission" which exist within most evangelical communions, it can be reasonably argued that an agnostic position (or even antagonism) toward the classical standards of the church's patristic Tradition serves to undermine its own aims.

Particularly noteworthy is the work of Thomas Oden, a United Methodist and professor of theology at Drew University, who forsook Protestant liberalism after a sustained reading of the Fathers. Oden announced his new orientation in an article entitled "Then and Now: The Recovery of Patristic Wisdom"[45] with a personal confession:

> We have lived through a desperate game: the attempt to find some modern ideology, psychology or sociology that could conveniently substitute for the apostolic testimony. That game is all over. . . . No political project is more urgent for society than the recovery of classic Christian consciousness through the direct address of the texts of Scripture and Tradition.

Oden unpacked his perspective through a substantial revision of his 1979 book *Agenda for Theology* by attacking the presuppositions of modernity which he says have for so long denied the ability of the Christian past to speak to the present, arguing that these have translated theological methodology into a search for novelty and exaltation of faddism. This "diarrhea of religious accommodation" is itself proof that modernity is in the process of dissolution. We are seeing the end of an era in which the methods of criticism are being applied to itself, the hermeneutics of suspicion are used of the hermeneut himself.[46]

With the demise of modernity, Oden calls for a "post-critical orthodoxy" (or "postmodern orthodoxy") which seeks a sustained companionship with the ancient Christian teachers: "The patristic stones the modern builders rejected must now become the major blocks for rebuilding upon the Chief Cornerstone, the unique theandric person, Jesus Christ."[47] The way forward for theology is to return to the orthodoxy or "classical Chris-

---

45. In *The Christian Century* 107 (1990): 1164-68.
46. *After Modernity . . . What? Agenda for Theology* (Grand Rapids: Zondervan, 1990), 104.
47. *Ibid.*, 106.

tianity," established by seven ecumenical councils, which produced what Oden terms the Christian consensus of the first millennium, and which left a legacy that has been accepted by the entire church as normative for almost two millennia.[48] Most church historians, especially Protestant ones, would hardly accept the validity of all seven councils and their creeds with equal authority, just as Luther countenanced the decisions of no council after Chalcedon (451). To this conciliar consensus, Oden adds the eight great doctors of the early church, as well as others in the patristic, medieval and Reformation periods, who have been perennially valued for their contribution to the ecumenical faith.

I applaud Oden's attempt to get Protestant conservatives to drink deeply from the wellsprings of Christian doctrine. The fact that most literature of the early church is *terra incognita* to evangelical leaders, apart from secondhand citations from Augustine's *Confessions*, makes it imperative that they should be confronted with the words of the theologians, biblical exegetes and preachers of the first five centuries. Oden's three-volume systematic theology reiterates and demonstrates how essential the contribution of the early church is to the enterprise of postmodern theology.[49] But are evangelical Protestants able simply to make such a return to the past as Oden prescribes? To expose readers to the ancient texts of the church's Tradition is a valuable introductory step, though the question remains, how is this continuity with the past ages supposed to work? How are we, in the postmodern era, able to incorporate the patristic thought-world into our own without due regard for some hermeneutical guidelines? Surely there was a development in the church's construction of orthodoxy, a development which implies orthodoxy is not an artifact of the church's past which need only be claimed by the faithful today in a static fashion. Undoubtedly, Oden would agree with this. The orthodox "solution" is no more valuable for us today than *how* the church arrived at its orthodox solutions.

My purpose here is not to offer a critique of Oden's work except to say that his amalgamation of patristic, medieval and Reformation texts provides impressive evidence for his consensual model of the church's faith, though his "steady state" theory of orthodoxy — note the repeated quotations of Vin-

48. *Ibid.*, 37.
49. Thomas Oden, *The Living God: Systematic Theology* (San Francisco: Harper & Row, 1987). "This effort . . . wishes nothing more than to identify and follow that ancient ecumenical consensus of Christian teaching of God" (xi). See also the other two volumes, *The Word of Life* (1989) and *Life in the Spirit* (1992).

cent's dictum of orthodoxy[50] — leaves the reader with a number of interpretative problems which still need to be addressed in order for Free Church evangelicals to claim early church doctrine as a necessary component for their own renewal. A good illustration of the problem was evidenced at the 1995 meeting of the American Academy of Religion in Philadelphia, where a session on evangelicalism concerned itself with the topic of evangelicals and postmodernism. As an invited panel participant, Oden presented his program of renewal through the theology and biblical exegesis of the ancient Christian Tradition with great fervor and passion. It became clear, however, from the direction of the ensuing dialogue and questions that the audience, comprised mostly of evangelicals, was either not comprehending Oden's proposal or not perceiving that it was something relevant to their concerns.

In dialogue with Gnostic opponents who had access to the same sacred texts as catholics (or "mainline Christians"), the late second-century writer Tertullian appealed to what he called a *praescriptio,* or a "prior principle" that had to be first acknowledged before anyone could faithfully interpret the Bible or expound on a proper view of God. In a similar way, I want to submit that before most evangelicals and Free Church Christians can reasonably be expected to translate the legacy of the pre-Reformation church into regular preaching and teaching practice, we must first address some "prior principles" that have to do with the relation of Scripture, Tradition, and the church. Since Tradition is the one that so often sticks in the throat of so many evangelicals, we need to establish a working definition and show that the Tradition is not an addition to the Christian message; it *is* the message and prime carrier of the faith.

The Tradition and Traditions

When it comes to understanding the ecclesiastical concept of "tradition," perhaps the biggest difficulty is the tendency to confuse it with "traditionalism." In my undergraduate classes on early Christianity, this is the first misperception that I try to divest from my students' thinking. Most of

50. "Quod ubique, quod semper, quod ab omnibus creditum est" ("that which has been believed everywhere, always and by everyone"). Vincent, *Commonitory* II.6. Even within the context of the mid-fifth century, Vincent's approach was rather idealistic. This is most apparent by the fact that the *Commonitory* was in part a refutation of Augustine's theology of grace. Ironically, the principle of orthodoxy stated here stems, even if indirectly, from Augustine's *On the Usefulness of Belief* 14.30.

them imagine that "tradition" has to do with former ways of doing things that have become honored simply because they have occurred over a (long) period of time and have remained roughly the same. When the young person asks, "Why do we observe this tradition?" we respond with the unconvincing answer, "Because we always have." The word "tradition" is thus used to express that observance given to these practices, beliefs or methods which are passed down in static form from one generation to the next, whether they are meritworthy or not. It is not unlike our use of the word "custom." "Tradition" is therefore placed in the category of old, crusty, and recalcitrant — a lot like my first car, a four-speed Ford Pinto — and often contrasted with what is recent, stylish and innovative.

Nothing could be more deceptive. When Paul wrote the Thessalonians to "stand firm and hold on to the traditions we passed on to you" he was thinking of an active and living process (2 Thess. 2:15) that he urged his readers to continue. The very word *traditio* (or in Greek, *paradosis*),[51] means a transmission from one party to another, an exchange of some sort, implying living subjects. As we will explore more fully in the next chapter, the language of passing and receiving repeatedly expressed in the New Testament became the hallmark of the church's understanding of "tradition." Half a century later, we can hear Clement of Rome invoke the "holy rule of our tradition" with the same Pauline emphasis — not something *dead* handed *down*, but *living* being *handed over*.

Traditio is as much a verb *(tradere)* as a noun. It was *that* which Jesus "handed over" to the apostles, and they to the churches, but it also meant the very process of handing over. In the verbal sense, or what is called the active meaning, we should think of the church's Tradition as a dynamic; it is a movement by which the Christian faith was deposited, preserved and transmitted. Harkening again back to my undergraduate classes, I often make the analogy of this dynamic to a football game. At the signal, the center hikes the ball, the quarterback receives it, and passes or hands it off to another player who then receives it. The entire event, or "play," is completely dynamic given its interactive nature. This was no less true of the apostolic proclamation of Christ, whose "play" occurred in living communities. We cannot appreciate the nature of the church's Tradition until we are confronted with that vitality, that which the church prayed, sung, preached and celebrated. The Tradition was the church's life.

---

51. A *traditor*, from which comes our word "treason," was one who had handed over copies of the Scriptures to the authorities in times of persecution.

My use of the term "Tradition," with a capital "T," as distinct from "tradition(s)," is nothing new. Most scholars accept some variation of these basic categories[52] in order to delineate the one apostolic and patristic foundation which is the common history we have as Christians, one that is longer, larger, and richer than any of our separate and divided histories (as stated by the resolution accepted at the Third World Conference of Faith and Order, 1952, in Lund, Sweden). All earthly forms of the church, that is, the plethora of existing traditions, purport that they mirror in a substantial way the Tradition. For in every one of these traditions there is that "critical" element: "They all claim to be, or at least wish to be, the vehicle of something which is over or beyond them and prior to them — to be servants of the saving message of Christ . . . [whereas] the Tradition is the essence in all traditions. Without it they lose all their meaning and substance."[53]

In the final analysis, then, the Tradition denotes the acceptance and the handing over of God's Word, Jesus Christ *(tradere Christum),* and how this took concrete forms in the apostles' preaching *(kerygma),* in the Christ-centered reading of the Old Testament, in the celebration of baptism and the Lord's Supper, and in the doxological, doctrinal, hymnological and credal forms by which the declaration of the mystery of God Incarnate was revealed for our salvation. In both *act* and *substance,* the Tradition represents a living history which, throughout the earliest centuries, was constituted by the church and also constituted what was the true church.

The integral and fundamental nature of the Tradition is, as I have said earlier, implicit in most doctrinal systems of Free Churches, even

52. Since the late 1950s, the Faith and Order Commission of the World Council of Churches has convoked a series of symposia with the aim of defining the essentials of the apostolic faith as the basis for interdenominational dialogue. While evangelicals have rejected the political and religious activities of the World Council of Churches, the working papers that have emerged from the special assemblies held in Lund (1952), Montreal (1963), and Lima (1982) have proven to be quite sensitive to the need for an unambiguous orthodox faith in light of the church's early history without attempting to blur the real distinctions between different denominations. At the conference in Montreal, the Tradition was distinguished from "tradition," which is the process or event of handing down the church's faith, and from "traditions," which are the various denominational or affiliated groupings of the universal church.

53. K. E. Skydsgaard, "Tradition as an Issue in Contemporary Theology," in *The Old and the New in the Church,* World Council of Churches Commission on Faith and Order (Minneapolis: Augsburg Publishing, 1961), 29.

though many historic expressions of the Tradition are rejected or marginalized. Free Church traditions may rarely make mention of the Nicene or Nicene-Constantinopolitan Creeds, or even the Apostles' Creed, or the teaching of the Fathers, and yet ironically the essentials of their Christology or theology of creation, or concept of original sin, or eschatology — in effect, the means of all biblical interpretation — are dependent upon this body of the Church's Tradition, or what Hilary of Poitiers called upon all pastors to preserve: "the right and catholic faith." Of course the problem has been that for some churches, the content of the Tradition is said to be much more extensive, involving liturgical practices, sacramental life, canon law and church orders. In part, this was the cause of the sixteenth-century Reformation and was the reason why the recovery of the ancient consensual doctrine lay at the heart of the "Protestant" desire to reform the church. What came out of the Reformation was not the abrogation of the Tradition in principle or reality, but a reassessment of what should constitute its form.

Change and Continuity

This last point leads us to consider a final element of the Tradition's dynamic nature. If it is true that the Tradition is what it is because of its active development within concrete, living communities, then the Tradition will itself be a construction of how the church addresses its present circumstances by utilizing what it has received. In other words, the Tradition is always in process of dialoguing with itself as it encounters each new crisis that confronted the church in history. Here I want to invoke again Alasdair MacIntyre and his theory of tradition, which he describes as an "argument extended through time in which certain fundamental agreements are defined and redefined in terms of two kinds of conflict: those with critics and enemies external to the tradition . . . and those internal, interpretative debates through which the meaning and rationale of the fundamental agreements come to be expressed and by whose progress a tradition is constituted."[54] Applying MacIntyre's definition to the early church,

---

54. Alasdair MacIntyre, *Whose Justice? Which Rationality?* (Notre Dame: Notre Dame University Press, 1988), 12. I am indebted to H. Jefferson Powell's study of MacIntyre's thought in *The Moral Tradition of American Constitutionalism: A Theological Interpretation* (Durham: Duke University Press, 1993).

one can readily see in the writing of the apologists and later theologians how the internal debates of "heresy" as well as the attacks of Roman paganism contributed to the formulation and reformulation of the church's teaching as it adapted its message as expressed in the Tradition. To take seriously the historical character of the Tradition means that it was received and handed on within concrete, temporal situations where the present was informed by and made intelligible by the past, and so incorporated into the church's ongoing understanding of God and its response to God. Both consensus and disputation make faithful reformulation possible. Without consensus, disputation degenerates into sectarianism and fragmentation; without disputation, consensus can easily lapse into an intractable authoritarianism.

The Tradition therefore is a matter of both *continuity* and *change,* and of development on the basis of the Tradition's past that leads to revision of that past in the present. This is the very reason why there are a number of ecclesiastical creeds before the sixth century. They are, in effect, milestones of the Tradition's argument with itself about the nature of orthodoxy as new doctrinal issues had to be addressed in light of what the church had always believed. As the faith was *de facto* a reflection of the living Tradition, so it would always be, in a certain sense, in an internal process of progression. Any invocation of the Vincentian canon of faith, "everywhere, always, and by everyone," must be viewed in this light, and not as a static equation of petrified orthodoxy.

Once we acknowledge that the Tradition is a matter of continuity and change, the door is always open for a renewal or reformation of that Tradition. Change is not a rejection of the continuity, but evidence of the fact that orthodoxy is achieved through both forces as Christians continue to ask what it means to be faithful to the apostolic teaching in each new age. The implications of this model for understanding the Tradition should be obvious by now. Since course correction is inherent to the dynamic of the church's Tradition, there is no need to cast the Reformation and the age of the Fathers into the roles of conflicting histories. The story of Protestantism is a redirection, not rejection, of the ancient ecumenical faith, an event entirely within the keeping of the faithful pliability of orthodoxy. And there can be no faithful Protestantism without the Tradition, even as the certain dimensions of the Tradition were reconfigured to an extent by Protestantism. No one can doubt that the Protestant Reformation posed breach points in the continuity of the church's Tradition, though it has been observed more than once that the points of that breach eventually had more to do with the sacramental and sacerdotal accretions that had developed in medieval Catholicism. More importantly, that same Reformation sought, by the Spirit's guidance, to vivify the church's Tradition through the points of faithful continuity.

Let me conclude this chapter by assuring the reader who is concerned that reception of the church's early Tradition means undermining the cardinal principles of their Reformational heritage such as "justified by faith alone," or the Scripture principle. We should not be blind to the fact that various doctrines have been put forth in the name of "tradition" that have no warrant in Scripture or in the consensual teaching of the church. But conservative Protestants have too quickly responded by throwing the (Roman Catholic) baby out with the (Tradition) bathwater. Or to use another metaphor, it is not necessary to act, as some later Protestants did, by jettisoning the guidance of the Tradition in order to escape the gravity of later corruptions or innovations of the gospel. As a result of these attitudes and practices, the evangelical spirit in its quest for articulating faithfulness to the apostolic message in each age has been cut off from a crucial part of its own identity. Luther without Augustine, Calvin without Ambrose, Zwingli without Chrysostom, Hoffman without Athanasius, and Menno Simons without Cyprian will only produce a fragmented and distorted picture of the church's theology and cannot do justice to the full treasury of the evangelical heritage.

CHAPTER 2

The Earliest Formation of the Christian Tradition

Our forefathers are witnesses of the entry of God into history. It is the fact of the appearance of Jesus Christ nineteen hundred years ago . . . that directs our gaze back to the ancients and raises in our minds the question of our historical inheritance.

Dietrich Bonhoeffer, *On the Jews*

I felt I had to write and urge you to contend for the faith that was once for all entrusted to the saints.

Jude 3

The authors of the New Testament did not write in a vacuum. Inspired by the Holy Spirit, who was the source of their originality and conviction, they were acutely aware that they were part of a continuum of preaching and teaching that stemmed back to Jesus and to the Old Testament prophets. The prologue to Luke's Gospel makes it clear that before the good doctor had begun to write, integrated summaries of Jesus' sayings and deeds were already circulating, since "many have undertaken to compile an account of things accomplished among us" (1:1). John too was only skimming the surface of available material and memories circulating among the earliest Christian communities; he observes twice that there existed many other deeds and interpretations of Jesus beyond what he penned (John 20:30; 21:25).

Of course the apostolic writers themselves added to the extent and shape of the gospel message given that their claim of firsthand exposure to the historical Jesus carried the highest authority (Gal. 1:11; 1 John 1:1-3). The apostolic pedigree rested on the fact that these men were the living media between Jesus and a knowledge of his words and deeds. Their testimonies became the basis of the Tradition which lay at the heart of the worshiping and didactic life of the churches. Like Polaroid shots of the church's living faith taken over a fifty-year period or so, the New Testament represents those still "moments" of the Tradition, captured in written form for the benefit of all subsequent generations of Christians.

What I want to do in this chapter is show first that the formation of the Christian Tradition, based as it was on the apostolic *kerygma* (preaching), was prior to and completely indigenous to the development of the New Testament, and secondly, show how the Tradition operated in the earliest church communities as witnessed through the New Testament documents themselves. There is nothing intentionally provocative in this twin thesis, and what follows may well be familiar to many readers. Nonetheless, it will become evident in this chapter and in chapter 3 that the tension often posed by evangelical writers between a canonical text and an extracanonical tradition has been exaggerated to the point of distortion, indebted to a subsequently dogmatic agenda rather than to the details of church history. For it is in the apostolic age that the language and category of "tradition" has its beginnings. A review of this process and how the Tradition both shaped and was shaped by the first and second generations of Christians is in order.

No matter how high a view of Scripture one accepts, the nonliterary and traditioned character of the original gospel has to be taken into account when reconstructing the beginnings of Christian thought and practice. Both evangelical Protestant and Roman Catholic scholars have long agreed that an oral tradition existed and preceded the editing of the Gospels.[1] "It was declared at first by the Lord," says the writer of the Hebrews,

---

1. F. F. Bruce, *Tradition: Old and New* (Grand Rapids: Zondervan, 1970), 39f.; Y. M.-J. Congar, *Tradition and Traditions: An Historical and Theological Essay* (New York: Macmillan Company, 1966), 8ff.

"and attested by us who heard him" (Heb. 2:3). Various modes of activity within the early church accounted for the preservation, shaping and transmission of the gospel tradition — preaching, controversy, worship and instruction — nicely summarized by F. F. Bruce.[2] These modes have been the subject of much inquiry, especially by "form-critical" and "source-critical" studies within German scholarship, into the origins of the New Testament documents as well as the religious life of the early communities. Long before there were written accounts, the "Christ-event" in its different versions provided the first followers of Jesus with the content of their mission and their unique identity. Evangelicals have often opposed some of the presuppositions of historical-critical scholarship, especially the view that the earliest preaching of Jesus' words and deeds had their origin in the needs and aspirations of the infant church rather than in the historical Jesus. With good reason has the old German liberal school been criticized for underestimating the abiding interest in historicity on the part of the early church when it came to Jesus. Surely the first Christians had strong motivation for preserving with the utmost care and exactitude the *memoria* of their Lord. The issue then is not rejecting historical criticism *in totum* but determining which methods will enable us to discern how the oral *kerygma* was faithfully transmitted over the years in its different forms and utilizing various sources.

Linking Old and New

The work of Birger Gerhardsson[3] has made an effective case for how the transmission of the written and oral Torah in Judaism set the precedent for early Christianity's delivery of the gospel tradition. Jesus' disciples faithfully preserved the teaching of their Master just as disciples of rabbis preserved theirs. In effect, the disciples became the first link in the chain of tradition — the one between Jesus and his disciples — a relationship characterized by instruction given and received. Lest we forget, there were no tape-recorders, video equipment, or a team of stenographers following Je-

2. Bruce, *Tradition*, 58-71.
3. Birger Gerhardsson, *Memory and Manuscript: Oral Tradition and Written Transmission in Rabbinic Judaism and Early Christianity* (Uppsala and Lund: C. W. K. Gleerup, 1961); *Tradition and Transmission in Early Christianity* (Lund: C. W. K. Gleerup, 1964); *The Origins of the Gospel Traditions* (Philadelphia: Fortress Press, 1977).

sus around. Whereas we may wonder how the oral transmission of Jesus' words and deeds could have been preserved with any accuracy for the decades before the writing of the Gospels, Gerhardsson points to the rabbinic pedagogical methods of the first four centuries of our era where the techniques of memorization, repetition and recitation were utilized in oral instruction. This was the primary means by which teaching was received, preserved, and handed on for others to do the same. It is not certain how closely Jesus and his disciples may have emulated the rabbinic style,[4] but reconstructed parallels from the late first and second centuries strongly suggest a proximity of practice. Nor is the active exercise of such methods ruled out by the probable existence of brief written summaries of Jesus' *logia* and *acta* which were already available by Luke's day.[5]

In our text-oriented culture, the idea of attributing significant authority to the oral transmission of important truths may seem completely unreliable, if not irresponsible. However, the dynamic nature of the Jesus tradition in its dissemination was no less a part of the church's faith development as was the use of written texts. Almost a century after the historical Jesus, the principle of oral succession was still regarded authoritatively. In a work unfortunately now lost, Papias (pastor of Hierapolis) is quoted by a later historian as saying, "I did not consider that I got so much profit from the contents of books as from the word of a living and surviving voice."[6] His comment does not imply that oral teaching was superior to the written, or that there were other sayings of Jesus not in the apostolic preaching that should be added, but it reinforces the idea that the early

---

4. Gerhardsson has been criticized for assuming that the memorization tactics of the rabbinical schools in the Tannaitic period (after the destruction of the temple in A.D. 70) were normative in the time of Jesus. He attempts to answer some of his critics, such as Jacob Neusner, in *Tradition and Transmission in Early Christianity.*

5. Luke 1:1. The existence of a written source "Q" of the synoptic Gospels that contained the sayings of Jesus is widely reputed, though still disputed. For a recent statement on the value of "Q" in historical Jesus research, see James M. Robinson, "The Real Jesus of the Sayings Gospel Q," *Princeton Seminary Bulletin* 18 (1997): 135-51. The hypothetical nature of "Q" document(s) is not beyond serious criticism, although arrangement of the Gospel of Thomas into a collection of sayings lends validity to the existence of such sources. There is also a reputed collection of miracle stories ("miracle source") which circulated presenting Jesus as a great miracle-worker. P. J. Achtemeier, "The Origin and Function of the Pre-Marcan Catenae," *Journal of Biblical Literature* 91 (1972): 198-221.

6. Quoted from his *Expositions of the Oracles of the Lord* by Eusebius of Caesarea in *Ecclesiastical History* III.39.4. Cf. C. E. Hill, "What Papias Said about John (and Luke): A 'New' Fragment," *Journal of Theological Studies* 49 (1998): 622-24.

church recognized how the unwritten testimony stood prior to documents, and that the documents were valued precisely because they were held to enshrine the preaching of the Tradition.

This was essentially the process of canonization for the New Testament. A writing was deemed canonical not solely, not even primarily, because of its apostolic authorship, for there was a multitude of books circulating by the middle of the second century which claimed apostolic origin. Some of the most popular of these were the Gospels of Thomas or Peter, and the Acts of John.[7] Canonicity was, from the beginning, a theological principle inherent to the church's Tradition; the "canon" (i.e., rule) of the church's faith was not a set of authoritative texts, but an authoritative teaching. Those texts which mirrored the canon (rule) of this faith, and had been received within the orthodox churches, were regarded as canonical.[8] Of course, given the active and unfolding character of the Tradition within living communities, we should expect that there was not entire agreement on the status of certain documents which had been received in some churches as canonical (such as Hebrews or James).[9] Moreover, other books reputedly written by those who were disciples of the apostles carried significant weight. Documents such as the *Shepherd of Hermas,* the *Epistle of Barnabas* and the *Didache* are treated in some early catalogues of scriptural texts as canonically received books. Eventually, these were accepted as deserving to be read in church, but not of the same status as the others. Governing the process was the gradual and hard-to-chronicle process of agreement among the churches about those texts which conformed to the principle of canonicity, as reckoned according to the canon or rule of faith. This principle of canonicity becomes more pronounced in the late second-century writings of Irenaeus, who struggled with the problem of refuting Gnostic interpretations of Scripture: "Even if the apostles had not left their writings to us, ought we not to follow the rule [canon] of the tradition which they handed down to those to whom they committed the churches?"[10]

---

7. Such texts are part of the collection commonly called the New Testament Apocrypha. See M. R. James, *The Apocryphal New Testament* (Oxford: Clarendon Press, 1924), and W. Schneemelcher and R. M. Wilson, eds., *The New Testament Apocrypha* (Philadelphia: Westminster Press, 1965).

8. E.g., Jerome, *Epistle* 129.3.

9. See Bruce Metzger, *The Canon of the New Testament* (Oxford: Clarendon Press, 1987), and F. F. Bruce, *The Canon of Scripture* (Downers Grove, Ill.: InterVarsity Press, 1988).

10. Irenaeus, *Against Heresies* III.4.1.

The most crucial point to make about the ongoing existence of an oral tradition or a shared understanding of theological canonicity is that these were not a set of theoretical principles expounded in an atmosphere of intellectual detachment, as the last part of Irenaeus's statement makes clear. Such concepts were, in practice, indissolubly hinged to the believing, worshiping, and responsive life of the churches. For "tradition," by its very name and existence, implies the "activity of the church living its belief and consequently elaborating it."[11] The *lex credendi* was not something received and transmitted in isolation from its exercise within the *lex orandi*, and vice-versa. There was no assembly of ecclesiastical officials or scholarly "think-tank" that laid down a slate of beliefs from on high, and then proceeded to hoist it upon the churches as worthy of their acceptance. Unlike the king in *Alice in Wonderland* who arbitrarily invented "Rule Forty-Two" in order to manipulate the proceedings of his court, the very nature of the Tradition, in all its tangible embodiments, reveals that it was completely indigenous to and developed within the beginnings of Christianity. It was not constructed as a kind of afterthought as an artificial means of enforcing uniformity.

Interpreting the Old Testament

The form of the Christian Tradition was developed after the pattern of its Jewish parent. This is most obvious in the church's claim on the Old Testament as its rightful Scripture according to the belief that God had acted and revealed himself in history through the Logos (Word) of God, Jesus Christ. Jewish tradition had served as the primary hermeneutic for interpreting Scripture and providing methods of application of the Law. What marked the unique entry of the gospel tradition was the christological interpretation of this Scripture and history. The preaching of Jesus himself had prompted this approach as seen, for example, in Luke 24:25-27: "Beginning with Moses and all the prophets, he explained to them what was said in all the Scriptures concerning Himself." It is understood here that Jesus laid claim to the whole of Hebrew Scripture as an explication of his person and mission. Both a sacred text and a hermeneutic informed the new church's teaching, and in this sense Geiselmann is correct to say, "If it is true that there has never been a Gospel without *paradosis* [i.e., tradi-

11. Congar, *Tradition and Traditions*, 5.

46

tion], it is equally the case that there was never an apostolic kerygma without Scripture."[12]

When Peter preached his first sermon in Acts 2, the earliest followers of Jesus were already drawing upon the Old Testament and utilizing a method of reading that Scripture. Repeatedly the apostle draws upon the texts of the prophets or the Psalms to substantiate his message that "in these last days" God performed wonders and signs through Jesus of Nazareth, who was delivered to death on a cross and was raised from the dead. The Hebrew king and prophet David himself spoke of the resurrection of the Messiah in Psalm 16:8-11, which Peter quotes (as Luke cites it) in order to vindicate his point that the sufferings and victorious redemption of Christ were new only in their occurrence but not in their acknowledgment by the writers of Scripture.

In all these instances, the texts of the Hebrew Bible were to be accepted as fundamental axioms for discerning divine truth. Used properly, they would lead the inquirer to a knowledge of the Messiah, Jesus, and culminate in the sequence of repentance, baptism and receiving the gift of the Holy Spirit (Acts 2:38; 3:19). It was through the reading of Isaiah 53:7-8 that the missionary Philip "preached Jesus" to the Ethiopian official who was sitting in his chariot (Acts 8:35). The Old Testament functioned like a prophetic map with the express purpose of uncovering what it revealed about the person and work of Jesus. As Christ was the very transformation of history, it was through his person that Christian believers assigned a definite meaning to all that had happened before the incarnation and all that will ever happen. It is on this basis, for example, that Justin (Christian philosopher and martyr of the second century) built his argument for the two advents of Christ:

> Since we prove that all things which have already happened had been predicted by the prophets before they came to pass, we must necessarily believe also that those things which are in like manner predicted, but are yet to come to pass, shall certainly happen. . . . For the prophets have proclaimed two advents of His: the one, that which is already past, when he came as a dishonored and suffering man, but the second, when, according to prophecy, He shall come from heaven with glory. . . .[13]

---

12. J. R. Geiselmann, *The Meaning of Tradition* (New York: Herder and Herder, 1966), 23.

13. Justin Martyr, *Apology* I.52 (trans. in Ante-Nicene Fathers, I.180).

There was no doubt that there existed a prophetic and historical continuity between the Old Testament and the apostolic preaching. The point of difference lay in the new Christian hermeneutic: the tradition of Torah was replaced with that of Jesus as the Messiah.

It was possible to find any central truth pertaining to the Christian faith in the pages of the Old Testament provided that one used the "lens" of the apostolic Tradition to read it. Should any conflict arise in the interpretation of the Scripture on points of doctrine, as often did among Christians, there was but one court of appeal. About A.D. 110, Ignatius of Antioch wrote the church in Philadelphia as he journeyed to Rome: "When I heard some people saying 'If I don't find it in the original documents [i.e., Old Testament], I don't believe it in the Gospel' I answered them, 'But it is written there.' They retorted, 'That's just the question.' To my mind it is Jesus Christ who is the original documents. The inviolable archives are his cross and death and his resurrection and the faith that came by him."[14] Any impasse encountered in scriptural hermeneutics was to be arbitrated by the rule of the gospel Tradition.

Jesus and the Language of Tradition

The New Testament contains numerous allusions to the Jewish tradition and to the terminology of the traditioning process. When the apostle Paul made his defense before the Jewish leaders in Rome, he declared that he had done nothing to violate "the customs of our fathers" (Acts 28:17). He uses the same comprehensive designation in Gal. 1:14 in describing his former life in Judaism and how he was extremely zealous for the "traditions of my fathers." As a former Pharisee, Paul is doubtlessly referring to the same authoritative tradition which Josephus declares the Pharisees, along with other Jewish sects, preserved and observed "by succession from their fathers" (*Antiquitates Judaicae* XIII.x.6).

In the Gospels, specific mention of the Jewish tradition is made in two parallel passages in reference to mealtime and purification customs. Some Pharisees and teachers of the Law from Jerusalem accused the disciples of eating without having ceremoniously washed their hands, thus breaking the "tradition of the elders" (*paradosin ton presbuteron*) (Mark 7:3; Matt. 15:2). A quasi-technical language of tradition is displayed in the

14. Ignatius, *To the Philadelphians* 8.2.

Markan account: "to maintain" (7:3); "to receive" (7:4); "walk/live according to" (7:5), and "to pass on" (7:13), all pertaining to the scrupulous care that the Jews were to show for "the tradition of the fathers."

It was this reverence for one's ancestors that made Judaism tolerable in the Romans' eyes, despite its monotheism. The golden rule for acceptable religion in the Graeco-Roman world is invoked by the Pagan interlocuter Caelius in the *Octavius* (c. A.D. 200): "As a general principle, the greater the age that ceremonies and shrines accumulate, the more hallowed these institutions become."[15] In an age that prized antiquity as the key criterion for intellectual reliability and social propriety, the Jewish linking of its identity to ancient traditions often helped mitigate, though not erase, Roman suspicion and persecution. For this very reason, Christian apologists would eventually argue that even though the coming of Jesus is a recent event, the testimony and arrangements for his appearing in the Old Testament are of ancient vintage. From an apologetical stance, at least, the Old Testament provided nascent Christianity with critical vindication for claiming ancient origination.

Why was Jesus so disparaging of the Jewish tradition? What did he mean by citing Isaiah 29:13[16] and accusing the Jewish leaders of letting go the commandments of God in order to hold on to the "traditions of men" (7:8)? Part of the Protestant suspicion of "tradition" is related to its various uses in the New Testament, especially the fact that Jesus' only references to the word are in a negative context. However, it would be faulty to see in these isolated remarks a general commentary on the role of oral tradition, or a conflict over the authority of text versus tradition.[17] There is no doubt that Jesus was criticizing the oral tradition, but his words were not a blanket condemnation of tradition as mere legalism which needed only to be

15. Minucius Felix, *Octavius* 6. The sentiment expressed by Minucius unmistakably echoes Cicero's influential dialogue, *On the Nature of the Gods,* in which traditional authority ought positively to persuade anyone who is skeptical of the existence of the gods.

16. "These people come near to me with their mouth and honor me with their lips, but their hearts are far from me. Their worship of me is made up only of rules taught by men."

17. See W. Lane, *The Gospel according to Mark,* New International Commentary Series (Grand Rapids: Eerdmans Publishing Company, 1974), who describes Jesus' reaction as a categorical rejection of the authority of oral law (p. 249). For C. S. Mann, Jesus is making a differentiation of the Law and the oral tradition, or human exigencies. *Mark,* The Anchor Bible Commentary Series (New York: Doubleday, 1986), 311.

rejected.[18] A systematic means of interpreting and applying the Law was inevitable, and Jesus stood the closest to the Pharisees (as opposed to the Sadducees) in the implicit admission of such a hermeneutic. In this instance, however, their interpretation of what constitutes "clean" and "unclean" demonstrated to Jesus that their tradition did not grasp the reality behind the legal precept. It was, in effect, a dead tradition, stultifying religious life rather than invigorating it. To be clean or not was foremost a matter internal to the human heart.

With the same point in mind, Jesus criticized another inert element of the oral tradition:

> For Moses said, "Honor your father and mother" [Exod. 20:12; Deut. 5:16], and, "Whoever curses his father or mother must be put to death" [Exod. 21:17; Lev. 20:9]. But you say that if a man says to his father or mother, "Whatever help you might otherwise have received from me is Corban" (that is, a gift devoted to God), then you no longer let him do anything for his father or mother. Thus you nullify the word of God by your tradition that you have handed down. (Mark 7:10-13)

What attracted Jesus' censure was an interpretation that allowed a man to avoid the duty of caring for his parents if he could claim that the resources which he might have used for that purpose were already "Corban." This application of the Law that vows made to God must by all means be fulfilled was allowed to abrogate the weightier obligation laid down in the fifth commandment. In this instance, the pharisaic tradition was not drawn up in conjunction with the teaching of the Law, and therefore found in conflict with the Mosaic precept. His own words serve not as a rejection but as a *corrective* of the oral tradition, for which Jesus introduced an understanding more in conjunction with the precepts of the Law's intent. To claim Jesus is overthrowing tradition in a wholesale fashion is a failure to appreciate sufficiently the Jewishness of Jesus' heritage, and to miss the point that Jesus' usual approach in his teaching was the inculcation of his religious culture with the redeeming message of the kingdom of God, not its abrogation.

---

18. The influential *Theological Dictionary of the New Testament* takes a decidedly (and predictably) negative view of Jesus' Jewish view of tradition (II.172), i.e., it was the legalistic accretion of the Pharisees toward the Torah which Jesus rejected.

Paul and the Jesus Tradition

It is not coincidental that Paul turned out to be the chief architect of a language of tradition for the church. Having been educated in Jerusalem under Gamaliel the Elder (Acts 22:3), he was thoroughly trained in the Law and was thereafter zealous to follow the "traditions of my fathers" (Gal. 1:4). Through his epistles, Paul either introduced or, more likely, expanded upon a terminology that articulated the process by which a uniquely Christian "tradition" was developed. While preserving the essential structure of the Jewish principle of "tradition," Paul brought new life into it by making it the vehicle of the gospel wherein Jesus Christ became both its content and the principle of its origin (authority).

According to Paul, the church possessed by his time a normative standard which he refers to as the *paradosis* (1 Cor. 11:2; 2 Thess. 2:15). He speaks of himself having "received" *(paralambano)* it from the Lord, using the dynamic language of the traditioning process, with which he also "delivered" *(paradidomi)* to his readers (1 Cor. 11:23; 15:3). Throughout the course of his correspondence, Paul shows that he was familiar with various teachings of Jesus, and he makes five explicit references to the "words of the Lord" (1 Cor. 7:10-11; 9:14; 11:23-26; 14:37; 1 Thess. 4:15-17), as well as a negative statement in 1 Cor. 7:25 that he has "no command from the Lord in regard to the unmarried."[19] Exactly how Paul came by his knowledge of Jesus' words is not clear, apart from his admission of having once met with the Apostles Peter and James immediately after his experience in the Arabian desert (Gal. 1:18). It is apparent therefore that these orally transmitted *logia* had already begun to shape the church's message and practice. Overall, scholars have found that Paul's understanding of the content of "tradition" is readily divided into three categories: kerygmatic tradition, church tradition, and ethical tradition.[20]

19. The teaching represented by each one of these can be found, directly or obliquely, in the canonical Gospels: (1) 1 Cor. 7:10-11 — Matt. 5:32; 19:3-9 (cf. Mark 10:2-12), Luke 16:18; (2) 1 Cor. 9:14 — Matt. 10:10 (cf. Luke 10:7); (3) 1 Cor. 11:23-26 — Matt. 26:26-28, Mark 14:22-24, Luke 22:17-20 (cf. 1 Cor. 10:16); (4) 1 Cor. 14:37 — Paul is not citing any specific teaching from the Lord here except to say that his instructions for proclamation in the church are directly dependent upon it and therefore should be received as authoritative; (5) 1 Thess. 4:15-17 — echoes may be found in the eschatalogical passages of Matt. 24:30-31and Luke 21:27-28, though Paul seems to be drawing on an otherwise unknown part of Jesus' teaching.

20. James D. G. Dunn, *Unity and Diversity in the New Testament: An Inquiry into*

Before we consider each of these categories, it is worth asking what Paul meant by the words "I received from the Lord" (cf. 1 Cor. 11:23). Because of his admission in Gal. 1:16 that he had come to know the Lord Jesus Christ through a personal revelation, and that he became an apostle "not through the agency of man but through the Lord Jesus Christ" (Gal. 1:1), the tendency has been to turn the apostle into something of a "lone ranger" when it comes to his version of the gospel message. The indication that Paul received the gospel through revelation would seem to negate the idea that the Tradition was the primary basis of his preaching. His remarks to the Galatians, that after his conversion on the Damascus road "I did not immediately consult with flesh and blood, nor did I go up to Jerusalem to those who were apostles before me, but I went away to Arabia" (1:16-17), bear out the fact that Paul attributed his calling as an apostle "set apart" to divine revelation. While Paul mentions this experience nowhere else in his extant correspondence, it is clear from the first chapter of Galatians that he had sustained heavy attacks on his authority as an apostle, making it necessary for him to defend the prophetic prerogative which had been bestowed on him by divine action (1:1, 11-17). His retreat into "Arabia," with no regard to the reception of the other apostles, further vindicated his calling in a manner strongly (purposely?) reminiscent of the prophet Elijah (1 Kings 17). But was his isolated experience in the desert the "received" source for his subsequent preaching that Jesus was the Son of God?[21]

In the first place, the gospel which Paul had received without mediation consisted in the revelation not of a set of facts, but of a person: "to reveal His Son in me, in order that I might preach him among the gentiles" (Gal. 1:16). Exactly what happened to Paul in Arabia is unknown, but it should not be overemphasized, following the apostle's own lead. In the book of Acts, Paul several times recounts his conversion experience (Acts 9, 22, and 26) without once mentioning it. Moreover, the chronology of events supplied in Acts allows a certain ambiguity concerning the time Paul spent in Damascus *before* he went into Arabia. Acts 9:19-22 tells us that Paul spent an unknown number of days ("certain days") with the disciples in that city, and immediately he began "to proclaim Jesus in the synagogues, saying 'He is the Son of God'" (cf. 26:20). It was also during this same time that the new convert was

---

the *Character of Earliest Christianity* (Philadelphia: Westminster Press, 1977), 66. A very similar scheme was established by R. P. C. Hanson in his *Tradition in the Early Church* (London: SCM Press, 1962), 10ff.

21. As Donald Guthrie hypothesizes in *The Apostles* (Grand Rapids: Zondervan, 1975), 75.

baptized (9:18). His messianic preaching had an immediate impact, and Saul himself is said to have increased in his proclamational abilities such that he consistently refuted his Jewish adversaries (9:22). All of this seems to have taken place prior to the Arabian interval which should be sandwiched in between Acts 9:22 and 23, whereafter Paul is said to have returned to Damascus[22] and later to Jerusalem (9:26). The implication is that Paul first "received" the gospel of the Christ who died, was buried, and rose on the third day within the context of the believing community where he was baptized and initially tutored in the faith.

In the second place, there is no need to propound a tension between the gospel as revelation and the gospel as Tradition. For Paul, there would have been only an artificial distinction between the two, since what was derived from the earthly Jesus and transmitted through the apostles was at the same time continuously validated by the exalted Lord who appeared to him. The result is that revelation and the Tradition are but two sides of one coin.[23] Thus, the Tradition was not only not antithetical to the inspirational process from which the New Testament evolved, but the gospel Tradition was a critical means by which the risen Lord had imparted his revelation through the working of the Spirit.

Certainly whatever Paul had acquired through special revelation was authenticated and expanded upon by the apostolic testimony that he learned of in Jerusalem from Peter and James (Gal. 1:18). This was doubtlessly a crucial part of Paul's message (1 Cor. 15.2ff.), being in the same vein as the Thessalonians who are said to have "received" *(paralambano)* the word of God's message from him, "not as the word of men, but for what it really is, the word of God, which also performs its work in you who believe" (1 Thess. 2:13). Both Paul and they were a part of the continuum of God's living Tradition in which they were called and in which they now stood. So Paul exhorts the Thessalonians to "stand firm and hold fast *(kratein)* to the traditions *(paradoseis)* which you were taught, whether by word of mouth or by letter from us" (2 Thess. 2:15).

(1) Kerygmatic tradition. It is apparent that this foundational element of the Tradition has to do with those summaries of the Christian message, focused

---

22. Gal. 1:17 does not say how long Paul spent in Arabia, only that he returned "once more" to Damascus.

23. Bruce, *Tradition,* 31-32, based on Oscar Cullmann's *The Early Church* (London: SCM Press, 1956), 66ff.

on the death and resurrection of Christ. Such a confessional summary is at work in Paul's discussion of sin and grace in Rom. 6:4, and located in "that pattern of teaching to which you were committed" (6:17). But the outstanding example of the Tradition's dynamism is found in 1 Cor. 15, where Paul reminds the Corinthians of the gospel which he preached to them, "which also you received *(paralambano),* in which also you stand" (v. 1). They had "received" what Paul himself had received and accordingly "delivered" *(paradidomi)* to them, namely, "that Christ died for our sins according to the Scriptures, and that He was buried, and that he was raised on the third day according to the Scriptures" (15:3-4). Here I must again resort to my football analogy in order to stress the interactive and processional nature of this language. Like the ball in motion, there is nothing static about the process as the apostolic preaching took concretized forms of confessional synopses and expressions of Christian worship that were "received" by the Corinthian congregation. Along with the process, the "kerygmatic tradition" also had a content of which Paul allows us a glimpse, besides providing a list of resurrection appearances (vv. 5-7).

Paul was not oblivious to the differences of nuance and emphasis in the apostolic preaching. As the "apostle to the gentiles," he was already acquainted with the fact that a certain amount of tension existed within the apostolic "pillars" over the substance of the preaching and its ethical demands (Acts 15; Gal. 2:11ff.). He was acutely aware that as one who was "untimely born" and "last of all" among the apostles (1 Cor. 15:8), he was bringing his own contributions to the articulation of the apostolic preaching. Nevertheless, Paul makes the important argument that there is a cohesiveness in the message which the Corinthians received: "Whether then it was I or they, so we preach and so you believed" (1 Cor. 15:11). Despite the diversity inherent among the Christian communities, and even among the apostles themselves, he can speak of an essential kerygmatic tradition which acted as a unifying strand linking the preaching and different churches together.[24]

(2) **Church tradition.** When Paul discusses the Lord's Supper in 1 Cor. 11 we encounter the fullest citation of Jesus' words, which Paul prefaces with the words, "I received from the Lord that which I also delivered to you" (11:23).[25] The expressions of oral tradition here are indisputable:

---

24. Dunn, *Unity and Diversity,* 70.

25. Paul goes on, "that the Lord Jesus in the night in which he was betrayed took bread, and when he had given thanks, He broke it, and said, 'This is my body, which is

paralambano (received) and *paradidomi* (delivered), implying that while the ultimate authority for the tradition is the Lord ("from the Lord"), the words of this institution had become the common property of the believing church and are the source of Paul's "receiving." But this element of the church's tradition had not remained stationary. The sequence of bread and cup is the same as that purported in the synoptic Gospels, though Paul's account demonstrates that both a certain amount of conflation and glossing has occurred, perhaps reflecting congregational practice. Whether Paul had made these alterations, or whether the words were already a part of what he had "received," is hard to tell. Paul's version most closely resembles the Gospel of Luke (22:19-20)[26] though he omits the words in the taking of the cup, "which is poured out for you," and he adds the phrase, "do this in remembrance of me," after the taking of the bread. It is quite likely that the parallel endings of bread and cup reflect liturgical usage and not simply Paul's own design.

(3) **Ethical tradition.** Paul uses the language of tradition just as frequently for corporate and personal Christian living as he does for matters of Christian belief. To the faithful in Colossae he writes, "Just as you have received [*paralambano*] Christ Jesus as Lord, continue to live in Him" (Col. 2:6). He sharply contrasts the Jesus tradition which they have been taught from "human traditions and the basic principles of this world," since the latter are based upon hollow and deceptive philosophy rather than on Christ (2:8). Instead, Paul draws heavily upon the life of Jesus as the model for a believer's deportment. Besides actual references to Jesus' statements (1 Cor. 7:10; 9:14), Paul, in numerous instances, entreats his readers to imitate his own conduct because he is imitating Christ (1 Cor. 4:16; 11:1; Eph. 4:20-21; Phil. 2:5; 4:9). As one who "delivers" the Christian teaching, Paul makes the claim that his very life is a vehicle of bringing Christ to the churches: "You know how we lived among you for your sake. You became imitators of us and of the Lord" (1 Thess. 1:5b-6).

In fact, Paul sternly admonishes his readers to avoid any brother who "does not live according to the tradition [*paradosis*] you received [*para-*

---

for you; do this in remembrance of Me.' In the same way He took the cup also, after supper, saying, 'This cup is the new covenant in My blood; do this, as often as you drink it, in remembrance of Me'" (vv. 23-25).

26. This is no surprise since Luke had joined Paul on his second missionary journey (Acts 16:10, note the "we") and remained in close relationship with the apostle and the churches that he founded (2 Tim. 4:11; Philem. 24). The likelihood of the matter is that Luke's version of the Lord's Supper is based on his experiences with Paul.

lambano] from us" (2 Thess. 3:6). Notice that both the noun and the verb of tradition language are being used, probably in order to stress that the activity of those who do not accept Paul's teaching have become adverse not merely to him, but to the teaching of the whole church. This is essentially the same tactic which Clement, an elder in the church of Rome, will use in his letter to the Corinthian church (A.D. 96-97). Exhorting them to discontinue the rivalry over leadership resulting in dissensions which still racked the life of the congregation, Clement urges these schismatics to give up such futile concerns and "turn to the glorious and holy rule of our tradition" (7.2). This is to be accomplished by fixing their eyes on Christ's sacrifice for them and responding with humility through repentance. Thus, it is the cumulative force of the "tradition" (and not Clement) which calls them to such a response (cf. 58.2).

It should be pointed out that the way in which scholars have divided the kerygmatic tradition from the tradition of church practice or ethics is, in fact, an artificial creation for their own purposes of explication. Such classification, in any strict sense, would have been foreign to Paul's approach. For the apostle consistently linked faith and practice together as the indissoluble twin of a distinguishable orthodoxy. Instruction in the preaching of the church meant living according to the mandates of that preaching, just as Jesus exemplified. So Paul will argue that being freed from slavery to sin and its lifestyle was the result of "wholeheartedly obey[ing] the form [or pattern] of teaching" to which the new believers in Rome had been entrusted (Rom. 6:17). The *paradosis* of Jesus, therefore, functioned as a dialectic between a pattern of belief and a pattern of conduct (cf. 1 Tim. 1:5; 4:3) which reinforced each other and identified the believer as a disciple of Christ.

Paul and the Freedom of the Spirit

An interesting phrase which Paul uses as a means of expressing the common heritage of the Jesus tradition, particularly with regard to Christian ethics, is the "law of Christ" (Gal. 6:2; 1 Cor. 9:21). There is a certain nonnegotiable quality in his choice of words, although it would be quite wrong to interpret it as though the apostle regarded the tradition as possessing a regulatory set of statutes which had a binding force on all his converts. Paul himself was too charismatic and conscious of the believer's freedom in Christ to enjoin an obligatory system of decrees and commandments:

"Where the Spirit of the Lord is, there is freedom" (2 Cor. 3:17). Faithful Christian living, according to the Pauline view, should be sensitive to and guided by the Spirit (Rom. 8:4, 14; Gal. 5:18, 25), free from the constraints of a legalistic mentality (Rom. 6:14; 1 Cor. 7:6), dependent upon the Spirit's gifts (Rom. 12:4-8; 1 Cor. 12; Eph. 4:11-13), and exhibiting the fruit of the Spirit (Gal. 5:22-25). Paul is therefore the last one to place another "yoke of slavery" around the necks of his congregations. And yet this same preacher describes his role as the bearer and deliverer of tradition by asserting that the very faith and life of the Christian is built upon such norms.

For most Protestants, especially those in the Free Church, the conjunction of an authoritative tradition and freedom of the Spirit appears, at first sight, to be a contradiction of concepts. Very often the believer's freedom in the Spirit through Christ is a defining feature of one's conversion experience, which seems completely antithetical to the adoption of a prescribed battery of beliefs and practices. After all, Jesus' only requirement for discipleship was to abide in his word, since it is the truth, "and the truth will set you free" (John 8:32). Such a tension recommended itself to certain church historians several generations ago, most notably Rudolf Sohm and Adolf von Harnack, who postulated that the earliest Christian communities were characterized by a Spirit-led existence, following the ways of Jesus, with a level of organization that was unsystematic, enthusiastic and spontaneous. This did not rule out the place of tradition, but such primitive spirituality would have entailed a limited amount of church structure, and its doctrinal content as a "canon of faith" was indeterminate, thus insuring the highest degree of freedom. Only in response to Gnosticism and other internal challenges to the Christian gospel did the formulation of doctrine(s) arise, which meant that inspiration and intuitional enthusiasm based on Jesus' model was being eclipsed by the formation of "catholicism." For von Harnack, it was an unfortunate but an inevitable process. When the diversity of teaching threatened to overwhelm the church's preaching, the simple spirituality of Christianity was transformed as the fixing of tradition became the supreme task.[27]

For Paul, however, the pneumatic, charismatic character of early Christianity never excluded the authority of the church's Tradition and its

---

27. Adolf von Harnack, *History of Dogma,* trans. N. Buchanan (New York: Dover, 1961), II.25.

development.[28] Though he does not use the word "catholicity," it would have harmonized with the promotion of the community led by the Spirit. The Christian was set free henceforth to "walk in the Spirit," but it was understood within the context of a specific and articulated faith which was transmitted for every congregation to accept and preserve:

> What you heard from me, keep as a pattern of sound teaching, with faith and love in Christ Jesus. Guard the good deposit that was entrusted to you — guard it with the help of the Holy Spirit who lives in us. (2 Tim. 1:13-14)[29]

Not only is there not a polarization between life in the Spirit and a concretized tradition, but both the content and the transmission of the Jesus tradition was superintended by the Holy Spirit.

Accordingly, the observance of that Christian Tradition which Paul had imparted was not optional for the believer. As the Thessalonians were instructed, their own sanctification was dependent upon their obedience to what they had "received" from Paul (1 Thess. 4:1-3). Spiritual growth is indeed accomplished through the inscrutable working of the Spirit in the life of the believer. It is at the same time guided and instructed by the external forms of the faith, forms which give a specific content to the preaching, confession and organization that identified Christians as the unique body of Christ.

Homologia

It is impossible not to find the Tradition manifested in process with varying content throughout the New Testament documents. Given the teaching and worshiping life of the earliest churches, it stands to reason that "the faith once delivered to the saints" (Jude 3) took practical forms of confessions which facilitated its expression and retention. That is to say, the beginnings of crystallization did not happen haphazardly. They were provoked by the needs of the believing communities as they evangelized,

---

28. Gerhardsson, *The Origins of the Gospel Traditions,* 29-32.

29. It should be plainly stated that I accept Pauline authorship for all three of the pastoral epistles as credibly argued by Luke Timothy Johnson, *Letters to Paul's Delegates: 1 Timothy, 2 Timothy, Titus* (Valley Forge, Penn.: Trinity Press International, 1996), 3-26.

baptized, nurtured, prayed, and formulated a Christian doctrine of God that made sense of Jesus as human yet as the Word of God. This does not mean that we encounter in the epistles and the Gospels a christological doctrine set out in its fullness: they rather suggest and hint at one. Even so, it is not difficult to point to those instances where the Tradition was becoming hardened into statements of confession *(homologia)* and short didactic summaries, and even hymns.[30]

If one operates on the principle of moving from the simple to the more complex, then the standard wisdom is that the earliest confessions of faith were one-clause Christologies. The most common seems to have been "Jesus is Lord," as Paul affirms in 1 Cor. 12:3, "No one can say Jesus is Lord *(Kurios Iēsous)* except by the Holy Spirit," and again in Rom. 10:9, "If with your mouth you confess Jesus is Lord and believe in your heart that God has raised him from the dead, you will be saved." We cannot be sure what occasion called forth these utterances, but the verse from Romans has generally been taken as an allusion to the acknowledgment of Christ's Lordship at the baptism of the new believer.[31] The repeated description in other texts of the New Testament (e.g., Acts 8:16; 19:5; 1 Cor. 6:11) implies that this declaration had a place in the rite and was used as part of a larger confessional context. A slight variation of the words also occurs in Phil. 2:11 and 1 Cor. 8:6 ("one Lord, Jesus Christ"), indicating a liturgical-like setting where such a confession was regularly affirmed (cf. Col. 2:6).

The apostle Paul makes it clear that "Christ Jesus as Lord" was a central point of his preaching (2 Cor. 4:5), and that the distinguishing mark of one speaking by the Holy Spirit was the proclamation of "Jesus as Lord" (1 Cor. 12:3). Ascribing Lordship to Jesus was a decided act of exaltation in a culture teeming with divinities, heroes and miracle-workers. Since the title "Lord" is used for God in the Old Testament, the inference (drawn from passages such as Ps. 110:1) makes it clear that the motivation for asserting Christ's Lordship was a setting apart of his divinity in terms previously reserved for the Creator.[32] Moreover, in light of the social and political context of the Roman Empire where Caesar was affirmed to be Lord, it is not hard to comprehend why this homologion would have figured so promi-

---

30. Paul Bradshaw offers a useful warning about the tendency to "read" credal and liturgical formulae into the apostolic era without a clear warrant. *The Search for the Origins of Christian Worship* (Oxford: Oxford University Press, 1992), 35ff.

31. J. N. D. Kelly, *Early Christian Creeds* (New York: Longman, 1972), 15.

32. I. Howard Marshall, *The Origins of New Testament Christology* (Downers Grove, Ill.: InterVarsity Press, 1976), 106-108.

nently in identifying authentic Christianity. In the stirring account of Polycarp's martyrdom (c. A.D. 155-56), the elderly pastor was urged to save himself from arrest and execution by making the admission that "Caesar is Lord." It seems to have been a direct negation of the Christian profession, as Polycarp's refusal to yield in the arena indicates: "Eighty-six years have I served Him, and He never did me any wrong. How can I blaspheme my King who saved me?"[33]

Another compact christological statement that stressed Messiahship was "Jesus is the Christ." The epistle of 1 John is most insistent that the one who denies that "Jesus is the Christ" is a liar and antichrist (1 John 2:22), but whoever loves the Father believes that "Jesus is the Christ" (1 John 5:1; cf. 2 John 7). As it might be surmised, this confession had its greatest impact among Jewish circles where, in the synagogue, it had become a test of heresy (John 9:22). When Peter preached his messianic sermon in Acts 2 to the diverse crowd of Jews who had come to Jerusalem for Pentecost, they were urged to respond by acknowledging that God had made Jesus "both Lord and Christ" and "to repent, and be baptized in the name of Jesus Christ for the forgiveness of sins" (2:36-37). It had been based on confession of Jesus as "the Christ" that Peter first expressed his own faith (Mark 8:29; Matt. 16:16). So too we find in Matthew's narrative, oriented as it was toward a distinctly Jewish audience, the frequent titular use of "Messiah" as the primary means for determining Jesus' identity (Matt. 1:17; 2:4; 11:2; 16:20; 23:10; 24:5; cf. "son of David," 9:27).

More common to the language of Christian profession as it moved out into the Hellenistic world and communities of the Jewish diaspora was the declaration of Jesus as the Son of God. A noteworthy though slightly later[34] example of its use as a baptismal confession is the account of Philip and the Ethiopian eunuch (Acts 8). The eunuch sealed his faith with the words, "I believe that Jesus Christ is the Son of God." It is with this declaration that Paul first began his preaching in Damascus (Acts 9:20), along with the defense that Jesus is the Christ (v. 22). The epithet functions in the Gospel of Mark as an important element of the writer's literary technique in order to elucidate his theological agenda: "the gospel of Jesus Christ, the Son of God" (1:1). Ironically, it is first and consistently found in

33. *The Martyrdom of Polycarp* 8.2; 9.3. Translated in *Early Christian Fathers*, ed. C. C. Richardson (New York: Macmillan, 1970), 152.

34. Verse 37 of Acts 8 does not appear in the earliest mss. and therefore may be a later interpolation. Its testimony, however, is not consistent with the kinds of faith professions which were already in use.

the mouths of demoniacs who were being exorcised (3:11; 5:7). Jesus never uses the title for himself, though there is a definite connection between it and his references to sonship, which are utilized in respect to Jesus' unique relationship with the Father (9:7; 12:6; 13:32). As the Gospel began, so it reaches its climax when the Roman centurion acknowledges at the foot of the cross, "Truly, this man was the Son of God" (15:39). That the title was used as a declaration of Christian faith is borne out by Heb. 4:14, which urges readers to recognize that Jesus, the Son of God, is their high priest and therefore, "let us hold fast our confession [*homologias.*]"

Fragments of the Preaching

The sheer abundance of these christological formulas would indicate that they were but the tip of the confessional iceberg. There is plenty of fragmentary evidence in the New Testament for more detailed formulas that operated concurrently. One must beware of applying the organic principle of the simple to the more complex without recognizing that it does not operate necessarily in a linear fashion when it comes to doctrinal growth. This would indicate that the so-called "one-clause Christologies" were not confessions isolated from the larger narrative of what God has done in Christ. We have seen in 1 Cor. 15:3ff. an extract from the church's preaching which Paul calls "the gospel." Its emphasis is obviously on the redemptive work of God through Christ, who "died for our sins . . . was buried . . . was raised on the third day."[35] The concentrated form represented here indicates that it was already functioning for catechetical or evangelistic purposes. Paul's mention of it was meant as a reminder of that gospel Tradition which they knew and practiced. Echoes of this *kerygma,* in which select incidents of Christ's redemption are recited, can be found in Paul's other letters (Rom. 1:3-4; 8:34; 1 Thess. 4:14; 2 Tim. 2:8).

In similar fashion, the salvific story is recounted in the letter of 1 Peter 3:18-22:

> For Christ died for sins once for all, the righteous for the unrighteous, to bring you to God.

35. This basic material functioned as the model upon which later creeds would be developed. One can see the pattern of these words from 1 Cor. 15:3-4 in all the versions of the Apostles' Creed and the Nicene Creed. For comparison, see Philip Schaff's *Creeds of Christendom,* vol. 2 (Grand Rapids: Baker Book House, 1983), 45ff.

He was put to death in the body, but made alive by the Spirit, through whom also he went and preached to the spirits in prison, who disobeyed long ago when God waited patiently in the days of Noah while the ark was being built.

In it only a few people, eight in all, were saved through water, and this water symbolizes baptism that now saves you also. . . .

It saves you by the resurrection of Jesus Christ, who has gone into heaven and is at God's right hand — with angels, authorities and powers in submission to him.

A baptismal context is clearly the occasion of these words,[36] and J. N. D. Kelly has suggested that this passage reads like part paraphrase and part quotation of an instruction preparatory to baptism.[37] The allegorical explanation inserted at verse 20 about the relation of "flood" water to baptismal water seems to vindicate the idea that it is based upon or taken from a catechetical scheme.

But perhaps the most striking example of the church's Tradition in liturgical practice is the well-known christological passage of Phil. 2:5-11. In all likelihood, Paul has incorporated a previously known hymn (or fragment of a hymn) in order to illustrate his precept about putting the interests of others before our own (2:3-4). The New International Version has rightly set off the lines of this passage into stanzas. Whether the Philippians were previously familiar with the hymn is uncertain, but it seems that it was arranged in rhythmic strophes for purposes of congregational worship and instruction before it came into Paul's hands.

Typical of other christological formulas, the passage presents a condensed summary of Jesus' sacrificial death and Easter triumph. There is discernible a two-stage pattern of (1) Christ's humiliation as the obedient servant despite being in the form *(morphe)* of God, along with his incarnation and death, and (2) his exaltation to the universally acknowledged position of Lord. The logic is evident: not through pretention but by sacrifice did Jesus demonstrate his true divine nature. Apart from the point as a whole, there is also the didactic value of each line which builds a composite sketch of Christ's identity, whose preexistent and divine nature is the basis upon which the rest of the declaration is built.

On the presumption that this passage used to be sung by ancient Christians, I asked the music director of the church where I once served to

36. Richard Longenecker, *Biblical Exegesis in the Apostolic Period* (Grand Rapids: Eerdmans Publishing Company, 1975), 85.

37. Kelly, *Early Christian Creeds,* 18.

put it to music. After some investigation, she found that the tune of "A Mighty Fortress Is Our God" was the most compatible. We used it in a Sunday morning service and it worked well, making for an eminently practical means of helping people remember the essential teaching of Christ's person and work. In effect, we had smuggled some fundamental elements of Christology into the congregation's understanding without having once used the word "theology." This, of course, was the early Christian purpose for arranging the apostolic Tradition into confessional or hymnic forms. By putting key elements of the orthodox faith to music or rhyme,[38] a highly effective means was established for preserving and transmitting that faith, making it easy to digest and harder to forget. Nor was there a need to assume the literacy of the worshipers, which would have been much more questionable than in Western societies today. Indeed, hymnody in the West has its origins in just this way. In the year 386 just after Easter, Ambrose of Milan and his congregation were held up for several days in a church surrounded by imperial soldiers intent on claiming the building for an emperor who was hostile to the Nicene faith.[39] An eyewitness account tells how the bishop taught the people "hymns and psalms *(hymni et psalmi)* after the custom of the eastern churches" as a means of relieving tension while maintaining their faithfulness.[40] The hymns introduced were meant not merely to provide an emotional and worshipful experience — Ambrose was too savvy to let an opportunity like this pass by. They also imparted theological truths about God as Trinity in accordance with the standards of "mainstream" catholic orthodoxy, thus reinforcing in the people an antiheretical consciousness in the face of their present siege. It was not the first time a theologian had set doctrine to metre in order to make it more palatable for and easily disseminated among believers. A number of hymns written by pastor-theologians from the 350s, such as the *Te Deum* perhaps by Nicetas of Remesiana, still survive. Lesser known is the set of intricate hymns defending the Nicene form of faith by Marius Victorinus. Already a famous rhetor in the city of Rome, Victorinus converted to Christianity late in life, and soon after wrote several technical philosophical works, which his contemporaries said could

---

38. Words in rhyme usually pertain to the arrangement of thoughts placed parallel to one another, not just to different words that sound similar.

39. For a reconstruction of events see D. H. Williams, *Ambrose of Milan and the End of the Nicene-Arian Conflicts* (Oxford: Oxford University Press, 1995), 210-15.

40. Augustine, *Confessions* IX.vii.15. "From that time to this day, the practice has been retained and many, indeed almost all your flocks, in other parts of the world have imitated it."

only be understood by the very learned.[41] His hymns (three are extant) were another matter, and on account of their profundity in simpler terms they probably did greater good for extending sound trinitarian teaching in the church. The "First Hymn" opens with the words:

> True Light, assist us,
>> O God the Father all powerful!
> Light of Light,[42] assist us,
>> mystery and power of God!
> Holy Spirit, assist us,
>> the bond between Father and Son!
> In repose you are Father,
>> in your procession, the Son,
>>> And binding all in One, you are the Holy Spirit.[43]

There is no proof, but we can imagine that this hymn was used by congregations in and around Rome so that they might realize more fully the object of their worship, just as Paul sought for the Philippians.

Before we finish this chapter, there are two other confessional fragments in the pastoral epistles that deserve mentioning. The first is in 1 Tim. 3:16 where the essentials of the *paradosis* are set forth in rhythmic form:

> He appeared in a body,
>> was vindicated by the Spirit,
> was seen by angels,
>> was preached among the nations,
> was believed on in the world,
>> was taken up in glory. (NIV)

These lines were applied by an unknown writer at the end of the second century, who rendered them in a kind of paraphrased version: "For this reason the Father sent the Logos to appear to the world — the Logos who

41. Jerome, *On Illustrious Men*, 101. It is for this reason, it is assumed, that these works are rarely employed by subsequent pro-Nicene writers.
42. This is a reference to the Son who is described in the Nicene Creed (which was itself based on earlier confessions) as "God from God, Light from Light, True God from True God."
43. *First Hymn* 1-7, *Marius Victorinus: Theological Treatises on the Trinity*, trans. Mary T. Clark (Washington, D.C.: Catholic University of America Press, 1981), 315.

was slighted by the chosen people, but preached by the apostles and believed in by the Gentiles."[44]

The poetic or hymnic origin of this passage becomes more evident when we observe that it is structured in three antithetical pairs. In each pair, a *datum* from the Jesus tradition is presented within a contrast of the heavenly/spiritual and earthly/material. The focus is clearly on the process by which God revealed himself in Christ:

1. related to the incarnation — God has come in the flesh/confirmed by the Spirit;
2. related to the gospel proclaimed — testified by angels (at birth or resurrection)/preached among nations;
3. related to the consequences of his coming — believed in the world/ ascends to heaven.

Like a neutron star, the kerygmatic content of this hymn is one that is densely packed in a small amount of space, imparting crucial truths about the equal realities of Christ's physical appearance in the real world and his heavenly origin and purpose. In just a few lines, the faithful confess the universal nature of Christ's person while avoiding the extremes of exalting Jesus' divinity at the expense of his humanity, not an uncommon problem by the middle of the first century, due to the influence of Gnosticism.

2 Tim. 2:11-13 is another instance of the apostle drawing upon an already-known liturgical source in order to substantiate his point. This is one of the rare occasions where the emphasis is not centered on Christ. Paul is encouraging his young disciple to endure suffering, as he has, for the sake of the truth of the gospel. Above all, Timothy is asked "to remember" by invoking a form of the church's preaching which he was taught: "Remember Jesus Christ, raised from the dead, descended from David" (2:8). It is at this juncture, as Timothy is prompted to think back to the gospel tradition which was the ground of his salvation, that Paul introduces a "trustworthy saying" *(logos)* in four couplets, each beginning with the conditional particle "if." The first couplet demonstrates the probability that the "saying" was part of a baptismal vow or a hymn sung at baptism:[45]

44. *Epistle to Diognetus* 11.3.
45. The first couplet starts with the words, "For if . . ." leaving the implication that some lines preceded the part that Paul has recorded here.

> If we died with Him,
> we will also live with Him.

It is a very Pauline kind of statement which closely adheres to the significance of baptism described in Rom. 6:8: "Now if we died with Christ, we believe that we will also live with Him." In this case, the believer is told to mortify his "old self" which has died in Christ through baptism, whereas in the 2 Tim. profession, the one being baptized is exhorted to endure and remain faithful by "living" in Christ. As a conditional vow, it is always possible for the new believer to "disown Him" by rejecting their confession such "that sin may reign in the mortal body" (Rom. 6:12). And yet the graceful stability of God is not annulled in our moments of faithlessness, and the final note of the passage is to encourage rather than provoke:

> If we are faithless,
> He will remain faithful,
> for He cannot disown Himself.

Triadic Confessions

There are a surprisingly large number of passages in the New Testament which show signs that the Tradition had already been and was becoming shaped into credal-like or hymnic expressions. Those passages which we have examined are, as in most apostolic writings, structured around a christological scheme that is often binitarian. That is, the focus is often built around the person and/or work of Christ in relation to God the Father (e.g., Rom. 4:24). Paul's salutation in the beginning of his letters is the best example of this: "Grace and peace be to you from the God the Father and our Lord Jesus Christ" (Rom. 1:7; 1 Cor. 1:3; Gal. 1:3; Eph. 1:2; Phil. 1:2; Titus 1:1), as are his benedictions (Rom. 16:27; Eph. 6:23; 1 Thess. 3:11). A binitarian scheme, it seems, was most deeply impressed on early Christian thought. The writer of the epistle of James describes himself as "the servant of God and the Lord Jesus Christ" (1:1), and 1 Pet. 2:5 speaks of "spiritual sacrifices acceptable to God through Jesus Christ" (cf. 2 Pet. 1:2; 2 John 3; Rev. 1:2).

However, a triadic articulation of God is also apparent in the New Testament, although it was less prevalent and its theological implications are not as clear. A triadic scheme, which is not a trinitarianism per se,[46] is quite discernable in 1 Cor. 12:4-6: "There are different kinds of gifts, but the same Spirit . . . different kinds of service but the same Lord . . . different kinds of working but the same God works in all of them" (see also Gal. 3:11-14; 2 Cor. 1:21; 1 Pet. 1:2). The two clearest formulations are found first in Paul's prayer at the end of 2 Cor. 13:14, "May the grace of the Lord Jesus Christ and the love of God and the fellowship of the Holy Spirit be with you all," and second, in the "great commission" passage of Matt. 28, "Therefore go and make disciples of all nations, baptizing them in the name of the Father and of the Son and of the Holy Spirit" (v. 19). The second passage may well have been used for baptismal purposes and thus provides the living context for Jesus' words as they were remembered and invoked within the church. This was the occasion for the Christian community whose religious affairs are reflected in a manual of church order known as the *Didache* (parts of which were written by the end of the first or very early in the second century). The Didachist seems to have known the Gospel of Matthew, and it was automatic that this formula was to be used at baptism:

> Now about baptism: this is how to baptize. Give public instruction on all these points, and then baptize in running water, "in the name of the Father and of the Son and of the Holy Spirit." If you do not have running water, baptize in some other. If you cannot in cold [water], then in warm. If you have neither, then pour water on the head three times "in the name of the Father, Son, and Holy Spirit."[47]

It seems that the actual manner of baptism was secondary to the fact that the proper confession of God was to be as Father, Son and Holy Spirit. Again, we must resist the temptation to imagine that the three-fold invocation presupposes a systematic rationale of God as Trinity. Prototrinitarian models do appear by the end of the second century, though there is little harmony of wording or concept among them. Not until the middle of the fourth century (a good quarter-century after Nicaea) can we reasonably

---

46. No "doctrine" of the Trinity will be published until the end of the second century with Tertullian, who also coins the word, *trinitas* (*Against Praxeas* 2). This does not mean there was no "trinitarian" understanding among Christian communities before this time, as references in Theophilus's *To Autolycus* II.10; Justin's *Apology* I.13, and others show.

47. *Didache* VII.1-4.

speak of a trinitarian theology whose articulation became universally accepted. Nevertheless, the "ground-floor" composition of the Tradition included such perceptions, demonstrating that the church was fully aware of the three-fold way God had revealed himself and could be approached.

Conclusion

We have seen that the earliest Christians would not have accepted the idea that the apostolic Tradition, as it evolved through the earliest preaching and teaching about Jesus, involved a deposit of revealed truth detached from Scripture, the Old Testament. The difference then between the Word proclaimed and the Word written was understood, but it had little significance. Doubtlessly, written collections of Jesus' sayings and deeds circulated among Christian communities before the writing of Paul and the Evangelists,[48] although it seems there was initially a preference for oral testimonies which were carefully preserved and transmitted. By the second generation of Christians, the apostolic documents had come to enshrine this Tradition as the Old Testament and the christological hermeneutic came together with it to form a new set of sacred texts (cf. 2 Pet. 3:14). There is no question that the Christian Tradition, expressed in the kerygmatic, ethical, and worshipful life of the churches, preceded the Christian writings, and functioned as completely authoritative before the advent of the New Testament.

Accordingly, Jesus did not reject the place of "tradition" categorically, though he was quick to attack unbalanced interpretations or areas where its development was in conflict with the sense of the written Torah. It is reasonable to suppose that Jesus' overall attitude is reflected in the ready acceptance toward the concept and language of tradition by the first generation of believers. Paul's correspondence reveals how the traditioning process was already underway, while he also participated in the fashioning of that process.

We have seen important evidence for the ways in which the apostolic Tradition had become incarnated within the believing and confessing church through baptismal professions, credal-like formulas, and hymns. Such vehicles were the primary means by which Christian teaching and

---

48. See J. C. O'Neill, "The Lost Written Records of Jesus' Words and Deeds Behind Our Records," *Journal of Theological Studies* 42 (1991): 483-504.

spirituality was conveyed to believers. One of the earliest glimpses we have of the worship of a Christian assembly is in the correspondence of a Roman governor named Pliny (the younger), who wrote to the emperor Trajan about the year A.D. 112 requesting guidance for the prosecution of those accused of being Christians. He states in the course of his letter that these Christians were in the habit of meeting on a fixed day before it was light, "when they sang in alternate verses a hymn to Christ, as to a god, and bound themselves with a solemn oath not to [commit] any wicked deeds, but never to commit any fraud, theft, or adultery, never to falsify their word . . . after which it was their custom to separate, and then reassemble to partake of food — but food of an ordinary and innocent kind."[49] It is not certain from the Latin *(carmenque . . . dicere)* whether they "sang . . . a hymn" or "recited . . . an arrangement of verses," but either way, a kind of liturgical-like utterance is being described, in which the worshipers alternatively *(invicem)* offered their profession to the divine Christ. Here is a singular picture of the Tradition in action; the apparent absence of a written text in no way prevented the sacramental and didactic ministry of the Word from taking root in the lives of these believers. The hearing, recitation and singing of the truth was all they had in that setting. And for them, possessing the truth of apostolic message was critical: some were tortured and executed by Pliny for their profession of faith.

To be within the Free Church does not mean that we are free from the historic Tradition of which various manifestations have been preserved by the believing church through the ages. Seeking the Spirit's power and leading in our lives must likewise not be governed by a disregard of the confessional parameters which Christians of the past furnished as the means for identifying a truly Christian faith. It is time for Protestant evangelicals to reconsider much more seriously the work of the Holy Spirit in the whole history of the church. This will mean that we will understand the ministry of the Spirit not as a privately emerging force in individuals as much as the primary Actor in the church's *actus tradendi,* the living transmission and acceptance of the apostolic message in the body of Christ. It is through this corporate and "horizontal" process that our individual ("vertical") encounter with the Holy Spirit is shaped and nurtured. Following

---

49. *Epistle* X.96. Pliny's reference to "food of an ordinary and innocent kind" underlines the suspicion Roman authorities had toward the aberrant practices of socially marginal groups. It was rumored that when Christians gathered for their agapé meals, they ritually murdered and devoured infants. Tertullian, *Apology* 7-9; Minucius Felix, *Octavius* 9.

the way of discipleship cannot function as *Christian* discipleship in isolation from the guidance which the Spirit has provided through Spirit-led men and women in the church's past. A dizzying array of options are available for anyone who seeks a privatized or small group spirituality, and some of these closely mimic Christianity. But only through Scripture and the consensual Tradition will the believer be enabled to find spiritual living that is within the shelter of the orthodox faith of the church.

CHAPTER 3

Defining and Defending the Tradition

For if the things which be first, after the rule of Tertullian, are to be preferred before those that be later, then is the reading of histories much necessary in the church, to know what went before, and what followed after; and therefore, not without cause "historia," in old authors, is called the Witness of Times, the Light of Verity, the Life of Memory, Teacher of Life, and Shewer of Antiquity, etc., without the knowledge thereof man's life is blind, and soon may fall into any kind of error.

John Foxe, *Acts and Monuments*
(or *Book of Martyrs*)

My own introduction to post-apostolic Christianity came through reading the surviving works of Tertullian (c. 155–c. 220), a brilliant though highly eccentric theologian, apologist and polemicist of the late second century. He lived in Carthage all his life and wrote in a convoluted style of Latin which served him perfectly as he engaged Roman pagans, Jews, Christian heretics and even fellow believers with the wittiest and most sarcastic of styles. Except perhaps for Augustine, Tertullian was the greatest genius the early Western church produced. When a later pastor of

Carthage, Cyprian, requested reading material with the words, "Hand me the master," everyone knew whose writings he meant. Historic Chrisianity is much indebted to Tertullian, who provided us with the fundamental articulation of the doctrines of the Trinity, of Christology, of anthropology; and of Christian practice such as baptism, prayer, and righteous suffering in the face of persecution. One of the most moving passages in patristic literature is Tertullian's address to those Christians who had been recently thrown into prison for their witness. He writes of their condition, "It is full of darkness, but you yourselves are light; it has bars, but God has made you free; unpleasant odors are there, but you are an aroma of sweetness; the judge is daily awaited, but you shall judge the judges; sadness may be there for him who sighs after the world's enjoyments . . . but the leg does not feel the chain when the mind is in heaven. Where your heart shall be, there shall also be your treasure."[1]

But there was a certain volatility in Tertullian's brilliance that led to imbalance. Toward the end of his life, he associated himself with a rigorist movement that called itself the "New Prophecy," which was then sweeping through the western parts of the Roman Empire. Its adherents claimed that the Holy Spirit, or "Paraclete," had only recently been revealed in its fullness through the prophecies of a certain Montanus and two women prophetesses. Their message was not anti-orthodox in any doctrinal sense, but the very nature of their self-professed prophetic authority, by which they advocated a stricter and purer Christian ethic, challenged other types of authority in the church. It was not long before Montanism was deemed to be a threat to the stability of the church, and condemned. This aroused Tertullian's fiery temperament only further as he sought to vindicate the legitimacy of its prophecies.

What intrigues me most about this figure is that he was a man on a quest — a quest for the certitude of authority: he wanted to ascertain beyond all doubt what the norms were for preserving the apostolic faith and where one should turn for the establishment of those norms. Not very unlike the concerns of today, Tertullian sought to address the problem of having the assurance of divine teaching in a religiously pluralist world.

One does not need to read very far in Tertullian's writings to find out that he had a passion for knowing and defending the truth. The Christian God was *deus verus* (the true God), and those who find him find the fullness of truth. Christ as True God was revealed in the flesh in

---

1. Tertullian, *To the Martyrs* 2.

order to lead humanity *in agnitionem veritatis* (to a knowledge of the truth).[2] Despite the fact that he was well learned in philosophy and literature, Tertullian took a dim view of any human reasoning when it was used independently of Scripture and the church, since it was too often abused by pagan philosophers and found in the ideas of heretics. Philosophical ideas were used no less in his own construction of theology, so that his much-quoted expostulation, "What does Jerusalem have to do with Athens?" should be taken with a grain of salt. Even so, he claimed the only sure ground for truth was to be found in divine revelation. But when one is looking to secure this truth through some tangible means, where should one look?

Should one turn to the succession of pastors in the churches, many of whom could trace a lineage several generations back to the apostles? Like his predecessors, Tertullian thought a demonstrable continuity of a shared faith within the churches offered strong testimony of apostolicity. At no point did he perceive the office of clergy as an automatic guarantee of orthodoxy, though he regarded the office as an authoritative one. The more Montantist Tertullian became, however, the less credence he gave to this argument. By the end of his life, he was convinced church leadership (not the church) had gone completely off the rails of faithful teaching regarding Christian practice. He now advocated longer and more stringent fasts, stricter penance, allowed no second marriages on any grounds whatsoever, and so on — all in accord with Montantist prophecies. And yet, despite his quarrels with the local clergy, Tertullian will never claim that true doctrine can be divorced from the context of the church.

Should one turn to the Bible for apostolic certitude? By the late second century, recognition of what we now deem to be the canon of the church's Scripture was more or less complete, though the list of inspired books varied in number from place to place, many collections containing books — namely, the so-called Apocryphal books — that are not found in the Protestant Bible today.[3] Translation was a problem too. In Tertullian's time, several Latin versions of both testaments were available, all of inferior quality in style and textual accuracy. The Latin Old Testament was a

2. Tertullian, *Apology* XXI.30.
3. One well-known example is the list of New Testament books given in the Muratorian fragment, which includes the Apocalypse of Peter, the Wisdom of Solomon, and the Shepherd of Hermas, the latter being recommended only for private spiritual reading.

translation, not from the Hebrew, but from the Greek Septuagint, itself a dubious though highly revered product, which had already been in use among Jewish communities for several hundred years.[4] Moreover, the Latin New Testament had an obscure origin and was subject to frequent revision, resulting in the proliferation of editions.[5] Scripture for Tertullian, nevertheless, was the indisputable witness of the apostles' preaching and testimony. It was the repository of all orthodox teaching, as he made clear when refuting an opponent's views: "If it is not in Scripture, let him fear the woe that was meant for all those who add or take away."[6] In Scripture, one found full divine authority.

But he also knew that anyone could get the Bible to say anything, and that it was being done by those with a Gnostic agenda as well as by naive Christians who were propounding some enormous heresies. A group known as the Marcionites cherished a particular reverence for the epistles of Paul and centered their theology on them to the exclusion of the Old Testament and the rest of the apostolic works (except for a expurgated version of Luke).[7] They were not alone in this bias. Not a few Christians were convinced that the Old Testament was no longer relevant for the preaching and application of the gospel. Others looked to the writings of the apostle John, which portrayed the wholly divine person and work of Christ. While there was no doubt in Tertullian's mind about the inspired character and complete authority of Scripture, as well as its inherent perspicuity, Scripture could not in isolation from the church's Tradition provide the refuta-

---

4. Not until Jerome's translation of the Old Testament were Hebrew manuscripts consulted for revising the Latin Bible. As a result of his new translation, many of the books commonly part of the Septuagint, such as Wisdom of Solomon, the Letter of Jeremiah, the Song of the Three Young Men and Bel and the Dragon (deemed parts of Daniel), Judith, and 1 and 2 Maccabees were not included in the new Latin Bible under the same canonical status as the others.

There was great resistance on the part of the fourth-century Christians to the displacement of the Septuagint in favor of the more accurate translation from the Hebrew. Augustine's attitude was typical when he referred to the authority of the Septuagint as "supreme," and refused to allow its emendation or substitution "even if we find in the Hebrew versions something that differs from what they wrote" (*On Christian Teaching*, II.55).

5. Catherine B. Tkacz, "*Labor Tam Utilis:* The Creation of the Vulgate," *Vigiliae Christianae* 50 (1996): 45.

6. Tertullian, *Against Hermogenes* 22. Cf. Rev. 22:18-19 for the allusion.

7. W. H. C. Frend, "The Gnostic-Manichaean Tradition in Roman North Africa," *Journal of Ecclesiastical History* 4 (1953): 21.

tion that was needed. In what context and on what basis was the Bible to be rightly used?

Let me warn the reader in advance that as we proceed with the answering of these questions a number of unfamiliar historical figures and terms will have to be introduced as we move into what is admittedly a more technical part of this book. It cannot be helped. Since the patristic legacy of the ancient Tradition is either not known at all or known in only a cursory fashion by most evangelicals (and, for that matter, most Roman Catholics), then it is important that we not gloss over important details and points of development, the implication of which will become clear later on. There existed concrete vehicles by which the Tradition was manifested in the church, and we need to explore what some of those vehicles looked like and how they functioned. This chapter will make it most apparent that the Tradition was not a body of particulars extrinsic to the apostolic faith, but was rather at the very doctrinal heart of what Christians believed and how they lived.

Defining Apostolicity

The credal-like fragments and simple confessions formulated in the apostolic era established patterns by which subsequent Christian communities strove to identify and transmit their faith. A primary issue for the early Christian movement was one of self-description; ever since the Jerusalem "council" of Acts 15, followers of Jesus had wrestled with distinguishing their faith from Judaism and gnostic doctrines. The very process of answering the question, "Who are we?" pushed believers for the next century or so to seek definition and to clarify the parameters of their own unique identity. For reasons internal and external to itself, the church was committed to the task of establishing norms of apostolicity which enabled it to distinguish true teaching and practice from the false.

Such norms found their expression in early teaching which served as guides for faithful reflection about God's revelation in Christ. These were a part of the doctrinal mosaic by which the churches in the second century sought to preserve the apostolic witness. We are probably hearing a portion of one such confession in Ignatius's letter to the Ephesians, "For our God, Jesus the Christ, was conceived by Mary, in God's plan being sprung both from the seed of David and from the Holy Spirit" (18.2). Another direct reference appears in his letter to the Trallians (9.1):

Jesus Christ, of David's lineage, of Mary; who was really born, ate, and drank; as really persecuted under Pontius Pilate; was really crucified and died. . . . He was really raised from the dead, just as his Father will raise us who believe on Him.[8]

The theological emphasis is christological, a point of focus which is frequently utilized throughout Ignatius's writings, providing the rudiments of what the faithful were taught and preserved about One who was the Son of God and Son of man. Trinitarian-type of statements seem also to have been a part of the church's worship and preaching (cf. *To the Ephesians,* 9.1; *To the Magnesians,* 13.1).

In many cases, these recitations of the apostolic Tradition intentionally functioned to define the boundaries of apostolicity in opposition to heretical notions. Ignatius's concern with gnostic teaching, especially docetism (that Christ only appeared to be human), as well as with "Judaizers," was the primary impulse for his doctrinal professions. Against the docetists ("wild beasts in human shapes"), who claimed Christ's passion was a sham and that resurrection was an exclusively spiritual event, he reiterated again and again what might be called basic gospel "facts": the reality of Jesus' human birth from a virgin, baptism by John, crucifixion in the flesh under Pontius Pilate, genuine suffering for our sakes, and physical resurrection.[9] In order to vindicate the reality of Jesus' complete humanity, which must not be obscured on account of his divinity, the utter historicity of the salvation story is emphasized. We will find Christian writers making the same kind of emphases against gnostic theosophy throughout the second century.

Against the Judaists, who were possibly part of a similar Judaizing movement attacked in Rev. 3:9,[10] and who represented the other extreme of christological error by exalting the humanity at the expense of divinity, Ignatius insisted that Christ is the Word of God, "who came forth from one Father, while still remaining one with Him" (*To the Magnesians,* 7.2). Christ was not only anticipated by the prophets, but he will raise them from the dead, just as he was raised.

---

8. Cf. Ignatius, *To the Smyrneans* 1.1-2.

9. All these points are treated in summary fashion in *To the Smyrneans* 1.1-2. See E. Glenn Hinson, "The Apostolic Faith as Expressed in the Writings of the Apostolic and Church Fathers," in *The Roots of Our Common Faith: Faith in the Scriptures and in the Early Church,* ed. Hans-Georg Link (Geneva: World Council of Churches, 1984), 116.

10. Rev. 3:7-13 is the message to the church in Philadelphia. It is surely no accident that Ignatius warns against a similar movement in his *To the Philadelphians* 6.1.

Closely tied to the church's need to distinguish orthodox from heretical teaching, the apostolic faith was related and clarified through the catechetical process as summaries of faith were drawn up for the purpose of instructing new converts. R. P. C. Hanson rightly declares that the church from the earliest moment of its existence was a teaching church.[11] We must not underestimate the importance which the preservation and transmission of the apostolic memory had for the churches of the post-apostolic period and on into the third century. The impartation of Christian teaching to inquirers and learners was a constant in the life of these churches. Allusions to this process of instruction in ethical and theological exhortations demonstrate that catechesis "served as a control with considerable effect on the understanding of the Christian faith."[12]

Evangelicals can learn much from the ancient church's focus on catechesis, that is, on carefully instructing converts or those preparing to join the church in the basic teachings of the Christian faith. In the preface to his manual of Christian instruction, Gregory of Nyssa declared "religious catechism is an essential duty of the leaders 'of the mystery of our religion' (1 Tim. 3:16). By it the Church is enlarged through the addition of those who are saved, while 'the sure word which accords with the teaching' (Titus 1:9) comes within the hearing of unbelievers."[13] No doubt Gregory would insist that the teaching of new Christians or new members must go well beyond an initiation into the church's leadership structure and polity of the congregation, issues of stewardship, acquaintance with the missions statement, or a brief denominational summary. To introduce the young or a novice to the church of Jesus Christ is to open for them treasures of the central points of the apostolic faith, a faith that is larger than any one denomination's or church's claims upon it, sharpened and transmitted through the ages. We too often assume potential church members already know the fundamentals of their faith, whereas in reality they are usually incapable of explaining the basics of "the pattern of sound teaching" (2 Tim. 1:13). This need for equipping cannot be displaced in favor of simply giving one's own testimony any more than to say a personal experience of the faith can be substituted for a reasonable grasp of that faith. If it is the case that the church, as the apostle phrased it, "is the pillar and foundation

11. R. P. C. Hanson, *The Tradition in the Early Church* (London: SCM Press, 1962), 52.

12. Hinson, "The Apostolic Faith," 117.

13. Gregory of Nyssa, preface to *An Address on Religious Instruction*.

of the truth" (1 Tim. 3:15), then ecclesiastical leadership must not shirk from the critical and time-consuming job of imparting Christian truth or catechizing those who profess to be Christian. Nothing can replace the formation of a theologically and biblically literate people. Nothing is more essential.

Fortunately, a great deal of evidence in the form of various formulae is recoverable from the surviving writings of the second and third centuries, which give us some idea about the content of what was taught in the churches. Like the passages of the New Testament that we looked at in the last chapter, the nature of catechetical instruction was fairly fluid, ranging from establishing norms of Christian behavior to Christian belief.

The Role of Catechisms

One of the earliest catechisms is one of Christian ethics known as the "Two Ways," which was circulating in the East by the mid-second century. Three versions of it have come down to us in the *Epistle of Barnabas* 18-19, in the *Didache*, and in book 7 of the *Apostolic Constitutions*,[14] beginning with the words, "There are two ways, one of life (or light) and one of death (or darkness); and between the two ways there is a great difference." What follows is a series of ethical injunctions, based on the Sermon on the Mount, directly quoting from Matt. 5 and Luke 6. Jesus' teaching on the lifestyle for the kingdom of God is taken at face value and embraced as authentic Christian living. The catechetical nature of these injunctions is made clear by the fact that they are issued within the context of a congregation: among other things the reader is urged to honor those "who preach God's word to you" (4.1), all forms of schism among believers are condemned (4.3), and the confession of sins in the church assembly before offering prayer is said to be "the way of life" (4.14). That the manual of "Two Ways" was immediately followed by baptismal instructions in the *Didache* and the *Apostolic Constitutions* underscores its original design as a catechism.

References to the dynamic and content of the Tradition that we found in Paul widely abound in this post-apostolic period. There was an acute

14. The *Epistle of Barnabas* and the *Didache* show close parallels, unlike the fourth-century *Apostolic Constitutions*, where the "Two Ways" instruction has been greatly expanded as the prolegomena to the preparation of candidates for baptism. All three versions show interpolations and glosses on the text, so we will never know exactly what the confines of the "Two Ways" document were.

sense that the teaching that Christian churches preached stemmed directly from the very teaching of the apostles. This is the meaning behind Polycarp of Smyrna's admonition to the Philippians, "Let us, therefore, forsake the vanity of the crowd and their false teachings, and turn back to the word delivered to us from the beginning."[15] Doctrine was the centerpiece of catechetical instruction, an instruction that was then related to a distinctive code of ethics and delivered to the convert as "tradition."[16] Just as we saw in the New Testament, this tradition was expressed in various summaries or formulae which had to do with both belief and practice. It was incomprehensible to the early church that these two could be severed, since there could be no authentic Christian living without authentic Christian doctrine. What one does was indissolubly linked to what one thinks. Right belief was always at the bottom of right action.

An acknowledged handbook of catechetical instruction from this period is Irenaeus's *Proof of the Apostolic Preaching,* a late second-century work that survives today only in a sixth-century Armenian translation.[17] The addressee of the work, a certain Marcianus, is told that its aim is to "set forth in brief the preaching of the truth" by providing "in brief the proof (or exposition) of the things of God," i.e., a concentrated explanation of God's unfolding plan for salvation. This condensed narration of God's redemptive activity was in keeping with a didactic format that naturally lent itself to catechetical purposes. In tandem with such a format, Irenaeus may have imposed or utilized a trinitarian framework on his presentation,[18] although the text *prima facie* suggests that he was just as interested in providing a biblical

15. *Epistle to the Philippians* 7.2.

16. So Justin will preface his description of the basic Christian teaching with the words, "But we have received through tradition . . . and have been taught" (*I Apology* 10).

17. The best translation with full discussion of textual history and analysis is by J. P. Smith, *St. Irenaeus: Proof of the Apostolic Preaching,* Ancient Christian Writers no. 16 (New York: Newman Press, 1952).

18. The breakdown of the text yields the following possible configuration:

Introduction 1-2
The Trinity, Creation, and Redemption 3-7
The Father 8-29
The Son 30-88
The Holy Spirit and the Church 89-97
Conclusion 98-100

From Everett Ferguson, "Irenaeus' Proof of the Apostolic Preaching and Early Catechetical Instruction," *Studia Patristica* 18.3 (1989): 127.

history centered on Christ as he is revealed prophetically in the Old Testament and historically through the incarnation.[19] Part of the difficulty in determining exactly how we should interpret Irenaeus's literary intentions is undoubtedly due to the case of the author employing the church's liturgy or confessions with a view of placing them within a larger pedagogical plan. Either way would be consistent with the content of the document.

Irenaeus begins by declaring that our faith "admonishes us to remember that we have received baptism for the remission of sins in the name of God the Father, and in the name of Jesus Christ, the Son of God, who became incarnate and died and was raised, and in the Holy Spirit of God" (c. 3). Doctrinal elaboration immediately follows this baptismal formula, evidently drawing on the profession of faith that was accepted in the Gallic churches. For Irenaeus here lays out the basis "of our faith, the foundation of the building, and the consolidation of a way of life":

> God the Father, uncreated, beyond grasp, invisible, one God the maker of all; this is the first and foremost article of our faith. But the second article is the Word of God, the Son of God, Christ Jesus our Lord, who was shown forth by the prophets according to the design of their prophecy and according to the manner in which the Father disposed; and through Him were made all things whatsoever. He also, in the end of times . . . became a man among men, visible and tangible, in order to abolish death and bring to light life, and bring about the communion of God and man. And the third article is the Holy Spirit, through whom the prophets prophesied and the patriarchs were taught about God . . . and who in the end of times has been poured forth in a new manner upon humanity over all the earth renewing man to God. (c. 6)

The trinitarian pattern, or "three articles," is not fashioned by Irenaeus; more likely he is incorporating a baptismal confessional form of faith already used in the West at that time.[20] Here it is employed as the doctrinal anchor for the rest of his catechetical manual, and it is on this basis that he will also conclude his work, warning his reader against doctrinal errors about "God the Father our maker . . . and the Son of God and the dispensation of his incarnation which the apostles transmitted to us . . . and the gifts of the Holy Spirit" (c. 99).

19. As Ferguson argues in "Irenaeus' Proof," 128-29.
20. In chapter 100, Irenaeus refers again to this passage as the "three articles of our seal," a clear indication that it was used as part of the pre-baptismal instruction.

Further and fuller evidence for reconstructing the content of teaching formulae comes from Aristides (of Athens), a little-known apologist of the second century, and Hippolytus, who was an eminent theologian and controversialist in Rome at the end of the same century (d. 235).[21] Aristides wrote his *Apology* as an address to the emperor around A.D. 125 or shortly thereafter,[22] exonerating the views of the Christians from false accusations by giving a true account of what they believe. One passage provides an echo of accepted christological teaching which Aristides claims was the "doctrine of the truth" preached by the apostles and still observed in his day: "Now the Christians trace their origin from the Lord Jesus Christ. And He is acknowledged by the Holy Spirit to be the Son of the Most High God, who came down from heaven for the salvation of men. And being born of a pure virgin, unbegotten and immaculate, He assumed flesh . . . and tasted death on a cross . . . and after three days, He came to life again and ascended into heaven."[23]

This is evidently not a fixed formula, and we can do no more than speculate whether Aristides is depending upon a more developed list of doctrines. It is reasonable to suppose that this summary of the Christian Tradition was derived from the oral teaching of contemporary churches, and that this teaching was presented in a form not unlike the manner stated here.

Among numerous works attributed to Hippolytus is one called *Apostolic Tradition (Apostolikai paradosis)*, which provides unique insight into the Church of Rome's worship and organizational practices. The perspective contained therein is intentionally conservative and even recalcitrant, since Hippolytus seems to have been writing against what he considered to be recent innovation in the church's teaching.[24] As a result, we cannot be exactly certain whether the teaching presented here represents the instruction given in the Church at Rome or the idiosyncratic views of one man. When comparing the *Apostolic Tradition* with the content of other Chris-

---

21. He was reputedly a disciple of Irenaeus, according to *The Library of Photius* CXXI.

22. Depending on how one should interpret the Syriac superscription of the work which was addressed, somewhat confusedly, to the emperor Hadrian (while he was in Athens in 125), and to the emperor Antoninus Pius (138-161), which places the date of writing after 138.

23. Aristides, *Apology* 15.

24. See G. Dix's masterful introduction, *The Treatise on the Apostolic Tradition of St. Hippolytus of Rome* (London: SPCK, 1937).

tian confessions and liturgies, we are probably justified in thinking that this document reflects the broader spectrum of Christian teaching, just as it claims explicitly to be recording only the forms and customs already long established.

After a period of instruction and probation that lasted three years, a catechumen was baptized by being asked to confirm his or her faith while standing in the waters and responding to the following questions:

> Do you believe in God the Father Almighty?
> Do you believe in Christ Jesus, the Son of God,
>> who was born of the Holy Spirit and the Virgin Mary,
>> who was crucified in the days of Pontius Pilate,
>> and died [and was buried],
>> and rose the third day living from the dead,
>> and ascended into heaven,
>> and sat down at the right hand of the Father,
>> and will come to judge the living and the dead?
> Do you believe in the Holy Spirit, in the Holy Church, and the resurrection of the flesh?[25]

This type of interrogatory format is derived from baptismal formulae which are different from the catechetical or didactic sort of instruction that we have seen above. It seems that Hippolytus's citation was a forerunner (or version) of what is known as the Old Roman Creed, an ancestor of the so-called Apostles' Creed. Most scholars believe that the evolution of the early creeds had a development distinct from that of the affirmative forms of teaching that existed. These latter, more fluid formulae of the faith, or catechetical summaries, are the predecessors of the rule of faith which was found in use by the middle of the second century as tests of orthodoxy. There is evidence that heretics were quite ready to borrow confessional statements from the New Testament or later creeds that celebrated the life-giving activity of the Father, Son and the Holy Spirit. However, what they could not use was the rule of faith which more precisely delineated the orthodox faith that the creeds represented in outline form. H. E. W. Turner points to a passage in which a gnostic named Theodotus makes reference to the triad of the Father, Son and Holy Spirit as "the names by whose power the Gnostic is released from the power of corrup-

---

25. *Apostolic Tradition* XXI.12-18.

tion."[26] The "bare-bones" of credal language could too easily be interpreted in a manner alien to the apostolic faith.

Distinction versus Discontinuity

In sum, when one traces the historical and theological developments after the death of the apostles, he or she discovers that the task of defining and teaching the faith had not essentially changed. The concern about preserving the apostolic truth was no less active and not contrary to the more concretized forms which the faith was taking. There has been, however, an unfortunate tendency among Protestant scholars and pastors to draw a thick line separating the "apostolic era" from the patristic era as if the doctrinal and structural complexion of early Christianity was suddenly and dramatically altered between the completion of the New Testament and the periods that followed. The drawing of this line is founded upon certain historical and dogmatic presuppositions — namely, that the New Testament period is one kind of "history" and the patristic is of a completely different kind. A material distinction is made between the apostolic and post-apostolic writings: the first has to do with divine revelation or with witnesses to that revelation, whereas the second does not; which means in practice that the first is absolutely vital to the Christian faith, whereas the second is optional. In part, this distinction served the needs of the Protestant Reformers, who were anxious to differentiate the superior nature of Scripture from its patristic commentators, who had also been deemed throughout the Middle Ages as authoritative. At the dogmatic level, the distinction was meant to emphasize the absolutely unique and *sui generis* nature of New Testament Christianity with respect to later modes of Christianity. That which is later must *a priori* be qualitatively different and inferior. This modulation, as Jonathan Smith astutely observes, is a version of the Protestant historiographic model: a "uniquely" pristine and original Christianity which suffered later "corruptions," and was therefore a different kind of Christianity.[27]

In itself, such a distinction is not unwarranted and is indicated in the

26. H. E. W. Turner, *The Pattern of Christian Truth* (London: A. R. Mowbray and Co., 1954), 154.

27. Jonathan Smith, *Drudgery Divine: On the Comparison of Early Christianities and the Religions of Late Antiquity* (Chicago: University of Chicago Press, 1990), 43. See chapter 4 below.

self-awareness with which post-apostolic writers submitted themselves to the authority of the apostolic documents. I know of no patristic writer who did not acknowledge the supreme and unique authority of the Scriptures. The problem, however, is the working assumption that the apostolic church was a singular entity, insular by means of its revelatory experiences, and therefore completely detached from the Christian faith that followed it. Such a scheme represents a deficient understanding about how the canonical process actually worked, and has implicitly caused many Protestant groups to disconnect the New Testament era from the rest of church history. Small wonder that numerous believers today regard the apostolic era in total isolation from the ensuing faith and life of the same church. The result is that they think of the Bible and its interpretation in isolation from the patristic age that followed it.

Just as significantly, the persistence of this dividing line is related to how scholarly disciplines within the study of theology have evolved (more or less based on the Protestant model) and become increasingly rarified and classified. Regardless of the fact that the "patristic" document known as I Clement was, like the last book of the New Testament (Revelation), written in the final decade of the first century (perhaps within a few years of each other), the scholarly research and secondary literature of the New Testament and of patristics have gone in different directions. One result has been the evolution of distinctive methods and biases that are peculiar to each field, such that in some universities or academic societies, "Scripture studies" have virtually no engagement with the work of those who pursue the study of church history. All parties agree that the demarcation between the two fields is contrived and non-historical, yet the line nevertheless acts as a kind of intellectual divide, impoverishing a truly integrated approach to Christian origins.

While few would argue against the unique inspirational nature of the apostolic documents, it seems that the New Testament's sacred character has been advocated at the expense of asserting an exaggerated separation between the kind and content of faith lived in the first century and what came next.[28] Certainly the Christians who lived the apostolic

---

28. In fact, most twentieth-century studies of early Christianity accept that a plurality of perspectives within Christianity was present from the beginning of the church's formation. It would be just as artificial to say that the transition from the apostolic to the post-apostolic meant a movement of uniformity to fragmentation. There is a useful summary in L. Goppelt, *Apostolic and Post-Apostolic Times*, trans. R. A. Guelich (Grand Rapids: Baker Book House, 1980), 146ff.

faith in the years after the death of the apostles would not have understood or appreciated the value of our compartmentalizing their history. For them, the apostles were the teachers *par excellence* whose authority set them in a distinct category, but this did not mean that there was a radical break in the way in which the churches were preaching, catechizing, and defending the Christian faith from the earliest days. We are able to observe those areas where there were developments in the church's doctrine and organization by the second and early third centuries (as I will note in the next chapter).

It is this increased theological sophistication and complexity in the church's authority structure that has been designated with the term "catholic," with the result that the church's history at this time is bifurcated into categories, "apostolic" and "catholic," or "biblical church" versus "episcopal church." These conceptual categories are indebted to a model of understanding church history that is still potent today, and is intent on proving that earliest Christianity was spiritually and organizationally simple in contrast to the religious technocracy that arose in its place.[29] Such a construal of history fails to see that the points of continuity from one century to the next were far greater than the differences, and that the line of division which moderns have drawn and treated as real is an artificial one, committing an injustice to the ancient church's integrity. We should instead think of a line that runs "through" the New Testament and the ensuing developments of canonization, doctrine and organization.

While post-apostolic Christian leaders in no way claimed for themselves the same authority as those first disciples of Christ, they did consider their faith and the transmission of that faith to be unified with them. The very basis for their claims to orthodoxy was grounded on the view that one could forge a tangible link between the apostles and themselves, just as Clement of Rome or Irenaeus most forcefully argued in their theories of apostolic succession.

For good reason was the period of the next two or three generations

---

29. For example, proponents of the so-called "Jesus Seminar" follow this pattern in their attempt to make a sharp distinction between the words and deeds of the historical Jesus and the early church that evolved. Robert Funk's *Honest to Jesus: Jesus for a New Millennium* (San Francisco: HarperSanFrancisco, 1996), a contemporary revision of nineteenth-century German liberal scholarship, is built on the assumption that the early church corrupted and distorted the intent and character of Jesus' preaching. The formulation of confessions of faith and the rise of doctrine represent alien elements which need to be purged as impediments to historical evaluation.

after the apostles eventually called the era of the "apostolic Fathers."[30] While we no longer assume that each author in this collection had known or been instructed by an apostle, certain connections between second-century communities and the earliest churches did exist. More than once it has been observed that the writings generated during the end of the first century and first half of the second century closely resemble the style, variety and pastoral character of the New Testament documents. The former attests to the fact that the early church continued to produce and share in pastoral correspondence, apocalyptic visions, homiletic instruction, and the need for antiheretical and antipagan defenses. Moreover, we have no reason to doubt that the pastor of Smyrna, Polycarp, whose letter to the Philippians and an account of his martyrdom survives in this collection, was a disciple of the apostle John.[31] Clement seems to have been the third pastor of Rome,[32] while Ignatius was the second pastor of Antioch,[33] that city where believers were first called "Christians" (Acts 11:26). Such personal links to the apostolic legacy were often emphasized, sometimes exaggerated, but all served to verify the church's claim that it indeed preserved the true gospel of Jesus Christ.

As one goes beyond the period of the apostolic Fathers, the overriding concern of the "catholic church" — a term first used by Ignatius and Polycarp around A.D. 115 — was no less one of doctrinal faithfulness to the biblical (Old Testament) and apostolic teaching. There was, of course, a certain fluidity in the formulation of message within catechetical, homiletic and polemical documents as one moves from writer to writer and from church to church. There was no grand uniformity in the understanding of doctrine. And yet the early church possessed, just like a center of gravity within a huge mass of manifold and diverse elements, an awareness of the "core" or essential elements of the Christian message. As one scholar

30. The title was not used by the ancient Christians and originates in the seventeenth century with the French patristic scholar J. B. Cotelier, who wrote *Patres aevi apostolici*, 2 vols. (Antwerp, 1672). A specific number of writings have figured in this category: I Clement, II Clement (which is really a sermon, not a letter, and by a different author), one letter of Barnabas (a pseudonym), seven epistles of Ignatius of Antioch, one letter by Polycarp of Smyrna, an account of Polycarp's martyrdom, and the Shepherd of Hermas. The *Didache* and the letter to Diognetus were added later.

31. Eusebius, *Ecclesiastical History* V.20.5.

32. *Ibid.*, III.15.34. Clement's acquaintance with the Apostles Peter and Paul is alleged based on his identification with the Clement mentioned in Phil. 4:3, but such associations are only conjectures.

33. Origen, *Homily VI on Luke*.

has noted, "The success of the second century was the affirmation that there was a true gospel; this was more important than any particular account of that gospel."[34]

The Rule of Faith

Now we must return to Tertullian's quest for the norms of authority. Rehearsing the lines of his quest is not simply an exercise of antiquarian interest. When he asked the question, "Where should one look for the apostolic faith?", it was because the pressure of adverse circumstances caused him to do so. Gnostic leaders did lay claim to the Christian Scriptures and Tradition, as we find evidenced in Ptolemaeus's letter to a disciple named Flora who was urged to to be found "worthy of the apostolic tradition which we too have received from a sucession . . . by the teaching of the Savior."[35] Within the context of a culture inimical to Christianity, it was critically necessary that the faithful be grounded in the essential doctrines of the apostolic faith against the threat of heresy and other forms of social-religious pressures. Long before the apostles' or ecumenical creeds, we find the regulating function of the Rule of faith in the churches, expounding the cardinal points of theology which evangelical Christians still believe and confess to this day.

For Tertullian, it was axiomatic that the rule was derived from the apostolic preaching itself. In *Against Marcion*, he claims Paul went up to Jerusalem after his conversion to compare the "Rule of his Gospel" with that of the other apostles.[36] That same "Rule has come down [to us] from the beginning of the Gospel."[37] It is the link between the apostolic past and the present; it refers to the original message of the apostles, going back to revelation itself, and to the message proclaimed by the churches of his day. It exists not merely to refute heresy, but as something positive, leading to the truth of what the faith claims and how it may be recognized.

The first time we actually hear of the "rule of faith" is from a younger

34. Eric Osborn, "Reason and the Rule of Faith in the Second Century AD," in *The Making of Orthodoxy*, ed. R. Williams (Cambridge: Cambridge University Press, 1988), 58.

35. Trans. Robert Grant, *Second Century Christianity: A Collection* (London: SPCK, 1946), 36.

36. Tertullian, *Against Marcion* V.3.1.

37. Tertullian, *Against Praxeas* 2.

contemporary of Tertullian named Irenaeus, who calls it the "Rule [or Canon] of truth," or sometimes just "the preaching," or "the faith," or "the tradition." In the opening of his *Proof of the Apostolic Preaching*, he claims Christians must adhere strictly to the "rule of faith" because it was handed down to us by the apostles and their disciples,[38] and because "it admonishes us to remember that we have received baptism for the remission of sins" in the name of the Father and of the Son and of the Holy Spirit (c. 3). It has been plausibly suggested, therefore, that the Rule of faith had its origination in the outlines of instruction for catechumens which pastors gave to their catechists.[39] These began as oral formulations of a common faith and pattern of teaching that came to serve a double-duty of defending the faith against heresy. For this reason, the Rule is not to be confused with the creeds, which scholars now believe had an interrelated but separate origination in the life of the ancient church.[40] The Rule was not a creed, nor a formula, but an abbreviated body of doctrine wherein the genuine articles of Christianity were articulated.

Several times Irenaeus refers to the Rule in one form or another in an anti-gnostic work entitled *Against Heresies*, where he confronts the gnostic claim of possessing secret and authentic teachings of Jesus. Considering the plane on which he will refute his adversaries, he is forced to make a distinction between Scripture and Tradition, given that they agree with neither (III.2.2). Even though Irenaeus is eager to show the falsities of the gnostic system through the authority of Scripture, he recognizes that their inconsistent hermeneutics may annul this approach. "They disregard the order and connection of the Scriptures, destroying the truth," he states (I.8.1). To illustrate the problem, he asks the reader to envision a beautiful mosaic of a king studded with jewels (i.e., the Bible) which is then perversely dismembered and rearranged to look like a dog or a fox (gnostic interpretations). Irenaeus concludes that one cannot proceed with proofs from Scripture without resorting to a reference outside of it.

Here Irenaeus asks the question where one would find the truth if he or she wished to see it. Supposing the apostles had not left us the writings

---

38. Irenaeus is doubtlessly thinking of Polycarp here.

39. L. William Countryman, "Tertullian and the *Regula Fidei*," *The Second Century* 2 (1982): 221-26. Ferguson has suggested that Marcianus, the recipient of the *Proof*, was not a catechumen, but a catechist and was therefore receiving further guidance as a teacher from Irenaeus ("Irenaeus' Proof of the Apostolic Preaching," 131).

40. P. Smulders, "The *Sitz im Leben* of the Old Roman Creed," *Studia Patristica* 13 (1975): 409-21.

— an imaginary and worst-case scenario — where would one locate the apostolic teaching (III.4.1)? His answer is that the truth is found in the Tradition of the apostles manifested to the world through the agency of the churches. In one passage, this Tradition as the Rule of faith is spelled out:

> The Church, though dispersed throughout the whole world, even to the ends of the earth, has received from the apostles and their disciples this faith: [she believes] in one God, the Father Almighty, Maker of heaven and earth, and the sea, and all things that are in them; and in one Christ Jesus, the Son of God, who became incarnate for our salvation; and in the Holy Spirit, who proclaimed through the prophets the dispensations of God, and the advents, and the birth from a virgin, and the passion, and the resurrection from the dead, and the ascension into heaven . . . and his [future] manifestation from heaven in the glory of the Father.[41]

It is characteristic of Irenaeus to lay stress on the centrality of the church in the faithful transmission of apostolic teaching.[42] There can be no revelation apart from Scripture and the Tradition, and only within the true church of Jesus Christ has this revelation been handed down. It is not merely that the church is the arbitrator of how one should understand and apply the faith, but that the church is the receiver and guardian of that faith through the succession of bishops.[43] For the apostles themselves instituted overseers (i.e., pastors or bishops) in the first churches, and it is

---

41. Irenaeus, *Against Heresies* I.10 (Ante-Nicene Fathers, I.330). For other citations of the rule with brief commentary, see V. Ammundsen, "The Rule of Truth in Irenaeus," *Journal of Theological Studies* 13 (1912): 574-80.

42. *Ibid.*, III.3.3; V.20.1.

43. Expanding on the views of Ignatius of Antioch, Irenaeus held that the purity of faith is maintained through the succession of ordained leaders. As the apostles instituted bishops (pastors) in the churches and entrusted to them their preaching or the gospel, so the apostolic message has come down untainted to the present day. Along with the unity of the preaching, the antiquity of the churches through the succession of their leadership ensures the immutability of the Christian truth proclaimed.

This theory of ecclesial uniformity, it should be remembered, was forged in the fire of polemics given the fragmenting effect which gnosticism was having on the church. For all its value in propounding a view of apostolicity, *Against Heresies* offers an idealistic view of the church and her message, even by Irenaeus's standards. The Gallic bishop knew well that tensions divided the churches in the West and the East, such as the controversy over the date of celebrating Easter, or concerning the relation of the gift of prophecy and the office of bishop (Eusebius, *Eccles. Hist.* V.7; 23).

through them that the apostolic preaching has come down to the present time.[44] Apostolicity is thus spelled out as the church's ability to trace its theological and historical lineage back to the apostles. As the two examples from the churches of Rome and Asia Minor show, the concept of succession of churches and their pastors had a very tangible quality for Irenaeus. A "spiritual-only" interpretation of succession would play right into the hands of his adversaries, who so stressed the spiritual transmission of truth for any enlightened Christian (i.e., gnostic). The chief implication is that the church is the only context by which the true faith can be properly expounded because the church is the original recipient of that faith. It is the visible manifestation of "where" the gospel can be found, and it is here that this faith is upheld.

Irenaeus's appeal to the sufficiency of Tradition alone, or to the vindication of apostolicity by tracing episcopal succession, were polemical tactics he used when pushed to the extreme. In fact, the ideal structure of authority for Irenaeus was multi-leveled: Scripture, Tradition and the church. Like a three-legged stool, these elements acted as the foundation for determining orthodox doctrine, and it was a platform for faith not at all unique to Irenaeus.[45] There was an inherent complementarity to the three parts, which was meant to secure the place of Christian truth and offer to each believer the means of locating this truth in space and time. Lest we forget, Irenaeus, like most Christian thinkers and writers of his day, was a pastor, and accordingly, he had pastoral concerns. His embrace of and articulation of Scripture, Tradition, and the succession of bishops in the church was not his attempt to forge a theory of ecclesiology, which is how Irenaeus's teaching has most often been used. His approach was rather an authoritative means by which Christians could be sure of the truth of their salvation in the face of competing schemes: "We have learned the plan of our salvation from none other than those through whom the Gospel has come down to us, which they did one time proclaim in public and at a later period, by the will of God, handed down to us in the Scriptures, to be the ground and pillar of our faith."[46]

Whatever claims to authority a Christian leader might make, they must be channeled through this tri-focal lens of the apostolic faith. Such

44. Irenaeus, *Against Heresies* III.3, 2.

45. Victor Walter, "Beyond Sola Scriptura: Recovering a More Balanced Understanding of Authority," *Touchstone* 4 (1991): 15-18.

46. Irenaeus, *Against Heresies*, III.1.1.

an arrangement acted like a spiritual system of "checks and balances" which guided the church in its decision-making and served to protect the church from those seductive voices who offered new or special revelation, or an alien interpretation of Scripture. The believer need never live in ambiguity when it comes to Christian truth; the veracity of his or her faith has been preserved and transmitted through the Bible, the church's Tradition, and its pastors.

Tertullian too would make the same argument about the constituents of apostolicity against heretical opponents. His problems were similar to those of Irenaeus. Gnostic teachers, like Valentinus, Basilides and Marcion, were busy proliferating a gospel Tradition based on a gnostic hermeneutic of Scripture[47] — in effect, another structure of authority allegedly based on divine revelation. Because scriptural interpretation was so often at issue between catholics (or "mainline" Christians) and various forms of gnosticism, it became clear to Tertullian that any appeal to the Bible alone for maintaining pure doctrine was impossible. Tertullian therefore addresses himself to the problem of authority. We must not be surprised, he says, that heresies utilize scriptural support for their positions. The stated purpose in *On the Prescription of Heretics* is to decide the question, "Who are the rightful owners of Scripture?" In order to answer the question, Tertullian declares,

> we must not appeal to Scripture . . . one point should be decided first, namely, who holds the faith to which the Bible belongs, and from whom, through whom, when and to whom was the teaching delivered by which men became Christians? For only where the true Christian teaching and faith are evident, will be the true Scriptures, the true interpretations, and all the true Christian traditions be found.[48]

No aspersion is being cast on the eminence of Scripture, but it was necessary to bypass it for the authority of the church's historic teaching because Scripture was itself the point of contention. Tertullian thus precludes any argument on the issue of Scripture or its interpretation by drawing our attention to the preliminary issue that must first be answered. It is necessary to show what ground of authority can be adduced which would entitle one to the access of Scripture. This prior point of order *(praescriptio)* must be proved before one can claim biblical authority.

47. The followers of Marcion were said to be following another "rule" (*Against Marcion* IV.17, 11).

48. Tertullian, *On Prescription of Heretics* 19.

It is very true that Tradition could not be alleged as an authority in anything that was ruled out by Scripture. Yet taken strictly on its own, "arguments about Scripture achieve nothing but a stomach-ache or a headache" since the Bible can be used to support any doctrine whatsoever. All agreed that Scripture could not be rightly handled without reference to the foundational teachings which resided within apostolic churches.

Those elements of what the church believed *(fides quae creditur)*, a kind of "mere Christianity," are discovered in the *regula fidei* or Rule of faith. As the name "Rule" implies, it functioned as the standard, or canon, for orthodoxy. To be more precise, the Rule did not function as a standard for the faith only; it was a distillation of the Tradition in the sense that it was deemed to be synonymous with the apostolic faith itself.[49] This is borne out by Tertullian's reference to the Rule as the "law of faith," or the fact that he defines an apostate as one who has "lapsed from the Rule of faith."[50] In effect, the rule was a product of, and at the same time represented, the Christian teaching in its totality. It follows then that all church offices, no matter how esteemed — bishop, deacon, widow, etc. — were subject to the Rule. To ignore or abandon it for one's own interpretation of the Bible or doctrine, Tertullian declares, is to depart from the Christian faith.[51]

As in Irenaeus, we find in Tertullian that the rule was an elastic summary of the fundamental doctrines of Christianity, which was not his invention but a preexisting body upon which he drew. Analogous to the four presentations of the Gospels, the arrangement of the Rule's content had some differences from one version to another without compromising its veracity. Moreover, it seems that the Rule was never fixed in a single or master version, but variable in its form and adaptable to the given didactic or polemical circumstances at hand. Three lengthy citations of the Rule are found in Tertullian's surviving corpus,[52] which possess few exact verbal similarities, vary in length, and whose content is clearly accommodating three distinct situations. At the same time, however, all three versions ex-

---

49. B. Hägglund, "Die Bedeutung der 'regula fidei' als Grundlage theologischer Ausslagen," *Studia Theologia* 12 (1958): 23.

50. Tertullian, *On the Veiling of Virgins* 1; *On Prescription of Heretics* 3.

51. Tertullian, *On Prescription of Heretics* 3.

52. Tertullian, *On Prescription of Heretics* 13; *On the Veiling of Virgins* 1; and *Against Praxeas* 2. There are also smaller, more particularized segments of the Rule which Tertullian mentions in passing, such as *On Prescription* 37; *Against Praxeas* 30; and *Against Marcion* IV.

hibit a basic shared structure that is bipartite in character, although *On Prescription* 13 and *Against Praxeas* 2 each include a clause about the Holy Spirit.[53] It would appear that the second and third centuries continued to reflect that association of binitarian and trinitarian confessional patterns that we saw in the New Testament documents. The passage from *On Prescription* 13 is the most comprehensive citation of the Rule:

> You must know that which prescribes the belief that there is one only God, and that He is none other than the Creator of the world, who produced all things out of nothing through His own Word, first of all things sent forth; that this Word is called His Son, and under the name of God, was seen variously by the patriarchs, heard always in the prophets, at last brought down by the Spirit and Power of the Father into the Virgin Mary, was made flesh in her womb, and, being born of her, went forth as Jesus Christ; thenceforth He preached the new law and the new promise of the kingdom of heaven, worked miracles; having been crucified, He rose again on the third day; having ascended into heaven, He sat at the right hand of the Father; sent the vicarious power of the Holy Spirit who leads the faithful; will come with glory to take the saints to the enjoyment of everlasting life and the celestial promises, and to condemn the wicked to everlasting fire, after a resurrection of both classes has been effected, together with the restoration of the flesh. This rule, as it will be proved, was taught by Christ. . . .

Exactly what was the source or common denominator of the Rule of faith is hard to say. The considerable latitude in the wording and flexibility in content disallows for the possibility that some fixed formulary lay behind it. Tertullian often speaks as if the rule were unalterable in any way whatsoever, whereas we know that this was not the case, given his use of it. The seeming contradiction may be explained. In the first place, Tertullian's penchant for hyperbole is undeniable, a factor to which we can attribute some of his language. Secondly, his citations of the Rule evidence certain freedoms taken in order to accommodate it to a polemical agenda or to his Montanism. And yet, this eccentric controversialist writes in a manner that acknowledges a general reverence for the Rule, a reverence that was evi-

53. Even so, Countryman has argued that the clause pertaining to the Holy Spirit is subordinate to the activity of the Son, which means a binitarian outline was predominant ("Tertullian and the *Regula Fidei*," 210). In Irenaeus, however, we found an essentially triadic pattern as is found in Origen, *On First Principles* I. praef. 4.

dently shared by his readership who looked to it as a point of stability. If the details of the Rule's localized forms were open to applied alterations, the basic Tradition that these forms represented was not. This suggests, thirdly, that Tertullian and his audience were familiar with the general and necessary structure of the Rule, and would therefore have some notion of which embellishments on it were acceptable and which were not. As L. William Countryman explains, "Tertullian expected catholic Christians to accept the idea that there were certain irreformable truths of the faith and that these are summarized in a brief, recognizable composition."[54]

Most of what has been said about Tertullian and the Rule of faith should not be segregated from the way in which the Tradition was manifested in other Christian communities. In the book *Tradition in the Early Church* (1962), which is still regarded as the foundational examination of this issue, R. P. C. Hanson has compared the contents of different citations of the Rule which are quoted in Irenaeus, Tertullian, Hippolytus, Origen, Cyprian, Novatian, Dionysius of Alexandria and the *Didascalia apostolorum*. There is quite a striking general similarity between these passages despite the external differences of language, location and time. At the same time, each writer is easily able to adapt the Rule for his purposes, whether it be speculative elaboration or as material for Christian instruction. Hanson concludes that the Rule could not have been a simple listing of proof texts, nor a static formula. Instead, it presents itself more as an oral account, divided into subjects, of the content of the preaching and teaching of the church.[55]

Certainly the Rule was not as static or fixed as the early apologists would have us believe because its very nature, as a dynamic movement, necessitates a process of growth, adaptability and sharpening of thought. Nor, on the other hand, was it simply a "stream which wanders where it will" or a mere unfolding of *Religionsgeschichte,* connected to the past only by the artificial design of polemical arguments. What we have in the rule is another example of the living and flexible nature of the church's Tradition which revealed itself as a set of doctrinal norms, a ready resource for catechetical teachers and apologists of the faith.

---

54. Countryman, 213. "Composition" is meant as a particular moment in communicating the Tradition, a performance, if you will, of transmitting the faith within the believing community.

55. Hanson, *Tradition in the Early Church,* 93.

The Rule and the Scripture

For years scholars have debated the relationship of Scripture to the Rule of the church, especially the question whether the Rule had a preeminence over Scripture. But the question tends to miscontrue the nature of the evidence. Neither Tertullian nor any of his peers would have imagined that the Rule can operate independently of Scripture no less than Scripture could act without the Rule and the church. The issue is rather one of context. When one examines their texts, one finds that the relationship between the authority of Scripture and that of Tradition exchange the primal position depending on what issues are at stake. As we have seen, Scripture was not sufficient alone for the refutation of heretical groups.

> What sort of truth is that which they patronize, when they commend it to us with a lie? Well, they actually treat the Scriptures and recommend their opinions out of the Scriptures! To be sure they do. From what other source could they derive their arguments concerning the things of the faith except from the records of the faith?[56]

This problem represents no tendency on Tertullian's part to subordinate the authority of Scripture to Tradition. Scripture is fully sufficient for declaring God's truth, and whatever it teaches is unconditionally true. But as he argues here and elsewhere, the exigencies of doctrinal heresy make it necessary to emphasize one over the other. In fact, there is an inviolable unity between the two such that to reject Tradition is to reject Scripture, and vice versa. One cannot use the Scriptures and refuse to submit to the teaching of the Tradition. Likewise, one cannot claim the Tradition in support of a teaching that is denied or not supported in Scripture.

Indeed, there was a symbiotic relationship between Scripture and the Tradition as they existed within the church. Doctrinal historians have a referred to this as "co-inherence" (or "coincidence")[57] since the content of the apostolic tradition co-inheres with the content of Scripture. Important for our understanding is that the Tradition manifested in the Rule was

---

56. Tertullian, *On Prescription* 15.

57. G. H. Tavard, *Holy Writ or Holy Church* (London: Burns and Oates, 1959); A. N. S. Lane, "Scripture, Tradition and Church: An Historical Survey," *Vox Evangelica* 9 (1975): 37-55, and Richard Bauckham, "Tradition in Relation to Scripture and Reason," in *Scripture, Tradition and Reason: A Study in the Criteria of Christian Doctrine*, ed. R. Bauckham and B. Dewey (Edinburgh: T. & T. Clark, 1988), 117-45.

something distinct, but not separate from or in addition to the Bible. Flessman van Leer makes the important point that the Rule of faith was thought to be not a formal principle for exegesis brought to the Bible from outside, but the real teaching of the Bible.[58] Another way to say this was that it was the purport of scriptural teaching. Irenaeus, Tertullian, Origen, and others were convinced that the authors of Scripture shared an agreement about the particulars of the church's Tradition or Rule of faith for the simple reason that they believed the Rule was the *ratio*, or what Athanasius would call the "scope," of scriptural revelation. As such, the Rule detected and represented the drift or burden of the main body of Christian truth. Those ancient writers who discuss the Rule, each exhibiting his own idiosyncratic version of it, all agree that its contents are in complete harmony with Scripture and when expounding it support it by an appeal to Scripture.

In historical terms, the Rule of faith was what the church was preaching. It was the Tradition in living color, just as we saw the preaching through the church's activity in the book of Acts — by word of mouth, in the synagogues, in the marketplace, on board ships, on the road. This was a preaching going on before the New Testament was completed and later canonized. But even when the New Testament was written, it had no automatic power of preaching and interpreting itself. The Bible is not like a video or a compact disc; it is far richer and more transcendent and, therefore, has to be preached. If we think of the Rule as a summary of how the church presents its faith and interprets its written texts, then it is quite correct to say that "The rule of faith of the Church is the faith as preached."[59]

The idea that there existed an authentic apostolic Tradition which was orally transmitted within the church yet never mentioned in Scripture or supported by the basic rule was unknown to the early church.[60] There was nothing in the various versions of the Rule to indicate that there was a dogma or doctrine held by the church not recorded or affirmed in Scripture. In effect, Tradition cannot be alleged as an authority for anything

58. E. Flessman van Leer, *Tradition and Scripture in the Early Church* (Assen: Van Gorcum and Co., 1954), 127.

59. R. P. C. Hanson, "The Church and Tradition in the Pre-Nicene Fathers," *Scottish Journal of Theology* 12 (1959): 27.

60. *Ibid.*, 25. Hanson says the only exception to this understanding in the second century was Clement of Alexandria, who claimed he had access to such a tradition. This can, in part, be explained by Clement's own and *sui generis* interpretation of "gnosis" as a truly catholic transmission of the faith.

ruled out by Scripture. This will be essentially the argument which the six-teenth-century Reformers will use against the medieval Catholic Church. As we shall see, the conflict between the early Reformers and Rome was not one of Scripture versus Tradition, but rather a clash over what the traditions had become, or between concepts of tradition.

To Conclude

We have seen enough evidence to state that the second- and third-century church was quite conscious of its responsibility to present a coherent message grounded upon the apostolic preaching that it had received. The Tradition in the form of the Rule of faith was not a novel set of practices made as an addition to Scripture. It was not from outside the faith. On the contrary, the Tradition had been kept "as a sacred deposit in the churches of the apostles"; as Tertullian maintained, "Let us see what milk the Corinthians drank from Paul; to what Rule (of faith) the Galatians were brought for correction; what the Philippians, the Thessalonians, the Ephesians read by it; what utterance the Romans give" (*Against Marcion* IV.5). No less than Scripture, the Tradition had been delivered from Christ to the apostles and the apostles to the churches. Tradition was an expression of the original apostolic preaching and could be sharply distinguished from human traditions that adorned the local customs of Christian communities. This is not to deny that certain ancient writers will defend a particular point of practice as "tradition,"[61] although they usually exhibited a sensitivity toward the differences which existed between that Tradition which has been received by the church from antiquity and those aspects which were more peripheral to its central teaching.

Nor was the Rule meant to function as an extracanonical source of revelation, since it was regarded as a summary of the essential content of faith to which the Scripture, Old and New Testaments, testifies. For this reason, it was decided how Scripture should be interpreted by using the

---

61. The best-known example is Tertullian's reference to the practice of triple-immersion and other practices of Christian devotion, of which he says, "If no passage of Scripture has prescribed it, assuredly custom, which without doubt flowed from tradition, has confirmed it" (*The Chaplet* 3). He goes on to defend these practices while acknowledging that the usual demand was that any countenance of Christian observances must be found also in Scripture. His protests would indicate that the norm was the joint sanction of Scripture and Tradition for doctrine and practice.

Rule as the canon of faith. As one scholar describes it, "The person who has a share in the faith (of the church), which is summarized in the 'rule of faith', also has a share in the Spirit, and is therefore qualified for interpretation of the Bible in its fullness of the Spirit."[62] The Rule was, as we have seen, a condensed version of the Christian faith that existed alongside the Scripture as an extension of its teaching and as its chief hermeneutic. This is Origen's point as he explains in *On First Principles* that working out a body of doctrine requires the guidance of "the tradition of the Church and the apostles" laid down in the Rule of faith, whose evidence is found in the Holy Scriptures or by those conclusions which are the logical consequences of scriptural teaching.[63]

Despite the recent attempts of a few evangelical writers to inculcate a theory of *sola scriptura* as the real intent of the early church,[64] there was no question in believers' minds that Scripture could or should function in the life of the believer apart from the church's Tradition. Were it to do so, there was scarce assurance that an orthodox Christian faith would be the result. While many parts of Scripture were inherently perspicuous and able to be understood with little outside assistance, post-apostolic Christians would have anathematized the principle set forth in Buswell's systematic theology, "The rule is then give the Bible an opportunity, in your own mind, to interpret itself,"[65] as setting the stage for heretical aberrations.

On account of the needs of discipleship through catechesis and defending the faith against heresy, it became obvious that the doctrinal substance which Christians were asked to believe in was not just the Bible, but the Bible interpreted by the church, which was the repository of the true faith. Tradition was (and is), in the formal sense, what holds the Bible together; it is what prevented Marcion from ejecting the Old Testament and part of the New; it is also what makes some biblical interpreters wrong and others right — indeed, it preserves the church's prerogative to claim that there is a right and a wrong. Not every method or interpretative approach to Scripture is valid or even useful, as ruefully substantiated by the vast multitude of modern publications in biblical exegesis. Where no interpre-

---

62. Peter Stuhlmacher, "*Ex Auditu* and the Theological Interpretation of Holy Scripture," *Ex Auditu* 2 (1986): 6.

63. Origen, *On First Principles* I. praef. 10.

64. See Appendix II.

65. J. Buswell, *A Systematic Theology of the Christian Religion* (Grand Rapids: Zondervan, 1962), 25.

tative guide exists as a theological "court of appeal," hermeneutical fragmentation can be the only result.

For the early church, the Rule served as the "plumbline of the truth" in that it was the truth as such concerning the facts of creation and redemption clearly evidenced in revelation.[66] It was the means of concretely establishing the norm of the Tradition, enabling one to rightly appropriate and understand Scripture in the Christian sense. Without such a plumbline, scriptural exegesis is left to the discretion of the individual interpreter or school of interpretation. Perhaps this is why a Baptist, a Quaker, a Charismatic and a Methodist all claim to believe what the Bible says, firmly holding to its complete sufficiency, and yet no two of them agree on what it is that the Bible says.

After the mid-third century we hear little more about the ongoing existence of the Rule as an oral body of truth distinguished from Scripture. In fact, any appeal to an oral-only tradition becomes strictly limited to matters of local church practice. The temptation to link this development with the growing prominence of a canonized body of sacred texts should be resisted as the only explanation. By no means had Tradition become outmoded in the wake of scriptural authority. Christian thinkers will still refer to the rule of faith and certainly to the role of the church's Tradition, but they will not mean exactly the same thing. By the fourth century, both of these concepts have become embodied in catechetical instruction, baptismal confessions, the language of worship and, later, in the great ecumenical creeds. In the next two chapters, we will see that the confessions of faith after the time of Constantine were no less formulated and defended as an extension of biblical teaching. Like the Rule of faith, these creeds of a later century were products of the life of the church and its faith as the very purport of Scripture.

---

66. Hägglund, "Die Bedeutung," 9.

CHAPTER 4

The Corruption of the Church
and Its Tradition

If the ancient Church was in error, the Church [of today] is fallen.

Blaise Pascal, *Pensées*

An evangelical with an ahistorical faith is a superficial one.

Bernard Ramm, *The Evangelical Heritage*

W hy is it that so many evangelicals who reflect on the heritage of their faith jump so easily from the New Testament to the Protestant Reformation with little concern or understanding for all that has taken place in between? How has it come about that one can worship for months or even years in many Free Church settings and hardly ever hear in the singing or the preaching express interaction with the message of the early Fathers? After all, hundreds of sermons, commentaries and hymns from the first five centuries have been preserved and translated into English. One may occasionally hear a quote from Calvin's scriptural commentaries, but never one from Origen's or Jerome's. On those very rare occasions when I have introduced patristic theology or spirituality within my own Baptist context, I have been met with a variety of reactions ranging from gratefulness for the exposure to new ideas, to curiosity combined with a wariness about promoting matters in church that are not biblical. Why are the ancient voices so muted?

I want to take up the idea again that a great deal of the Free Church and evangelical suspicion about the viability of the church's patristic Tradition is directly related to a negative or an ambivalent view of post-apostolic Christianity. First-century believers are given high marks for preaching and preserving the original gospel message, but in the ages that followed, the faith of the church is thought to have become corrupted by adhesion to practices and rituals which were foreign to the New Testament. The ensuing history of the church, therefore, is a history of something having gone wrong.

In this chapter, our focus will be on the evidence that has supported this perception of the church which became prevalent during and after the sixteenth-century Reformation, namely, that the church "fell" at some point after the apostolic era, and that from this fallen condition emerged an alien charter of faith (usually seen as the Roman Catholic Church, replete with its hierarchical priesthood, creeds and councils, holy days, sacraments, etc.). During these intervening centuries of ecclesial degeneration, all was not lost, however. A remnant of true believers, often rejected by the institutional church, could be found here and there in every age carrying on the torch of the gospel. Finally, in the bursting forth of the Protestant Reformation, the biblical faith of the New Testament was restored and set on its originally intended course.

For a great many clergy and laity, this description is ecclesiastical reality; it is the way that they conceive of the church and her history, if only implicitly. A key factor, however, is often not taken into account with the above sketch, namely, that it is a *paradigm* — a constructed pattern or model — of interpreting church history, which itself has a history determined by certain motivations which gave rise to it and caused it to flourish. As a paradigm, therefore, it is not the only way of looking at the church's past, and as a paradigm, it should always be subject to correction.

There are a number of assumptions at work in this paradigm of which contemporary Protestants may not even be aware, but which have resulted in effectively (1) creating a gulf between Protestantism and its patristic foundation, and (2) spawning ahistorical interpretations of church history that are based on a kind of spiritual successionist model that connects the Day of Pentecost (Acts 2) directly with the present-day church by transcending the external (outward) institutions of the historic church.

The first assumption leaves the false impression that Protestant Christianity is a development independent of, or even despite, the patristic (and medieval) church, while the second proposes a counter-historical solution to the claim for continuity — how we are connected to the age of the apostles — on the basis of our spiritual connection to the "true church" of history. We will find in this and the next chapter that these perspectives are neither warranted by a firsthand knowledge of the early sources themselves, nor do they better secure an orthodox understanding of the Christian faith. Moreover, the role of church history itself is seen, quite erroneously, as an expendable commodity in the way one ought to appropriate faith in Christ and pursue discipleship for today. Until the "fall" paradigm of viewing church history is revamped, or at least put in a more limited perspective, it will be exceedingly difficult for evangelicals to accept the "consensual tradition" of the early church.[1] For as long as a negative view of most of church history persists, there is no good reason to be reconciled with our pre-Reformation inheritance. Simply being introduced to the foundations and vitality of the early Christian Tradition is not going to be sufficiently convincing unless it is accompanied by a realignment of the church's past. To accomplish such a realignment, we need to take a more detailed look at certain historical dynamics at work in the late medieval and the Reformation periods as they relate to the early church. We will find that the points of theological and historical disjuncture between the Reformation and its patristic-medieval precursors have been highly overrated for too long.

The "Fall" of the Church

The concept of the fall of the church has always been perceived as axiomatic for the Protestant identity. Already in the first half of the sixteenth century, opinions varied as to the moment when the decline began in the post-apostolic period. For some of the early Anabaptist Reformers, such as Thomas Müntzer, the Christian church lost its virginity and became an adulteress soon after the death of the disciples of the apostles because of

---

1. As advanced by the writings of Thomas Oden. See his *After Modernity . . . What? Agenda for Theology* (Grand Rapids: Zondervan, 1990), esp. 106, 160-64, and the preface to vol. 1 of his systematic theology, *The Living God* (San Francisco: Harper & Row, 1987), or major projects like The Church's Bible, forthcoming from Eerdmans Publishing Company, designed to encourage evangelicals to reclaim their ancient heritage.

corrupt leadership,[2] manifested in the predominance of a clergy who cared more for the amassing of property and power than for the acquiring of spiritual virtues. Spiritualist Reformer Sebastian Franck heartily agreed, arguing that the outward church of Christ was wasted immediately after the apostles because the early Fathers, whom he calls "wolves" and "antichrists," justified war, power of magistracy, tithes, the priesthood, etc.[3] Franck knew firsthand what he called the writings of the "doctors of the Roman church," but (unlike the majority of his contemporaries) he utterly scorned them. That they are "wolves" within Christ's flock is, he claims,

> proved by their works, especially [those] of Clement, Irenaeus, Tertullian, Cyprian, Chrysostom, Hilary, Cyril, Origen, and others which are merely child's play[4] and quite unlike the spirit of the apostles, that is, filled with commandments, laws, sacramental elements and all kinds of human inventions. . . . What they have written is nothing but a shame and a disgrace.[5]

Although most leaders of the various Free Church movements did not share such a dim view of the earliest centuries, Franck's portrayal of the early church had a weighty influence on subsequent Free Church historiography.[6]

For the bulk of the Middle Ages and later reform movements, however, the critical transformation of the church as an institution occurred

2. Thomas Müntzer, "Sermon Before the Princes" (Allstedt, 13 July 1524), in *Spiritual and Anabaptist Writers,* ed. G. H. Williams, vol. 15 of Library of Christian Classics (Philadelphia: Westminster Press, 1957), 51.

3. Sebastian Franck, *Letter to Campanus,* in *Spiritual and Anabaptist Writers,* 151-52. Written in 1531 or 1541.

4. A different manuscript of the text says, "full of ravings and alien nonsense."

5. *Ibid.,* 148-49.

6. Particularly influential was a historical chronicle of Sebastian Franck, *Chronica. Zeitbuch vnnd Geschichtbibell von anbegyn bisz in diss gegenwertig* (Stuttgart, 1536). It is mentioned in 1560 by Obbe Philips as a reference work for the teachings of leading Anabaptists (although Franck was very critical of all organized churches, including the Anabaptists), and for providing historical guidance for author of *The Chronicle of the Hutterian Brethren* (1665). Anabaptist writer Pilgram Marpeck cites the *Chronica* as useful for its view of the Fathers (*The Writings of Pilgram Marpeck,* trans. and ed. W. Klassen and W. Klaasen [Scottsdale, Penn.: Herald Press, 1978], 285), as does Menno Simons in his 1539 "Foundations of Christian Doctrine," in *The Complete Writings of Menno Simons c. 1496-1561,* trans. L. Verduin and ed. J. C. Wenger (Scottsdale, Penn.: Herald Press, 1956), 138.

once Constantine became emperor and embraced Christianity. The moment seemingly so beneficial for the life of the church was the very point of its downfall. The famous John Wesley was most insistent upon this point in his sermon, "The Mystery of Iniquity":

> The grand blow was struck in the fourth century by Constantine the Great, when he called himself a Christian. . . . [j]ust so, when the fear of persecution was removed, and wealth and honour attended the Christian profession, the Christians did not gradually sink, but rushed headlong into all manner of vices. Then the mystery of iniquity was no more hid, but stalked abroad in the face of the sun. Then, not the golden, but the iron age of the church commenced.[7]

Ever since the death of Constantine in 337, Christian historians have wrestled with the implications of his rule for the church. He was not the first emperor to proclaim toleration for Christianity, but by 312,[8] the Roman world beheld an emperor who was identifying himself with the Christian faith in such a way that he believed the proper worship of "the Deity" was of vital importance for the welfare of the empire, and regarded himself as God's servant.[9] The social and political ramifications of Constantine's "conversion" were highly significant: Christians were reimbursed from the imperial treasury for their losses during the previous persecution, Christian clergy were exempted from the onerous burden of public obligations and could not be tried in civil courts, Christian nobility were more likely to be elected to high office, Christian basilicas — some of them very lavish in Jerusalem and Constantinople — were built from public funds, individuals were allowed to will their property after death to the

---

7. John Wesley, *Sermon* 61.27, in *The Works of John Wesley*, vol. 2, ed. A. C. Outler (Nashville: Abingdon, 1985), 463.

8. October 28, 312 was the battle of the Milvian bridge where Constantine was victorius over Maxentius for the control of the Western empire, which is also the approximate time, according to the differing accounts of Eusebius and Lactantius, that Constantine experienced a theophany convincing him to embrace the Christian religion. Exactly how this experience was a "conversion" must be taken into account with the evidence that Constantine was already refusing to persecute Christians and eschewed polytheism, as his father Constantius I had done in Britain and the Gauls.

9. The more useful studies on this subject are A. H. M. Jones, *Constantine and the Conversion of Europe* (Toronto: University of Toronto Press, 1978); T. D. Barnes, *Constantine and Eusebius* (Cambridge: Harvard Press, 1985); and H. Pohlsander, *The Emperor Constantine* (London and New York: Routledge, 1996).

church, councils of bishops were convened using imperial means for their transportation and accommodation, decisions promulgated by major councils were enforced by the authority of the state, all pagan symbolism and inscriptions were banned from Constantinople, and finally, Constantine became fully immersed in the Christian faith by being baptized in Nicomedia just before his death.[10] Whatever darker shadows his political agenda may have cast on his Christian sympathies,[11] and there has been much ink spilled on this, Constantine sincerely believed that God had given him a mandate to convert the Roman Empire to Christianity.[12] More significantly, the church's relation to the empire would never be the same again, as Christianity eventually moved from being a persecuted sect to the preeminent religion of the Mediterranean world, and its leaders became the chief arbiters in juridical matters and military conflicts.

In her play, *The Emperor Constantine,* Dorothy Sayers may have been right in thinking that it was inevitable for Christianity to cease from being a minority cult, if not by Constantine then by some other means, such that "the power of the purse and sword" must come into Christian hands.[13] As rapidly as Christianity was growing and permeating all the strata of Roman society, it was just a matter of time before Christianity would be embraced by an emperor and come to dominate the religious and social world of the empire. But at what price did such a transformation occur? What would the social and political triumph of the church mean for its role in the world as the incorporation and herald of the gospel of Jesus Christ?

10. Putting off baptism until later in life was quite common among Christians in the fourth and fifth centuries, especially among the nobility (e.g., Ambrose of Milan and his brother Satyrus), unless a serious illness intervened.

11. For example, Constantine continued to incorporate the worship of Sol Invictus (the Unconquerable Sun) in his public images on coins, in the famous triumphal arch erected in his honor in 315, being religiously neutral in both its symbolism and inscriptions (which may in part be explained by the fact that the Roman senate sponsored its erection), and in the pagan honorary title of Pontifex Maximus which was maintained until his death. Exactly how Constantine understood the Christian message is not clear, although one can certainly trace a development in the emperor's grasp of his Christian commitment from the victory in 312 to his conquest of the Eastern empire in 324. Moreover, the emperor's presence at some church councils, most notably Nicaea, indicates a veritable interest in theological matters.

12. *Oration to the Saints,* 11.1.

13. Dorothy Sayers, *The Emperor Constantine: A Chronicle* (London: Gallancz, 1951), 5.

The answer to these questions generated varying responses and is directly related to how the patristic legacy would eventually be regarded.

The Formation of the Paradigm

The idea of Christianity's corruption after Constantine and need for reform was hardly a novel idea with Protestantism, having taken less divisive forms already in the preaching of Francis of Assisi or Jean Gerson. A host of reforming initiatives swept through the twelfth and thirteenth centuries[14] (aimed mainly at the clergy and monastic institutions), characterized by a heightened understanding of the Bible and an emphasis on returning to the faith of the apostolic church. Central to these initiatives was the contention that the pristine and simple character of the original church was opposed to what the church had become. The very fact of the church's present corruptions implied that a discontinuity between the apostolic era and the post-apostolic church existed. Such a view can be found affecting a wide variety of thinkers in the high Middle Ages such as the Spiritual Franciscans, William of Ockham, Joachim of Fiore, and more popular protest movements as the Waldensians or the Apostolic Brethren. Theirs was an appeal to history that introduced a critical attitude toward the church as an institution in the sense that the church was no longer regarded as having existed the same for all time. Instead of an ongoing continuity between the earliest church and the present hierarchy, there had been a break and a subsequent decline.[15] This approach to history and the primitivistic ideal of a "return" to the apostolic faith will become one of the main weapons in countering papal claims to legitimacy during the fifteenth and sixteenth centuries. But for the time being, this view, employed as a critical perspective of ecclesial reform, was not a call to reject the traditions or the essential structure of the Roman church. It was rather an attack upon deviations from the true Tradition of the primitive church, which was to be found in Scripture. For such thinkers with Franciscan ideals, such as Peter John Olivi, the Roman church may have been identified as the "carnal church," or "Babylon," or the reigning pope associated (in

14. Christians living in this period were convinced that they were living in an age of reform. See Giles Constable, *The Reformation of the Twelfth Century* (Cambridge: Cambridge University Press, 1997).

15. G. Leff, "The Making of the Myth of a True Church in the later Middle Ages," *Catholic Historical Review* 68 (1968): 1-2.

varying degrees) with the Antichrist,[16] yet his apocalyptic images of a future apostolic church still included a pope at its head, albeit in an idealized form. Even Peter Waldo and his disciples (Waldensians) were from the very beginning bound by the traditional concepts of the church, despite their autonomy through the creation of independent worshiping communities. Their intent only was "to give greater space within the true church to the hearing of the Gospel, and this they initially had wanted to do within the body of the Roman church."[17] However much the papacy had polluted itself, the church was for the Waldensians, as it was for Hussites, the Roman church, whose sacerdotal hierarchy continued to communicate, if only in muted ways, the ancient faith of the apostles and the Fathers.

It remains to be seen why so many medieval sources traced the reasons for the moral and spiritual decadence of the church back to the accession of Constantine in the fourth century. One can find, for instance, in the opinions of John Wycliffe (c. 1325–1384) and John Hus (1369–1415) that the church's glad adoption of Constantine's patronage was perceived as the beginning of its degeneration from its original apostolic character, involving the accretion of unbiblical practices and the desire for temporal power. But exactly how the Constantinian era was considered a chief accessory to the downfall of the church's purity and the rise of Roman papal supremacy has, in fact, only partly to do with the fourth century. Instead, it was fueled in large part by the pervasive influence of an eighth-century decretal that came to be inserted in canon law known as the *Donation of Constantine*.[18] It was one of the greatest literary hoaxes of the Middle Ages.

The fascinating story behind this document begins with a legend that was already circulating about Sylvester (the *Life of Sylvester*), who became bishop of Rome in 314. At that time, Constantine was said still to be a worshiper of pagan idols and was persecuting Christians in the city. For his wickedness against God's people, the emperor contracts an incurable case of leprosy. He is advised by pagan priests to wash himself in the blood of three thousand infants, but cannot not bring himself to kill so many hapless innocents. Because of his clemency, Constantine is directed by a

16. *Ibid.*, 7-9.

17. A. Molnar, *A Challenge to Constantinianism: The Waldensian Theology in the Middle Ages* (Geneva: World Council of Churches, 1976), 43.

18. For the most comprehensive survey of the Sylvester legend and the *Donation*, see J. J. Ign. von Döllenger, *Fables Respecting the Popes of the Middles Ages*, trans. A. Plummer (London: Rivingtons, 1871).

heavenly vision to send for Sylvester, who had gone into hiding with his clergy during the persecution. The Roman bishop arrives, converting the emperor to Christianity, and heals his leprosy through the washing of baptism, whereupon the whole of Rome, senate and people, believe in Christ.

This legendary account was then later utilized in a public decree attributed to the emperor Constantine which he supposedly issued four days after his baptism. An unknown party sometime in the middle of the eighth century took the *Life of Sylvester* and turned it into the occasion by which Constantine, as a reward for healing him from leprosy, granted to Sylvester of Rome and his successors a number of comprehensive ecclesiastical and political rights.[19] The more significant of these privileges granted to the "Chair of Peter" and its successors was the imperial Lateran Palace in Rome (wherein Constantine was supposely baptized), sovereignty over the city of Rome, the provinces, cities and towns of the whole of Italy and the West; and most all, supreme authority over all churches in the world, including the chairs of Alexandria, Antioch, Jerusalem and Constantinople. The *Donation* was, in effect, a sweeping bow to the authority of the papacy, in realms both sacred and secular. Whereas attributing to the bishop of Rome religious and civic jurisdiction had nothing to do with the historic Constantine or the realities of the fourth-century episcopacy, it had everything to do with reinforcing early medieval Roman papal theory that governing the empire ought ultimately to rest with the head of the church.[20] So Constantine is said to have conferred upon Sylvester the symbols of the empire — the diadem, the purple robe, and the scepter.

Whether Owen Chadwick is correct in thinking, "The forger [of the *Donation*] must have known that to make the pope into the king of Spain, France, the Rhineland and Britain was a wild dream,"[21] is beside the point. Its influence during the Middle Ages and into the sixteenth century was extensively felt. That the *Donation* and its legend did not square with any known historical details always troubled some of the more astute.[22] Never-

---

19. "Edictum Domini Constantini Imperatoris," *Patrologiae Latinae* CXXX. 245A-252B (first incorporated in what is called the Pseudo-Isidorian decretals about A.D. 850). Extracts from it are later found in most medieval collections of canon law that governed ecclesiastical and social life, but in whole form in the *Decree of Gratian*. The *Donation* is found in part 1, division 96, chaps. 13-14 of the *Decree of Gratian*.

20. W. Ullmann, *The Growth of Papal Government in the Middle Ages: A Study in the Ideological Relation of Clerical to Lay Power* (London: Methuen, 1970), 416-17.

21. Owen Chadwick, *A History of Christianity* (New York: St Martin's Press, 1995), 60.

theless, the story appears ubiquitously in the literature of the Middle Ages, most prominently in the biographical account of Sylvester in the *Liber Pontificalis (Book of the Popes)*,[23] and in the extremely popular *Golden Legend* of Jacobus de Voragine.[24]

Though many were prepared to grant the historicity of the *Donation*, its grim implications for the amalgamation of the church with secular power and wealth were all too apparent. One can hear echoes of its fateful consequences in canto 19 of Dante's *Inferno*:

> Ah Constantine, what evil marked the hour —
> not of your conversion, but of the fee
> the first rich Father took from your dower!

Strong papal supporters, like Bernard of Clairvaux in the twelfth century, acknowledged that the moral decadence afflicting Christianity should be traced back to the *Donation*.[25] For the Waldensians, the moment of the church's spiral into decadence occurred at the beginning of the fourth century when Pope Sylvester and Constantine made themselves the architects of a pseudo-Christian unity of the world. Wycliffe too, in his *De ecclesia*, repudiates papal authority and the entire papal system on the grounds of having been founded by Constantine and not Christ.[26]

Despite the published findings of the Italian humanist Lorenzo

22. Constantine never had leprosy, nor did he persecute Christians before his "conversion," which was in 312 — two years before Sylvester became bishop! Nor was Constantine baptized in Rome by Sylvester, but in Nicomedia in 337 by an "Arian" bishop of that city, Eusebius. The real irony of the legend is that Sylvester made little or no lasting impact on the church or on the papcy itself. "Indeed," says Richard McBrien, "it is what he did not do as pope that is more significant than what he did do." *Lives of the Popes: The Pontiffs from St. Peter to John Paul II* (San Francisco: Harper, 1997), 57.

23. L. Duchesne, ed., *Liber Pontificalis,* vol. 1 (Paris: E. de Boccard, 1955), 170-87. It may be that this account is based partly upon the "sixth ecumenical" council of 680 which knows of the *Life of Sylvester* and expressly asserted that the Council of Nicaea was summoned by the Emperor Constantine and Pope Sylvester.

24. A narration of saints' legends organized according to the church calendar year, probably completed in 1260. Of the seven laws that Constantine supposedly issued as a result of his healing by Sylvester, the fourth was that "as the emperor is the ruler of the world, so the Pope of Rome should be the ruler of all the other bishops."

25. M. D. Chenu, *La théologie au douzième siècle* (Paris, 1957), 81.

26. Of his "Forty-Five Articles" (condemned on 10 July 1412), article 33 reads: "Silvester papa et Constantinus imperator erraverunt ecclesiam dotando" ("Through his endowment, Pope Sylvester and the emperor Constantine led the church astray").

Valla[27] in 1440 which showed that the *Donation* was a complete forgery and fraud, the momentum of eight hundred years of ecclesiastical custom was not so easily dismissed. A century later, Calvin was still obliged to refute the validity of the *Donation* against its supporters (*Institutes,* IV.11.12). The eminent Roman Catholic historians Bellarmine and Baronius would continue to credit the story with historical respectability for obvious reasons, though by the end of the Enlightenment its illegitimate nature had been sufficiently unveiled so that there could no longer be any doubt about its spuriousness. Nevertheless, permanent historical "damage" had been done: the reactionary basis of many reform movements was built upon an image of post-Constantinian Christianity that had been partly or largely informed by a distorted view of the fourth century and beyond. A dividing line was drawn between the true apostolic faith and the false hierarchy that had arisen as a later mutation, between the church of Jesus Christ and the one forged from the human power and traditions incarnated as the Roman institution. Such an image only served to exacerbate the abuses of ecclesiastical power and practices which were truly present in the medieval church and required reform.

As far as many Anabaptist reformers were concerned, what had happened to the church under Constantine began a chronicle of mounting apostasy in which Christianity stood in need of radical revision or restitution. Melchior Hoffman (c. 1530), who was also probably influenced by the eschatology of Franciscan spirituality,[28] construed his church history in seven periods, each represented by the seven churches in Revelation 2–3. The first church, that of Ephesus, is designated as the time of the apostles, and then Smyrna is the "church of the martyrs," referring to the persecuted

---

27. See C. B. Coleman, *The Treatise of Lorenzo Valla on the Donation of Constantine* (New Haven: Yale University Press, 1922). Valla knew only too well the ecclesiastical repercussions that his accusations would have, as he himself says in the preface, "For I am writing against not only the dead, but the living also, not this man or that, but a host, not merely private individuals, but the authorities. And what authorities! Even the supreme Pontiff himself. . . ." Cf. R. Fubini, "Humanism and Truth: Valla Writes against the Donation of Constantine," *Journal of the History of Ideas* 57 (1996): 79-86.

28. Most notably, the *Readings on the Apocalypse* of Peter John Olivi (1248-1298) and the apocalyptic interpretations of Joachim of Fiore. See W. O. Packull, "A Reinterpretation of Melchior Hoffmann's Exposition against the Background of Spiritualist Franciscan Eschatology with Special Reference to Peter John Olivi," in *The Dutch Dissenters: A Critical Companion to Their History and Ideas,* ed. I. B. Horst (Leiden: Brill, 1986), 49-50.

church of the second and third centuries. The church of Pergamon (Rev. 2:12-17), however, is symbolic of the reprobate church and the beginning of the church's degeneration. Hoffmann saw particularly the Constantinian legacy as the cause of spiritual decline. He seems to know of the *Donation of Constantine,* which of course he accepts as genuine, and is perceived as the link between pagan Rome and the anti-Christian papal church.[29] It is on account of this link that the Roman church arose and brought about the degeneration of the church through its acceptance of celibacy, replacement of the Lord's Supper with the Mass, and the introduction of infant baptism.

The Chronicle of the Hutterian Brethren (an Anabaptist account begun in the late 1560s) pinpoints the moment when the early church moved from its apostolic origins as the suffering church to the Roman church:

> Sylvester testified to Constantine the Great, the forty-third emperor, and won him over with many flattering words, accepting him as a Christian through baptism. . . . Here the pestilence of deceit that stalks in darkness and the plague that destroys at midday swept in with force, abolished the cross, and forged it into the sword. All this happened through the old serpent's deceit.[30]

The unfolding of history was accordingly molded to this pattern. Roman bishops gained absolute power over the rest of the churches and over kings, and whoever spoke out against them was condemned as a heretic and put to the sword. Such misalignment of the original apostolic initiative thanks to post-Constantinian Christianity called for a radical reevaluation of the concept of the church of Jesus Christ.

Just as central to the conception of the fall of the church is the development of what I will call a counter-church history that insisted the post-apostolic corruption did not result in a total loss of the gospel witness, but was in fact preserved through movements peripheral to, and often persecuted by, the institution of the Roman church. If the Roman church had become the cause of discontinuity between the New Testament church and the time of the Reformers, then another means had to be located which insured that continuity.

---

29. *Ibid.,* 53.

30. *The Chronicle of the Hutterian Brethren* or *Das grosse Geschichtbuch der Hutterischen Brüder,* trans. and ed. by the Hutterian Brethren (Rifton, N.Y.: Plough Publishing House, 1987), 31. The *Chronicle* accuses the popes of throwing out the Holy Scriptures and using "the Papal decretals" as the basis of their authority.

It was this "rewriting" of sacred history that has come to define the identity of many Protestants and their view of history unto the present day.

Returning to *The Chronicle*, those who were considered heretical by the church are depicted as dissenters of the Roman establishment by the very fact that opposition to Rome and the pope was itself a prototype of reformation. That the theology of these "dissenters" might be deemed heretical, or that no papacy existed in the fourth century, or that infant baptism was rarely practiced, is not taken into consideration. Such a philosophy of doctrinal (counter-)history provides very surprising results indeed! A third-century schismatic in Carthage named Donatus[31] is said to have taught and written against the pope as the greatest abomination. No less praiseworthy is the infamous Arius, whose views on the divine nature of Christ condemned at the Council of Nicaea (325)[32] are completely glossed over; he is called an "outstanding scholar" who "came forward to attack the Roman church for its errors. . . ."[33] Both of these men are honored for the fact that they rebaptized those who left the Roman church "with a true baptism," and that they were in turn reviled by the Pope. They are the forerunners of a long line of dissenters — Peter of Aragon, Dolcino of Novara, Peter Waldo, John Hus, John Wycliffe — wherein the light of truth had been preserved throughout the centuries before it was fully incarnated again within the churches of the Reformation. As one views the treatment of each of these figures, particularly the early patristic ones, it is apparent that the writer's agenda has completely overwhelmed the value of taking into account the historical and theological context in the task of interpreting church history.

31. "Donatism," taken from the name of Donatus, who was appointed bishop of Carthage by a dissident majority about 313, was a purist or rigorist movement within catholic Christianity. It refused to acknowledge the legitimacy of any bishop, or anyone ordained by such a bishop, who had surrendered the Scriptures *(traditor)* in times of persecution. Congenial to the stringent temperament of North African Christianity, Donatist churches often represented the majority in many towns, including Augustine's in Hippo. Whereas Donatists harbored more hostile attitudes toward the state, they were just as episcopally oriented as their "catholic" counterparts, affirming a succession of (Donatist) bishops from the apostle Peter.

32. Supposely citing fragments from his letters, the closing anathema of the Nicene Creed evidently wanted to shut out all theology related to Arius: "And those who say 'there was when he was not,' and 'Before his generation he was not,' and 'he came to be from nothing,' or those who pretend that the Son of God is 'of another *hypostasis* or substance,' or 'created,' or 'alterable,' or 'mutable,' the Catholic and Apostolic Church anathematizes" *(Letter of Eusebius of Caesarea to his Church)*.

33. *The Chronicle*, 43.

A very similar course of interpretation was pursued by the widely read *Martyrs' Mirror*,[34] which was compiled in the seventeenth century in order to show how the Anabaptists, not the Roman church, were the true church and linked to the age of the apostles. It is a thesis of spiritual successionism. The introduction contends that a remnant of "Anabaptists, or those who maintain such a confession as they do, have existed through every century, from the days of Christ to the present time." Wholly circumventing the institutional church of history, the true church is that which has regularly exhibited two signs: believers' baptism and persecution for its profession of faith. A long line of personalities is chronicled from the first to the sixteenth centuries as proof of the antiquity of Anabaptist views — the apostles, Donatus of Carthage (who "was called an Anabaptist, and his followers, Anabaptists"), various Fathers of the fourth century,[35] The Poor of Lyons, Albigensians, Waldensians, John Hus, John Wycliffe, and others. Not interested in a theory of dissenters, *The Martyrs' Mirror* seeks to stress that continuity in each age from the time of the apostles until the present was secured through a succession of doctrine, namely the Anabaptist beliefs regarding congregationalism, believers' baptism, and participation in the suffering at the hands of the Romanists. More than any one writer of the Reformation, it was these historiographic-like renderings of the church's past that left the most enduring mark on fostering the "fall" paradigm.

The Autonomy of the Paradigm

It often happens that a characterization of a past event becomes more influential in its later reception than the historical occurrence itself. We are familiar with the typical fishing stories in which the catch grows larger

34. Thieleman J. van Braght, *The Bloody Theater or Martyrs' Mirror of the Defenseless Christians Who Baptized Only Upon Confession of Faith, and Who Suffered and Died for the Testimony of Jesus, Their Saviour, From the Time of Christ to the Year A.D. 1660*, trans. J. F. Sohm (Scottsdale, Penn.: Herald Press, 1938).

35. Unlike Franck and the Hutterite Chronicle, *The Martyrs' Mirror* attempts to reclaim many of the patristic authorities by remolding, often drastically, their contributions in conformity with Anabaptist polity. Despite the fact that papalism is said to have commenced in the fourth century, Constantine is declared to have had a believers' baptism, and Sylvester is said to have been in agreement with Anabaptist perspectives on this point. It is important to note, however, that all of the chronicler's information about the earlier periods is second or thirdhand.

with each telling of the story. There is no question about how influential and utterly pervasive the "Constantinian fall" model of understanding church history has been in one form or another on subsequent Free Church identity. This is chiefly so because the model, which purported to originate from the ancient sources, came to acquire a dynamic existence of its own that served as an overriding hermeneutic for how one interprets those sources. Once the assumption was accepted as "historical," it was easily expanded and elaborated upon in subsequent years.

Succeeding interpretations of the church will regularly draw on the fall model and its correlative, a restitutionist sense of church history.[36] The Protestant Reformation, as a result, becomes construed not as a reform of what had come before (Catholicism), but as a retrieval of the apostolic "golden" era that either bypasses the intervening ages or so selectively chooses events and figures according to the restitutionist agenda that the effect is virtually the same. An even sharper dualism between the institutional ecclesiastical history and that of the church of true believers becomes promulgated.

Thus, the Pietist historian Gottfried Arnold (who subscribes and expands on the Hutterite thesis) taught in his *Impartial History of Church and Heresy* (1699)[37] that a radical redefinition of Christianity took place by the fourth century as powerful clerics came to believe that only they upheld the truth with the result that anyone who spoke against them, or their abuses, was branded as a heretic. Such heretics were the true believers who upheld the simplicity of Christ's teaching, and along with the persecution they suffer for standing against the ecclesiastical establishment, they show themselves to be authentic witnesses to the apostolic succession. This was the succession of the true church, fashioned and animated by the power of

36. Dennis Martin offers the following definition of "restitutionism": "It rejects traditional pre-modern history in order to restore 'true history' and locates 'true history' not in tradition or the mystery of the church but in a lost yet supposedly recoverable body of 'facts.' It assumes that one group or person can be closer than another (corrupted) group or person to the original Jesus or the true Jesus or the true Paul solely by studying the documents of the New Testament." "Nothing New Under the Sun? Mennonites and History," *Conrad Grebel Review* 5 (1987): 5.

37. *Unparteiische Kirchen- und Ketzer Historie vom Anfang des Neuen Testaments bis auf das Jahr Christi 1688* (Frankfurt am Main, 1699). I am indebted to Peter Erb's fine introductory discussion of Arnold in *Pietists: Selected Writings* (New York: Paulist Press, 1983); and in his *Pietists, Protestants, and Mysticism: The Use of Late Medieval Spiritual Texts in the Work of Gottfried Arnold (1666-1714)* (Lanham, Md.: Scarecrow Press, 1989).

the Spirit. In contrast, the bishops of the Constantinian corporation forged their theologies into narrow and stultifying definitions, building not on the Scripture, but on symbols and conciliar statements according to which all truth must be judged.

Reflective of the thesis in the *Martyrs' Mirror,* Free church historian Ludwig Keller developed his own successionist interpretation from the early church to the Reformation,[38] which in turn inspired Ernst Troeltsch to take up a dualistic rendering of church history in his magisterial *Social Teaching of the Christian Churches* (1911). Likewise, Baptists have generally followed a similar pattern in accordance with one of their precursors, John Smythe, who repeatedly denied belief in an outward succession — i.e., popes, bishops, etc. — claiming that "there is no succession in the outward church, but that all succession is from heaven. . . ."[39] Continuity of faith resides in the succession of divine truth, not in the usual tokens of the institutional church. Although a predominant number of Baptist historians have taught (accurately) that the Puritan context of seventeenth-century England and Holland marks the origination of modern-day Baptists,[40] no less influential have been those who claim their lineage should be traced back across the centuries to New Testament times. According to this latter scenario, Baptists are not a species of Protestantism, but predate it, being found in every previous age since the apostles.

The popularity of this opinion was enhanced by the wide dissemination of a small booklet earlier this century by J. M. Carroll, *The Trail of*

---

38. Ludwig Keller, *Die Reformation und die älteren Reformparteien* (Leipzig, 1885). The origins of the Waldensians, who were the direct precursors of the Free Church, could be traced back to the Jesus and the apostles, and throughout the succeeding centuries, whenever those who opposed the policies of Pope Sylvester and Constantine were deemed heretics on that account. This approach was countenanced in the works of Eberhard Arnold (d. 1935), himself a member of the Bruderhof (Hutterian Brethren) in Germany.

39. Quoted in W. M. Patterson, *Baptist Successionism: A Critical View* (Valley Forge, Penn.: Judson Press, 1969), 15. Eventually, Smythe comes to the conclusion that the restitution of the church had been effected in the Mennonites with whom he joins. The practice of finding a remnant of true believers in each age of the church has been particularly favored by Baptist and Disciples of Christ historians. D. F. Durnbaugh, "Theories of Free Church Origins," The *Mennonite Quarterly Review* 41 (1968): 85f.

40. Robert Torbet, *History of the Baptists* (Philadelphia: Judson Press, 1950); H. Leon McBeth, *The Baptist Heritage: Four Centuries of Baptist Witness* (Nashville: Broadman Press, 1987); William Brackney, *The Baptists* (Westport, Conn.: Greenwood Press, 1988).

Blood Following the Christians Down through the Centuries.[41] Despite the fact that apostolic succession is discredited (as an episcopal institution), Baptists can point to an unbroken line of churches since Christ, identified chiefly through congregational polity, believers' baptism, separation from the state, and persecution — the "trail of blood." Corruption of the apostolic church commenced soon after the apostles as "the original democratic policy and government of the early churches" was eclipsed by the rise of the episcopal hierarchy and infant baptism. But it was when Constantine became a Christian emperor that the church was wedded to the Roman Empire and brought about an exchange of spiritual and temporal power.

> To effectually bring about and consummate this unholy union, a council was called. . . . The alliance was consummated. A Hierarchy was formed. In the organization of this Hierarchy, Christ was dethroned as head of the churches and Emperor Constantine enthroned (only temporarily however) as head of the church.[42]

This "hierarchy," whose development is signified by conciliar activity, is the beginning, according to Carroll, of the Catholic Church. It is important to note that the "council" mentioned above, presumably Nicaea, represents not biblical Christianity, but a compound of state and church, replacing the apostolic faith and charisms with legislative enactments. Those who refused to attend the ancient councils, thereby rejecting the marriage of the episcopacy with the imperium or any exaltation of a centralized government over the individual congregation, are described as "Baptists." In keeping with the successionist model, "Baptists" can be found, if not in name, in every age since the the apostolic era. Moreover, the number of dissenting groups that are identified as proto-Baptists was enlarged as the paradigm became a fix-

41. The full title of this book is worth noting: *The Trail of Blood Following Christians Down through the Centuries, or The History of Baptist Churches from the Time of Christ, Their Founder, to the Present Day* (Lexington: Ashland Avenue Baptist Church, 1931). Enclosed is a two-page chart which traces development of both the hierarchical or "Catholic" church and that of the true Christians from Christ to the present day.

This publication seems to be a twentieth-century popularization of the same theory put forth by an English Baptist minister, G. H. Orchard, *A Concise History of Baptists from the Time of Christ, Their Founder, to the Eighteenth Century* (Lexington: Ashland Avenue Baptist Church, 1838), whose work was reissued in 1855 as *A Concise History of Foreign Baptists . . . from the Establishment of Christianity to the Present Age.*

42. *Trail of Blood,* 16.

ture in historical interpretation. Modern theorists identify groups from every epoch — Montantists, the so-called "Novations," Donatists, St. Patrick, the Bogomils, the Albigenses, the Lollards, the Waldensians and, of course, the Anabaptists — as doctrinal precursors.[43]

A nearly identical model is followed by the Independent Christian Church historian, James DeForest Murch, who argued that Rome's claim to supremacy was aided and abetted by the rise of Constantine to power. Just as the chief founder of the Disciples' (Christian Church) movement, Alexander Campbell, had opined in the previous century,[44] ecclesiastical hierarchy and organization were regarded as a substitute for the church's life in the Spirit. The move was a clear departure from New Testament Christianity.

> In self-defense came the first creeds, definitions of dogma and official norms for church teaching. The eventual tendency was for faith to be placed in doctrinal statements to such a degree as to obscure individual commitment to and communion with Christ. Men well versed in theology and church tradition came to occupy positions of prominence far beyond their local churches.[45]

Nevertheless, Murch declared, "The Free Church has had an unbroken existence in Christendom from the first Christian Church in Jerusalem, A.D. 30, to the present day."[46] Most noticeably — and strikingly reminiscent of

43. The enduring influence of Free Church successionism is demonstrable by the continued publications of historical refutations. Patterson, *Baptist Successionism*; J. E. McGoldrick, *Baptist Successionism: A Crucial Question in Baptist History* (Methuen, N.J.: Scarecrow Press, 1994).

44. "Spirituality and true charity amongst the leaders expired in the council of Nice [Nicaea], when the first creed received the imperial subscription." *The Christian Baptist*, 5.1 (6 August 1827): 7.

45. J. D. Murch, *The Free Church: A Treatise on Church Polity with Special Relevance to Doctrine and Practice in Christian Churches and Churches of Christ* (Louisville: Restoration Press, 1966), 29. To what degree Disciples' and Christian Church historians subscribe to Murch's scheme is impossible to determine at the present time, since there seems to be no prevailing attitude toward the applicability of the early church. The want of a "longer" view of church history within this Free Church tradition is obviously problematic.

46. *Ibid.*, 36. For successionist theology in the Plymouth Brethren and Seventh-Day Adventism, see respectively, E. H. Broadbent, *The Pilgrim Church* (London: Pickering and Inglis, 1931); Ellen White, *The Great Controversy between Christ and Satan* (Washington, D.C.: Review and Herald Publishing Association, 1911).

Arnold's approach — the links in this "unbroken" chain of existence are drawn from heretical groups: Montanists, Marcionites, Priscillians, and so on, all on the (mistaken) basis of their congregational polity and persecuted status. Virtually no heed is given to the respective historical contexts of these earlier groups as they are liberally drafted into the Free Church paradigm. Certainly no self-respecting biblical scholar would allow Old or New Testament texts to be treated in such a fashion!

William Patterson's critique of the successionist model is not overstated when he argues that such theories show an excessive use of and dependence on secondary sources,[47] and, exhibiting little knowledge of the primary works themselves, utilize past groups or associations with no regard to historical context in order to suit their presuppositions. As the secondary sources cited become unquestioned authorities, a facade of "historical" evidence is established that acts as proof for the fall of the church and successionist theses. That these theses are dependent on or derived from a paradigm seems not to be noticed. Another way to say this is that the paradigm has become self-evident enough that testing it against the original sources for validity is no longer necessary. In either case, the fall paradigm has acquired the power of its own authentication which remains active to this present day.

Rival Versions of the Past

An important motivation in the promulgation of the paradigm is revealed when we acknowledge that it evolved largely as a Protestant polemical device. As a central feature of the anti-Roman Catholic theological arsenal, the "fall" and "restitution" of the church became an indigenous part of Protestant historiography that was preserved and augmented over the cen-

47. Patterson, *Baptist Successionism*, 24. If anyone should complain about my use of less contemporary sources to define Free Church attitudes toward early church history (e.g., Carroll, Murch, etc.), I would simply reply that they are symptomatic of a general state of affairs that continues to govern Free Church self-perception when viewing history and theology. There are signs of an awakening to the seminal role which the early church plays in the fashioning of the Free Church identity; see the forthcoming collection of essays, *The Free Church and the Early Church: Bridging the Historical and Theological Divide*, ed. D. H. Williams. Nevertheless, the usual absence of integration with the patristic sources and early church history within the communitarian life of most Free churches, tells us that we have a long way to go.

turies. In other words, the idea of church renewal through a revival of patristic scholarship, outside of Christian humanist circles, was rapidly polarized into "Protestant" and "Roman Catholic," each side claiming descent from the apostolic church as the notion of the church's reformation became translated into rival versions of the past.

In a fascinating book entitled *Drudgery Divine*, Jonathan Z. Smith shows how much the appeal to Christian origins in the post-Reformation period was transformed into a matter of Protestant anti-Catholic apologetics. The working assumption for Protestant scholarship in the seventeenth and eighteenth centuries was that pernicious doctrines, philosophies and practices had crept their way into the primitive gospel of Jesus which had become thus transmuted, incarnate as the Roman church, or for that matter, as any highly organized form of religion. As Smith explains,

> The German reformation is imperfectly described as an appeal to scripture versus tradition. It was rather an appeal to history. The discovery had been made that the church, as it existed, was an institution which no longer corresponded to its original, that it was a corrupted, degraded, perverted institution. The appeal to scripture was not itself the moving spring of the reformation, it was the consequence of the sense of decay and degeneracy. As the doctrine of the fall of man was the key of human, so the doctrine of the corruption of the church was the key of ecclesiastical history.[48]

We have already seen a similar principle at work in *The Martyrs' Mirror*, a prime example of the ideological forces that were shaping Free church historiography. This lengthy document is much more than a chronicle of martyrs of the true faith. It is an attempt to rewrite church history in acccordance with the original marks of the true church of Jesus Christ in contrast to the origins which marked the institutional church of Roman Catholicism or other Protestant groups. Such revisionist history was not unique to Anabaptists. Various reconstructions became endemic to the early development of Protestant historiography, especially as charges of novelty were inveighed against Protestants by Roman Catholics. One

---

48. *Drudgery Divine: On the Comparison of Early Christianities and the Religions of Late Antiquity* (Chicago: University of Chicago Press, 1990), 73, quoted from M. Pattison, *Isaac Casaubon: 1559-1614*, 2nd ed. (Oxford: Oxford University Press, 1892), 322.

can see these forces at work in John Foxe's *Actes and Monuments* (1554),[49] the first English attempt to establish the continuity of a proto-Protestant piety from apostolic times to the Reformation. His point in reviewing the cases of hundreds of believers who suffered for their opposition to a corrupt church was both to show Roman Catholicism's ecclesial degradation and to trace a succession of pre-Protestant groups, most notably the Albigensians and Waldensians, whose faithfulness throughout the centuries provided an alternative link to the apostolic church.[50] The seventeenth-century Puritans/Dissenters also condemned most of church history as anti-Christian popery, given that the church's hierarchy had precipitously fallen into spiritual decline ever since Constantine. Origins of the true church had to be found elsewhere. A succession, not of bishops, but of pre-Protestant dissenters whose origins stretched back before Constantine was the means of establishing the Puritan claim to antiquity.

In what was the earliest constructed Lutheran history of the Reformation, the *Ecclesiastica Historia* (1574), supervised by Matthias Flacius Illyricus (later called the *Magdeburg Centuries* from its third edition in 1757 because of its treatment of each century of church history as a discrete unit),[51] maintained that by the beginning of the second century the church had begun already to fall away from the apostolic truth in her constitution and in specific doctrinal elements, what he calls the *mysterium iniquitatis*, the first phase of Catholicism (II.109). But not until the fourth century, namely, the alliance with the Roman Empire via Constantine and his successors, did the church witness the rise of rituals and ceremonies that were borrowed more from paganism than from the New Testament. The tone of the entries is overtly polemical, its intent being to refute Roman Catholic claims to authenticity and to show that Lutheranism is a return to the apostolic faith.

It is a recurring theme that can be found in numerous translations of the early Fathers published by Protestants. This is not the place to catalogue

49. The full title is *Actes and Monuments of these latter and perilous days touching matters of the Church, wherein are comprehended and described the great persecutions & horrible troubles, that have bene wrought and practised by the Romishe Prelates*, or popularly known as the *Book of Martyrs*. The first English edition was published in 1563.

50. S. J. Barnett, "Where Was Your Church before Luther? Claims for the Antiquity of Protestantism Examined," *Church History* 68 (1999): 15-16.

51. For an insightful commentary on the historical reconstruction of the *Historia*, see Auguste Jundt, *Les Centuries de Magdebourg, ou la Renaissance de l'Historiographie Ecclésiastique au Seizième Siècle* (Paris: Librairie Fischbacher, 1883).

the variety and distinctions of works produced, apart from mentioning by way of example Wolfgang Musculus's 1540 Latin translation of Basil of Caesarea's *Ascetica magna,* which sought to show that the Cappadocian was a direct precursor of the Reformation, or Théodore Béze's 1570 Greek-Latin edition of *The Five Dialogues on the Holy Trinity* (which he wrongly attributed to Athanasius), arguing that the trinitarian teaching of the Reformers is more in line with that of Athanasius.[52] It is clear enough that the writing of church history or translations of texts during this time was very often prompted by confessional aims that fueled contemporary disputations, among both Protestants and Roman Catholics. Whether such interests in the early church were driven by an aim to recapture the "golden age" of theology or as means of reforming the present church mattered little in the overall quest on all sides to claim sole continuity with New Testament Christianity in the face of longstanding corruption.

Some Implications

There is no question that the above perspectives on the "Constantinian fall" of Christianity have percolated their way into contemporary theological thinking for different reasons and in different ways, scholarly and popular, with examples too numerous to count. Jürgen Moltmann draws on the paradigm when he cites the beginning of the Constantinian era as the Christian church taking over the role of political religion, i.e., a delimiting of the church to the political order of the Roman Empire.[53] Likewise,

52. Irena Backus, "Some Fifteenth- and Sixteenth-Century Translations of Basil of Caesarea and Justin Martyr," *Studia Patristica* 18. 4 (1990): 305-21.

53. Jürgen Moltmann, *The Passion for Life: A Messianic Lifestyle* (Philadelphia: Westminster Press, 1978). In this book, Moltmann exalts the church polity of congregationalism as that which best fulfills the Reformation's idea of universal priesthood. All the internal structures of the church exists for the sake of the congregation. However, he says, "[w]ith the christianization of the Roman empire the church sacrificed its peculiar and visible form as the congregation. Thus the church was no longer formed through voluntary and independent congregations, but belonging to regions, zones, parochial territories, provincial churches, cultural churches, and national churches" (like the German national church which he criticizes) (121). Moreover, the separation of the clergy from the laity became final; faith was practiced by participating in public events; instead of the sacraments being celebrated by the believing community, they became official acts of the priests; diakonia was dissolved into the state's general welfare system, and with this the church also lost its mission (122).

Malcolm Muggeridge makes the distinction between Christianity and "Christendom": "Christendom began with the emperor Constantine. Christianity began with the Incarnation."[54] Thus Christendom, a calcified and politicized version of God's original work, came about in the fourth century through an absorption of Christianity into the state.

No less has Stanley Hauerwas, an ethicist working from a Methodist background (who has referred to himself as a "high-church Mennonite"), incorporated the Constantinian paradigm into his thought as a means of criticizing contemporary Western culture, especially American Protestantism. Like those ancient Christians who associated the Roman Empire with the kingdom of God, so have many American Christians conflated the democratic and capitalist policies of their country with the plan of God's salvation.[55] Any time the church and its theological identity become interwoven with the ideology of the system or state, Hauerwas argues, we have an instance of "Constantinian Christianity." This occurs whenever Christian universality has been embodied in Western civilization or the state, and not in the church. "The church thus no longer signified an identifiable people, but came to mean primarily the hierarchy and sacramental institution."[56] Instead, Hauerwas claims, the church is meant to be a colony of resident aliens, functioning as a contrasting society or *polis*,[57] where the best interests of the church do not coincide with those of the state.

None of my observations thus far are meant to deny that the structure of the Christian faith was deeply impacted by the end of the fourth century as it moved from being a marginal sect to the primary religion of the Roman Empire by the time of Theodosius I (379–395). It is also obvious that Constantinianism has come to mean much more than the series of events that played themselves out during the fourth century. I quite agree with the criticism that the temptation of the church in seeking to identify its mission and the meaning of its history with the function of the state in any age or culture is a chronic problem that Christians have had to confront in their

54. Malcolm Muggeridge, *The End of Christendom* (Grand Rapids: Eerdmans Publishing Company, 1980), 14.

55. "What Could it Mean for the Church to Be Christ's Body?" in *In Good Company: The Church as Polis* (Notre Dame: University of Notre Dame Press, 1995), 58.

56. A. Rasmusson, *The Church as "Polis": From Political Theology to Theological Politics as Exemplified by Jürgen Moltmann and Stanley Hauerwas* (Notre Dame: University of Notre Dame Press, 1995), 222.

57. Stanley Hauerwas and William Willimon, *Resident Aliens* (Nashville: Abingdon Press, 1989), 69ff.

calling to "go into all the world and make disciples" (Matt. 28:19). The great irony in the success of christianizing any society is that the faithful must inevitably wrestle with Jesus' claim that his kingdom is not of this world. For the church's unity with the host culture results in the church's loss of self-identity and ability to speak prophetically to that culture.

It may be that a limited version of Constantinianism is a useful model for moral theology and for confronting the gnawing questions about the changing role of the church in contemporary society.[58] As a Baptist whose heritage is committed to maintaining a separation of church and state, I certainly have no quarrel with this. But then, as Hauerwas has rightly put it, "Constantinianism is a 'given',"[59] which is precisely the difficulty. What exactly are Christians renouncing if they renounce Constantinianism? The fact that Constantianism has been historically connected with the "fall" of the church has meant for most Free Church Protestantism much more than a problem of political theology; it has served as the grounds rather for an abdication — tacitly or explicitly — from the theological and spiritual history of the post-apostolic church. The Constantinian model has come to indict all of fourth-century Christianity and subsequent ages as seriously flawed and having abandoned their biblical moorings. Those who would walk the path of Christian faithfulness must therefore go around it to stay on the path.

One of the strongest cases for the problematic nature of Constantinianism and its alien legacy in comparison to biblical Christanity has been made by the late John Howard Yoder, a Mennonite scholar, whose work has definitively shaped the direction of Free Church studies in this century. On one hand, Yoder does not identify with the kind of restitutionism that traces the true church through a series of covert links with martyrs or dissenters. The temptation of this counter-historiography is "to imagine genetic connections where there were none, thus short-changing the study of proximate real causes."[60] Another problem is to assume all suffering dissenters agreed on all points; they did not, including infant baptism. But more fundamentally, Yoder criticizes the ahistorical

58. See, as another example of this, Loren Mead's *The Once and Future Church* (New York: The Alban Institute, 1991).

59. *Ibid.*, 231. The fall paradigm is functional but not in the polemical, anti-Catholic sense for Hauerwas, who prizes his Methodist heritage as "the rediscovery of the Catholic substance of John and Charles Wesley."

60. John Howard Yoder, *The Priestly Kingdom: Social Ethics as Gospel* (Notre Dame: University of Notre Dame Press, 1984), 133.

nature of restitutionism: "If it is not the public institutional succession which accredits the faithfulness of the mainstream church, then why should it be a clandestine institutional succession which accredits the faithful church?" Any skirting of the church's whole history shuts the door on responsible criticism. In order to be able to offer any revisionist alternative to church history, one must be history oriented. A dualistic perspective of the church's history cannot suffice.

On the other hand, Yoder identifies the "fall" of the New Testament church with what he calls the "Constantinian shift," that great negative watershed in Christian history which turned the church from a critical, prophetic and suffering minority to its new role as legitimator of power, wealth and hierarchy. To put it simply, the gospel norm — the story and claims of Christ — was betrayed in the Constantinian era when the fourth-century "fall" produced a new ecclesiology and concomitantly, a reversal in Christian ethics. Imperial values and social and legal structures came to be identified with Christianity, "the Constantinian wedding of piety and power," so as to create a Christian Roman Empire. Before Constantine, violence and coercion were morally abhorrent; after Constantine, there was a growing acceptance of imperial violence as a Christian duty, to the point of repressing other Christian groups deemed heretical. What the church accepted in the Constantinian shift is what Jesus had rejected, moving from Golgotha to the battlefield. Yoder's own position in defense of Christian pacifism is most apparent in his arguments here.

In this new ecclesiology, the lines between state and the church were no longer clear; Roman society was the church at large. There was no way to clearly distinguish the true church anymore. The very meaning of the word "Christian" was altered: its earliest moral and intellectual meanings were reversed through sociological and political pressures. This had profound implications for the church's internal structure:

> The definitions of the faith could thus no longer take the assembly of believers as its base. As a result, therefore, the eyes of those looking for the church had to turn to the clergy, especially to the episcopacy, and henceforth, "the church" meant the hierarchy more than the people.[61]

"Constantinianism" is, therefore, directly related to the rise of the church as a hierarchical institution and the eclipsing of congregational polity. In

61. Yoder, "The Constantinian Sources of Western Social Ethics," in *The Priestly Kingdom*, 136.

effect, a contemporary political-social agenda took over the development of doctrine from the believing and confessing churches.

As its identity was transformed, there was likewise an impact on the church's doctrine as expressed in the major formulas of faith. In a commentary on Yoder's perspective of the fourth-century church, A. J. Reimer claims that it is not entirely clear whether Yoder considers the Constantinian shift and trinitarian orthodoxy as defined at the Councils of Nicaea (325) and Constantinople (381) to be part of the same movement, though the general trend in Yoder's thought is that the two are intrinsically linked together. The Apostles' Creed, for example, which was already in place by the third century, is perceived as a deviation from the biblical narrative since its lacks specific allusions to the life and teachings of Jesus: a kind of "leap" is made from birth to the crucifixion. Nor is there a sense of urgency to call people to repentance and seek forgiveness of sins, despite the fact that the creed affirms Christian belief in the "forgiveness of sins." "Instead," says Reimer, "there is reflected in the creed the beginnings of the sacramentalism and metaphysical speculation so prevalent in the medieval church with the Catholic church itself becoming an object of belief."[62]

Although there are many nuances in the constructions of Yoder's thought that cannot be presented here, it is accurate to say that the basic structure of the fall paradigm is being asserted with full rigor: Anabaptist Christianity restored the normative state of the church as found in the New Testament which had been obscured in the clouds of authoritarianism and politico-doctrinal manipulation since Constantine. Despite Yoder's justifiable protestations against the validation of counter-church histories, one is nevertheless encouraged to jump from the New Testament over centuries of a corrupt establishment to find radical renewal in the sixteenth century. This is not unlike Harold Bender's famous essay, "The Anabaptist Vision," wherein he also rejected spiritual successionism. Anabaptism is depicted as the culmination of the Reformation, the fulfillment of the original vision of Luther and Zwingli, and is therefore a recreation without compromise of the New Testament church and the vision of Christ and the apostles. It is preferable, Bender claimed, to make a radical

---

62. A. James Reimer, "Trinitarian Orthodoxy, Constantinianism, and Theology from a Radical Protestant Perspective," in *Faith to Creed: Ecumenical Perspectives of the Affirmation of the Apostolic Faith in the Fourth Century,* ed. S. M. Heim (Grand Rapids: Eerdmans Publishing Company, 1991), 136-37.

break with 1500 years of church history and culture than to break with the New Testament.[63]

Repercussions and Implications

Now we must return to the question I asked in the beginning of this chapter. Did a breach occur in the ways by which the faith was defined and defended in the fourth century and afterwards? Do we find the ecclesial vitality of apostolic Christianity and its proclamation of the evangelical truth increasingly abandoned or even repressed in the centuries that immediately followed? As we have seen, Free Church Protestantism, despite a lack of uniformity in its doctrines and historical developments, answers these questions with a story of the church that is primarily negative. It is a story of increasing degeneration that has served to devalue theological formation between the end of the apostolic age and the Reformation. In particular, the later (patristic) Tradition becomes suspected of superimposing alien interpretations on the simple biblical revelation, replacing the straightforward narrative of Jesus' life and death with credal formulas politically motivated, producing an elitist type of theology. The result is that the christological and trinitarian formulations which became Christian orthodoxy are thought to reflect the power structures and understanding of the Constantinian church instead of a Christian one.[64] As creeds, liturgies, dogmas, and ecclesiastical offices became the antitheses of the apostolic era, the external or "Catholic" church obscured the means by which the true faith was transmitted to succeeding generations of believers. And thus, the fall paradigm is complete.

In a highly tendentious interpretation of the Constantinian era, Alistair Kee unequivocally argues that Constantine was never really a "believer" and his alleged conversion meant that the church's values were substituted for Constantine's, which were governed by a political ideology of power and wealth. The church simply became incorporated into the imperial plan and became an instrument in the unification of the empire. "The values of the historical Jesus are now replaced by the values of Constantine," and thus,

63. Harold Bender, "The Anabaptist Vision," in *The Recovery of the Anabaptist Vision*, ed. Edward G. Hershberger (Scottsdale, Penn.: Herald Press, 1957), 37-41.

64. For other examples of the Constantinian "fall" and restitutionism, see G. J. Heering, *The Fall of Christianity* (New York: Fellowship Publications, 1943); Henry Townsend, *The Claims of the Free Churches* (London: Hodder and Stoughton, 1949).

He [Constantine] conquered the Christian church. The conquest was complete, extending over doctrine, liturgy, art and architecture, comity, ethos and ethics. And this is the greatest irony, that Constantine achieved by his kindness what his predecessors had not been able to achieve by force. Without a threat or a blow, and all unsuspecting, the Christians were led into captivity and their religion transformed into a new imperial cult.[65]

Once the driving forces of the Christian Roman empire became transformed into the politics of power, the formulation of Christian doctrine and ethics would swiftly mirror its environment. The very mechanism of church councils and decisions made by enclaved bishops bespeaks the secularization of the church's organization. Both doctrine and practice were becoming polluted, since the church was moving away from its New Testamental and sub-apostolic origins. This meant that the major creeds of the fourth century, the Nicene and the Constantinopolitan (381), and Chalcedon (451) in the fifth, could be seen as symptomatic expressions of the corrupt legacy of Constantine, and therefore not relevant to the task defining orthodox Christianity.

Such a perspective casts a dark shadow on the origination of doctrinal creeds and is translated as a general suspicion about creeds in general. It is hardly surprising that those denominations which are part of the historic Free church consider themselves anticredal — "no creed but Christ" — cleaving only to the Bible and the working of the Spirit.[66] Since ancient creeds are a reflection of the rejected hierarchical and imperial institution, they are held of little account when it comes to marking the road of orthodox belief. Whereas they may function implicitly in marking the parameters of theological orthodoxy, as does the Nicene Creed, they are also perceived as manifestations of the political and social changes within the church that had come upon Christianity in the fourth century. That

65. Alistair Kee, *Constantine versus Christ: The Triumph of Ideology* (London: SCM Press, 1982), 154.

66. E. Glenn Hinson, one of a handful of patristic scholars writing today from a Baptist perspective, has shown that despite Baptists' disavowal of creeds and doctrinal formulae, they have in fact historically affirmed their faith through "confessions," and that these statements have acted as succinct summaries of the Christian essentials. "Creeds and Christian Unity," *Journal of Ecumenical Studies* 23 (1986): 25-36. From a Mennonite perspective with the same aim, see Howard Loewen, *One Lord, One Church, One Hope and One God: Mennonite Confessions of Faith* (Elkhart, Ind.: Institute of Mennonite Studies, 1985).

such creeds are used at all, or at least thought of as a doctrinal baseline, has more to do with the fact that such confessions were valued by the Reformers rather than with the historical pertinence of the patristic era in itself.

More important for our present task, however, is the tendency of the paradigm (intentionally or not) to discredit or minimize the value of the late patristic era as normative in defining the true faith. Again, the staggering irony of this position is that most evangelicals subscribe to a Nicene-Constantinopolitan Trinity and a Chalcedonian Christology, and read their Bibles with these theological "lenses" as the truth. The Tradition articulated in this era is nevertheless perceived in practice as discontinuous with either the apostolic age or the first three centuries. It only stands to reason that the ecclesial establishment (e.g., "hierarchy") and the deposit of faith formulated in the later patristic period must be completely subordinated to a biblical notion of the church and its faith, and in some instances, even repented of.

Despite the ostensible care and attention given to doctrine and history by evangelical scholarship, the long term effects of the fall of the church paradigm have caused a compartmentalization of church history in very select and ahistorical ways. By discounting the intrinsic theological value of the fourth century and beyond, the only "real" history that counts is a truth-only or a spiritual successionism that has come to typify the history of evangelical theology and biblical exegesis. One may hear occasional appeals to the Nicene or Apostles' Creeds; nevertheless, the doctrinal history and theological architects of Christianity in the Constantinian era are not essential parts of today's preaching and teaching. As indirect as it may seem for today, I maintain that the fall paradigm (with or without Constantine) has been functionally discreet and highly successful in preventing evangelicals from claiming the foundational centuries of the faith as their own.

What this means is that the heritage of the ancient Tradition has been sufficiently discounted such that the training of pastors and scholars in many Protestant institutions receive minimal, if any, exposure to it. Making room for courses in historical theology in most seminaries is difficult enough as it is, with general surveys and denominational histories receiving the lion's share of available space. There are very few scholars from Free Church communions in the United States who are conversant with the literature of the Fathers, though the growing number of graduate students specializing in patristics would indicate that their number is on the rise.

Theologically speaking, the widest part of the rift in Free church thought, which presupposes that patristic (and medieval) theology was constructed along the lines of conformity with an imperial or hierarchical model rather than a biblical one, is that Scripture and Tradition are two different and conflicting authorities in the sense of being mutually exclusive of each other. The interpretation of the Tradition as a nonbiblical and purely human artifice designed to reinforce the institution of the episcopacy has deep roots within the Free Church mentality, as we have seen. If the goal of restoration is a return to the Bible or apostolic Christianity, then the Tradition of the church becomes not an ally in the process of restoration but an impediment as a byproduct of the church's "fall."

An Alternative Approach

At issue in this chapter is how the fall paradigm has been cultivated to the point of distorting the ecclesiastical and political forces which composed the fourth century in order to supply a stronger case for the church's need of radical restitution. Central to this distortion is how the conception of "Constantinianism" has operated to reduce the development of the early church's doctrine to an epiphenomenon of imperial politics. What is nearly or entirely ignored in this paradigm is the vitality and continuity of the worshiping and confessing church throughout the patristic era — including the period after Constantine. The faith professed and practiced in the early churches was not determined by the political machinations of emperors and episcopal hierarchies. The essential formulation and construction of the Christian identity was something that the fourth century *received* and continued to expand upon through its biblical exegesis and liturgical life as reflected in the credal Tradition. In other words, I am postulating that the continuity between the post-apostolic period and the kind of Christianity articulated in fourth and fifth centuries was more complex and durable than Free church typologies of ecclesiastical history have been willing to allow. Most criticisms of the Constantinianization of Christianity tend to draw their conclusions from a one-dimensional model that is so focused on how political-conciliar authority affected the whole that it ignores the multiple ways which Christian leaders and churches faithfully preserved doctrinal orthodoxy apart from, and sometimes in opposition to, prevailing imperial power. As with any century of Christian development, the historical evidence of the later patristic age is richer and less uniform than our models would indicate.

The negative regard with which too many in the Free Church have approached the pre-Reformation church has prevented them from seeing that Christ's promise to build his church and cause it to prevail against the "gates of Hell" (Matt. 16:18) pertains no less to this period of church history. This promise was meant not merely for evangelical churches! Christ is himself the head of his body which is the church (Eph. 4:16). This is the church which Christ loves and for which he gave himself up in order "to make her holy, cleansing her by the washing with water through the word, and to present her to himself as a radiant church without stain or wrinkle or any other blemish, but holy and blameless" (Eph. 5:27). To understand these words in solely spiritualist or eschatalogical terms would do an injustice to the present sense of the passage, by refusing to see that Christ's establishing the church in holiness is a part of the process of every age since his ascension.

Declaring our faith in the "holy and catholic church" is just that: a statement of conviction that must be integrated with whatever view of the church's corruption we take. To claim that the church fell into near total apostasy, with the exception of a tiny remnant, from the time of Constantine until the Reformation strips these passages of their meaning and calls into question Christ's provision for his church, his bride. We may agree with the dangers of what the ethicists call "Constantinianism," and yet we ought to expect God's providential rule in the Roman Empire, visibly impacting his church through its strengths and weaknesses. What we choose to emphasize in church history should not be confused with the promised working of the Spirit in every age, or the lack thereof. As John Howard Yoder has rightfully observed, if apostasy was real, faithfulness must also be possible. In the next chapter, let us see how this faithfulness was at the same time preserved and transformed.

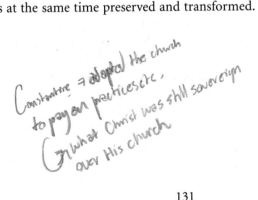

131

CHAPTER 5

Tradition through Church Councils and Creeds

[T]he deepest respect should be paid to the emperor because, in-deed sovereignty comes from God, nevertheless his ruling is not being adopted passively by episcopal judgements, because what belongs to Caesar should be rendered to Caesar, but to God what belongs to God.

Hilary of Poitiers, *Against Valens and Ursacius*

Just as all men under Roman rule serve you as emperor and lord of the world, so you, too, are a servant of the omnipotent God and holy faith.

Ambrose of Milan, *Epistle to Valentinian II*

In the 390s, a church called St. Pudentiana (now Santa Pudenziana) was built in Rome, and its apse[1] was decorated for the worshipers with a

---

1. The apse was a semicircular space at the end (front) of the nave, usually the area reserved for the altar or sanctuary of the church. It was a common element of the basilica-style of architecture during this period.

huge and majestic mosaic of Christ sitting on a high-backed throne. He holds an open book which reads "(I am) the Lord, the preserver of the church of Pudentiana." The apostles sit lower down on either side, against a background of some sort of portico, beyond which appears the cityscape of Jerusalem. Above all this looms a large cross on a hill and four winged creatures, probably symbolizing the four Gospels. It is altogether an awesome sight for the congregation to face. But like a great magnet, the figure of Christ is placed in the very middle of the mosiac, drawing all attention to himself, like one who sits in the center of heaven and earth.

Because Christ is enthroned and garbed in golden Roman dress with his "court" in attendance — a striking image of regal pomp and circumstance — most art historians have interpreted the figure as an appropriation of emperor symbolism, thus re-imaging the scene as a visual instance in which the church was usurping the insignia of the Roman emperor as a means of bolstering its claims to authority over the empire. Here again we meet the kind of assumptions at work which we confronted in the last chapter, namely, that caesaro-papal politics had come to dominate the thought and aspirations of Christianity since Constantine.

And again we must address the problem of whether such assumptions do adequate justice to the variety and complexity of data from the time of early Christianity. The mosaic of St. Pudentiana offers a prime example of the ancient church's internal expression of its faith set within the context of the Roman Empire. There is no doubt that the representation of Christ and the apostles, even of Jerusalem, is dictated by the cultural standards of the late fourth century. But it is another matter to claim that Christ is an intentional emulation of the emperor as further demonstration that the patristic church was embracing imperial ideology. In a landmark book on the interpretation of early Christian art entitled *The Clash of Gods*, Thomas Mathews argues against what he calls "the emperor mystique," or a general tendency among historians to attribute post-Constantinian Christianity's widespread acceptance in the Graeco-Roman world to its ability to closely absorb and mimic the opposition. The problem, according to Mathews, is one in which such reigning presuppositions have so dictated scholarly analyses of early Christian artifacts that the many irregularities and just plain contradictions in the evidence have been dismissed.[2]

2. Thomas Mathews, *The Clash of Gods: A Reinterpretation of Early Christian Art* (Princeton: Princeton University Press, 1993), 11-22. "The imperial structure of Chris-

Art historians have generally seen the fourth century as the period of the "establishment" of the Church and its assimilation into the orbit of the imperial court, and have tried to bend images to fit this perception. But historically, the most notable achievement of the fourth century in church-political terms was the definition of the *separation* of church and state.[3]

If we dismiss the presuppositions of which Mathews speaks with regard to the apse of St. Pudentiana, one is able to notice that the Christ figure lacks the most significant marks of imperial ornamentation, that the throne looks nothing like the usual seating place of emperors, and that the alleged "court" of apostles are featured in sitting positions alongside of Christ, something that the Roman senate or the imperial consistory (similar to a presidential cabinet) were never permitted to do in the presence of the emperor.[4]

Overall, the attributes assigned to Christ here are not meant to make an emperor of him but to signal his complete divinity, as the Nicene Creed proclaimed of Christ against Arianism, "God of God, light of light, true God of true God, begotten not made, of one substance with the Father." By the end of the fourth century, Nicene Christians were engaged in understanding and defending how the incarnate Christ is no less than God, not an earthly (and inferior) ruler. The motivation of the mosaic, then, is a theological one, perhaps an anti-imperial one, by depicting the exalted Christ in all his authority as the philosopher-teacher (the Word of God) and "preserver" of the believers at St. Pudentiana against any, including hostile Arian emperors, who would violate the orthodox faith.

To repeat, the conflicting interpretations of St. Pudentiana offer a model for our own task of accounting for the variegated evidence of locating the post-Constantinian church within the Roman Empire. Did the church of this period suffer a "fall" such that an episcopal hierarchy began to impose its authority upon the doctrinal and spiritual prerogatives of the believing congregation? Did the christological and trinitarian creeds which became orthodoxy in the fourth and fifth centuries reflect the new power structures and perspective of the Constantinian church instead of a

---

tian imagery is a dogma too sacred to tamper with. Incorporated into handbooks of art history in English, French and Italian, as well as German, it still represents the prevailing opinion on the rise of Christian art" (21).

3. *Ibid.,* 89 (emphasis mine).

4. *Ibid.,* 98-114.

Christian one? Like the past portrayals of the mosaic, I suggest that there are serious defects with the paradigm which has so informed the Free Church historical understanding, and that it requires rebalancing.

A couple of propositions must be established at the start of this chapter. First, every historical age of the church contains elements within its response to the gospel in the world that are both more and less faithful to the gospel of Christ. This principle applies to the post-Constantinian era as much as any other era in church history. We can be certain that apostolic teaching was both preserved and distorted in the doctrines that were produced in the late patristic period. Likewise, if we are going to speak about a "fall" of the church in moral and political terms, then we will ultimately be forced to find it no less in the earliest generations of Christianity, including the time of Paul. One hard look at the problems afflicting the Corinthian church reveals evidence for institutionalism versus Spirit-led freedom (1 Cor. 1, 12, 14), doctrinal strife and heresy (chap. 15), using the state to prosecute other believers (chap. 6), the abuse of authority, and rejecting Christ's call to love our neighbor (chap. 13). The generation of believers contemporary to the historical Jesus was in a critical position as eyewitnesses and mediators of the gospel; the gospel's *manifestation* was not, however, immune to the struggles of a fallen human nature and its effects on Christian communion. As glorious as the gospel message was, it was launched in the full mundanity of history.

To this we might add the observation that the potency of the "Constantinianism" theory is less impressive when we see how Christianity had been, since the age of the apostles, already assimilating as well as transforming the Roman cultural world. Second- and third-century apologists argued that Christianity was quite compatible with the noblest ideals and virtues of Greek culture.[5] Intellectuals like Justin (the Martyr), Origen and Clement of Alexandria depicted Jesus Christ as the fulfillment of what the ancient philosophers, particularly Plato, could only partially envision about God and the world. As Robert Markus has pointed out, the attitude among Christians toward pagan secular culture was by no means uniform, and had had a checkered history.[6] There was always a need for

5. There were, of course, exceptions to this attitude toward Graeco-Roman culture. Early Christian writers such as Tatian and Tertullian were not as accommodating (despite their own excellent training in pagan literature and philosophy), and decried those practices among believers that they believed to be objectionable compromises.

6. Robert Markus, *The End of Ancient Christianity* (Cambridge: Cambridge University Press, 1990), 27.

believers to define their separate identity in the midst of secular society and to decide which of the values of their pagan contemporaries were acceptable and which were not. Constantine's embrace of the church may have ushered in an era of respectability and social advantage for Christianity, but the new situation also had an effect of exacerbating tensions between church and culture that were already present.

Secondly, and more importantly, we will see that the doctrinal and ecclesiastical formulations of the fourth and fifth centuries cannot be attributed to a series of political power plays on the part of imperially directed bishops. On the contrary, the theology that emerged from the pens and great councils of the patristic church exhibited sensitivity to New Testament teaching and terminology, to the authority of faith found in local church confessions, and to the prevailing needs which congregations faced as they sought to address their cultural and intellectual context with the implications of the gospel. Post-Constantinian Christianity was just as quick, if not more so, to reexamine its loyalty to the Christian identity regardless of whether or not one believed that the fortunes of the empire were somehow tied up with the advance of Christianity.[7] If anything, the very assertion that there existed a relation between state and church tended to make such self-searching all the more necessary, just as one finds in Augustine's enormous volume *The City of God*.

Doctrine as Living Tradition

The Tradition of the early church, as I argued in chapter 1, was not static and thus subject to emendation. In the fourth century the degree of its flexibility was sorely tested within the church, wracked by severe theological discord. Necessity produced significant modifications or alterations of previously articulated doctrinal positions. By the late patristic period very few would have been happy with Justin's second-century description of Christ's being as "a second" (in relation to the being of the Father), or as "an angel." Likewise, Athanasius's early construal of Christ's humanity was

7. There was no monolithic position among Christian historians about this subject. Following the pattern of Eusebius of Casearea's *Church History*, writers such as Rufinus and Orosius interpreted the empire as a providential vehicle for the propagation of the Christian message. Others, such as Augustine and Salvian, were eager to distance the waxing and waning of the empire from the history and future of the kingdom of God.

deficient when contrasted to the creed of Chalcedon (451), though no one raised the point. We must not forget that the doctrines of the Trinity, of Christology, and of pneumatology were not more generally coherent and universally received until the late fourth and fifth centuries.[8] What was considered orthodoxy in earlier centuries was in a few cases regarded as heresy later on because of the very dynamic character of the Christian Tradition. The most faithful doctrine is itself the result of a process and progression by which the Bible is read and the apostolic message is incarnated in the world, as Jaroslav Pelikan explains:

> Christian doctrines are ideas and concepts, but they are more. Christian doctrine is what the Church believes, teaches and confesses as it prays and suffers, serves and obeys, celebrates and awaits the coming of the kingdom of God. It is also an expression of the broken state of Christian faith and witness, the most patent illustration of the truth of the apostolic admission is 1 Corinthians 13:12: "Now we see in a mirror dimly. . . . Now I know in part.[9]

The point here is that as we consider the faith and confessions produced by the post-Constantinian church, we must avoid the extremes of thinking of doctrinal continuity between the centuries as a uniformity, or conversely, endorsing a historical model which glorifies diversity and heterogeneity. Continuity of doctrine does not imply that it is an ever-expanding, unbending succession of growth for the very reason that Christian doctrine is not an abstract set of principles and speculation. Because doctrine has always grown out of the life of the churches, its continuity is never tidy; it is one of preservation but also of alteration, of fulfillment but also of correction. R. P. C. Hanson once hinted that the best way to think of doctrinal continuity was like a ship tied with a length of rope to an anchor. The wind

---

8. The basic language and self-understanding of Christian orthodoxy is derived chiefly from the four "ecumenical" councils: Nicaea (325), Constantinople (381), Ephesus (431), and Chalcedon (451). These are the four councils (and their creeds) which Luther accepted as truly catholic and faithful. Other sources of confessional authority which did not originate from councils and guided the belief of the early churches were the Apostles' Creed and the so-called "Athanasian Creed." For a handy compendium of these creeds in English translation, see Philip Schaff's *The Creeds of Christendom*, vol. 2: *The Greek and Latin Creeds* (Grand Rapids: Baker Book House, 1983).

9. Jaroslav Pelikan, *Development of Christian Doctrine: Some Historical Prolegomena* (New Haven: Yale University Press, 1969), 143-44.

and waves of contemporary issues may set it moving in various directions that alter its course in beneficial and unfortunate ways, but never farther than the length of rope. There may and should be periods in church history of "reduction, retrenchment, reformation and reconsideration as the anchor-line of Scripture and the Church pulls back the adventurous ship" of development.[10]

With this caveat in mind, I want to argue, quite unoriginally, that the post-Constantinian period in accordance with God's providence played a foundational part in the development of biblical exegesis and the church's most pivotal teachings. In more vigorous terms, I am claiming the late patristic period functioned as a kind of doctrinal canon by which all subsequent developments of theology were measured up to the present day. The great creeds of the period, the development of trinitarian and christological theology, the finalization of the biblical canon, doctrines pertaining to the human soul and being made in the image of God, to the fall and redemption, to justification by faith, and so on, find their first and (in many cases) enduring foothold in this period. All theological steps later taken, in confirmation or denial, will begin on the trail marked by the early Fathers.

If we say that the church fell, then we must realize it was because the church was already fallen, just as the same church was called to be holy, and was therefore still holy in this period. The theology that developed after Constantine was not a movement radically subversive to Scripture and to the apostolic faith. On the contrary, the major creeds and doctrinal deliberations were a conscious extension of the earlier Tradition and teaching of the New Testament while attempting, in light of new challenges, to articulate a Christian understanding of God and salvation. We cannot, therefore, discount the standards that an orthodox Christianity established as doctrinal norms for future generations. Quite apart from any agenda conceived by the National or World Council of Churches, patristic Christianity offers a coherent and faithful ecumenicity that provides "roots" of identity that the Free Church must recover. No branch of the Christian church, Protestant, Roman Catholic or Orthodox, can afford to ignore this inheritance without great cost to its future mission.

---

10. R. P. C. Hanson, *The Continuity of Christian Doctrine* (New York: Seabury Press, 1981), 83.

Taking Stock of the Sources

Perhaps most problematic in the task of interpreting Constantine and his legacy is how he was represented in the writings of a Christian contemporary and ardent admirer, Eusebius of Caesarea. Most of what we know about the famous emperor is due to this pastor's efforts. Under his pen, Constantine is installed as an integral part of God's salvation history, "as a general bishop constituted by God,"[11] and one whose career is comparable to the life of Moses.[12] Because he is divinely appointed, Constantine is God's vice-regent on earth, designated for the welfare of both the affairs of humanity and church (II.28; IV.24). An alliance between Christianity and empire is thus forged.

To say that Eusebius's influential *Life of Constantine* speaks for the general aspirations of the church or of the church's actual relations with Constantine must be squared with the fact that the work is an unabashed panegyric, celebrating "in every way the praises of this truly blessed prince."[13] The picture that emerges here may be confidently said to represent the writer's own ideal of the new Christian empire, and only approximates historical actualities. The response of the church is no less idealized than the portrait of its emperor. Furthermore, it cannot be demonstrated that Eusebius was read widely by Christians in the fourth and fifth centuries, other than by other historians.

What is most striking in Alistair Kee's work, referred to in the last chapter, is that Eusebius's panegyrical accounts are utilized as accurately representing the mind of the fourth-century church. Kee assumes that the attitude exhibited in Eusebius is a reflection of the wider Christian understanding of church and empire, despite the mixed opinions of later historical chronicles.[14] This sort of monolithic interpretation of the early

---

11. Eusebius, *Life of Constantine* II.44.

12. Michael Hollerich, "Myth and History in Eusebius's *De Vita Constantini:* Vit. Const. 1.12 in its Contemporary Setting," *Harvard Theological Review* 82.4 (1989): 421-45. Claudia Rapp, "Imperial Ideology in the Making: Eusebius of Caesarea on Constantine as 'Bishop,'" *Journal of Theological Studies* 49 (1998): 685-95; "Eusebius clearly pursued a deliberate strategy of evoking Moses as the Old Testament exemplum which Constantine imitates at every turning-point of his career" (*ibid.,* 689).

13. *Ibid.,* I.11. The same can be said of Eusebius's *Oration,* in which Constantine is called the "friend and interpreter of the Word," whose aims are to recall the whole human race to the knowledge of God (*The Oration of Eusebius of Pamphilus in Praise of the Emperor Constantine* II.4).

14. For the plurality of historiographical accounts within Latin Christianity, see the massive account of H. Inglebert, *Les Romains Chrétiens face à l'histoire de*

TRADITION THROUGH CHURCH COUNCILS AND CREEDS

church is necessary for critics to be able to dismiss it so readily. So broad are the implications drawn from the Eusebian portrait that later historians, ancient, medieval and modern, "filled in" the gaps to create a portrait about the church's supposed embrace of Constantinian Christianity. The process is rather like that which John Henry Newman once described about attributing any mythical representations to the ancient church:

> If the alleged facts did not occur, they ought to have occurred (if I may so speak); they are such as might have occurred, and would have occurred, under circumstances; and they belong to the parties to whom they are attributed, potentially, if not actually. . . .[15]

Mennonite theologians John Toews and J. Denny Weaver commit a similar fallacy in their generalizations about the early church from its credal statements. They are right to point out the limitations of the great creeds, namely, that they were addressing the relevant issues of their time, and therefore do not confront the kinds of problems which affect our own quest to grasp the historical Jesus. Both, however, claim the Christ of the patristic credal Tradition is so indebted to a philosophical orientation that the biblical presentation of the suffering and redemptive Christ was lost.[16] For Weaver, the impact of Constantine brought about a dramatic reversal: "Parallel to the shift from church to empire as the institutional bearer of God's providence was the shift from Jesus to the emperor as the norm by which to judge the behavior of Christians."[17] Now that Christianity had became the "religion of the empire," the operative question was no longer "What would Jesus do?", or "WWJD" as the popular bracelet reads, but "WWED," "What would the emperor do?" The result with regard to ethics, Weaver states, was that Christians believed it was more important to preserve the empire than to live by the teachings of Jesus. Moreover, the Nicene and Chalcedonian Creeds became the re-

---

Rome. Histoire, christianisme et romanitas en Occident dans l'Antiquitie tardive (IIIe-Ve) (Cambridge: Cambridge University Press, 1998), 421ff.

15. John Henry Newman, Sermon XV.35, cited in Fifteen Sermons Preached before The University of Oxford (Notre Dame: Notre Dame Press, 1997), 343.

16. John Toews, "Jesus Christ, the Convener of the Church," and J. Denny Weaver, "Christology in Historical Perspective," in Jesus Christ and the Mission of the Church: Contemporary Anabaptist Perspectives (Newton, Kans.: Faith and Life Press, 1990), 33-55, 83-105. Yoder's influence is clearly perceptible in both essays.

17. Weaver, "Christology in Historical Perspective," 95.

ligious platform of the new imperial church, the symbols of a new ecclesiastical establishment.[18] One sort of norm for defining the Christian faith has replaced another.

It is imperative to note that the means of evaluating the character of the later patristic church we have encountered here and in the last chapter is based on a limited and somewhat myopic approach to the ancient sources. Such a one-dimensional view of an exceedingly complex and diverse body of data from the post-Constantinian era can hardly be said to offer an adequate account of the church's ancient Tradition nor convincingly demonstrate that it took such a drastic turn in the fourth century. Even if we were to accept the theory that the first four major creeds of the church obscured biblical and congregational faithfulness, we should also have to observe that the critics' heavy reliance on credal or dogmatic formulas inevitably creates an unbalanced interpretation. It is like trying to paint a whole forest landscape using a single tree branch as a model. The great creeds were, after all, just creeds that acted as "fences" delimiting the faith, not exhaustive statements of Christian belief and practice. It is better said that the kind of criticisms Weaver and others extrapolate from the material is based on a caricature of the period which is more indebted to their "reading" of the early church through the lenses of post-Reformational syntheses than from the sources themselves.

The necessity of taking into account the various types of evidence for one's appraisal of the post-Constantinan church, such as sermons, hymns, letters, biblical commentaries, and treatises on Christian virtues, is extremely significant and usually overlooked in grand schemes of evaluating ancient Christian perspectives. Using just a fraction of this wealth of literary evidence, in the rest of this chapter I want to expose the reader to patristic "voices" by responding to the main theses, artificially worded for purposes of presentation, utilized in the fall paradigm of the post-Constantinian Church.

---

18. *Ibid.*, 96, 89. Weaver claims (erroneously) that it was Constantine who proposed and argued for the controversial word in the Nicene Creed, *homoousios* (the Son is the *same substance* as the Father). Thus, "the Christological formulations traditionally accepted as orthodox reflect the understandings of the Constantinian church, the church which did not make Jesus' life and teachings normative for the Christian life" (104).

1. THE EARLY FATHERS MARSHALLED THEIR ACTIVITY IN ACCORDANCE WITH THAT OF THE CHRISTIAN EMPEROR AND THE ROMAN PAPACY.

One of the misguided sides of the Constantinian paradigm is that it tends to depict the Fathers of the later patristic period in accordance with the Roman papal pattern. There at are least two problems with this view, both of them historical. First, the role of the bishop of Rome during this time is usually conflated with that of the high medieval period. As the leader of the largest metropolitan area in the West, the Roman bishop was certainly treated with great deference and honor. But he was a *primus inter pares*, a leader among equals (i.e., other bishops). Cyprian of Carthage, another metropolitan bishop in the west, felt no compunction in recognizing the importance of Rome as the seat of Peter for the sake of stressing the unity and confidence that exists between the Roman and Carthaginian churches. At the same time, Cyprian declares Peter's authority was "exactly as the rest of the apostles,"[19] and will later renounce the Roman bishop's (Stephen) willingness to accept believers who were baptized by heretics.[20]

After the fourth Nicene canon gave greater authority to a metropolitan bishop in the matter of episcopal elections — and there were far fewer metropolitan sees in the West than in the East — the authority of the Roman bishop increasingly and expectedly became a court of appeal in times of conflict between other churches and bishops.[21] Nevertheless, the eminence attributed to the Roman see did not mean that the bishop's authority was unilateral. When the emperor Theodosius issued an edict on 28

---

19. Cyprian, *On the Unity of the Church* 4. The manuscripts include another reading of this chapter in what is known as the Textus Receptus version, or the Primary text. It is so called because this version stresses the primacy of the Roman see to a greater extent as the basis of Christian unity in the faith. M. Bévenot argues that both versions may have originated with Cyprian, but at different stages of his relationship to Rome. *"De lapsis,"* and *"De ecclesiae Catholicae unitate"* (Oxford: Clarendon Press, 1971).

20. At a council held in Carthage in 256, the North African bishops agreed that every bishop was free to decide each case for himself without outside intervention.

21. In the case of such conflicts, the fifth canon of the Council of Serdica (343) resolved that the Roman bishop could intervene on the behalf of bishops who he deemed were wrongly accused of misconduct. Even so, when bishop Zosimus of Rome attempted to intervene in case of a North African clergyman in 424 (citing the Serdican canon as the basis of his authority), a collective letter of African bishops rebuffed his claim to do so. See H. Bettenson, ed., *Documents of the Christian Church* (Oxford: Oxford University Press, 1977), 81-82.

February 380 in support of Nicene orthodoxy, he stipulated that ortho-doxy should be measured by the standard of faith held by bishops of Alex-andria (Peter) and Rome (Damasus).[22] And the decisions of a collective of bishops always took precedence over any individual bishop, just as the Ro-man bishop's resolutions on doctrine or practice (including ordinations) had to be affirmed by other fellow bishops in council.

The second problem with molding the disposition of patristic clergy according to the papal pattern is that the early bishops are made into power brokers and political schemers, not the pastors and preachers which most of them were. Interpreting and proclaiming the true faith to their congregations was a major preoccupation with nearly every one of the early church theologians.

Unlike our post-Enlightenment age of categorizing all knowledge and its application into tighter and tighter specializations, the role of theo-logian and that of pastor often coalesced. This is not to say that every pas-tor or bishop in late antiquity was an intellectual, much less had training in the liberal arts or was even literate. But in the many cases where a classical education and Christian faith were united, the arduous work of theology and of shepherding Christ's flock were perceived as corollary tasks for church leaders. Indeed, there are very few examples in the patristic era where the writer of surviving scriptural commentaries, apologetics, theo-logical hymns, or doctrinal treatises was not a pastor. In the case of Ambrose of Milan, the vast majority of his theological writings were an edited version of what he first presented orally in sermons or in teaching new converts. It was this sort of pastoral output which so impressed and attracted the young Augustine, before his conversion, to attend Ambrose's sermons and discover the resources he lacked for interpreting the Bible and comprehending the nature of God.

Compounding the dubious image of patristic bishops, moreover, it has become something of a trend in early Christian scholarship to situate fourth- and fifth-century bishops in their social and political roles so that their concerns for faithfulness to Scripture and obeying the precepts of the gospel are minimalized. We have moved from the excessively romantic portrayals of episcopal heroes half a century ago to men notable for their shrewd and cunning management of inter-church affairs, episcopal elec-tions, or headstrong emperors. Powerful bishops are celebrated as accom-plished manipulators, reinforcing their position through propagandizing

22. *Codex Theodosius* XVI.1.2.

and posturing so that their success was really a matter of effectual stagecraft.[23]

There is no question that many episcopal figures, such as a Basil of Caesarea or Epiphanius of Salamis, must be interpreted within the rough and tumble world of ecclesiastical and imperial politics, which often meant the usage of their considerable rhetorical or diplomatic skills for representing themselves in the best possible light or their opponents in the worst. We can also single out church leaders in sheep's clothing whose quest for personal aggrandizement outweighed the consideration due to their office. The anti-Nicene bishops Valens of Mursa and Ursacius of Singidunum were often accused by their fourth-century contemporaries of currying the emperor's favor for their own purposes. No doubt such criticism was doctrinally motivated, but their seemingly constant presence at the imperial court bears out some of its truth. Pointing to such instances, however, is hardly satisfactory grounds for maligning the whole framework of authority that served the church so well.

Important Roles of the Bishop

Long before Constantine, bishops of major cities were already socially substantial figures of influence, which explains why the Decian and Valerian persecutions of Christians in 250-51 and 257-58 targeted Christian bishops (such as Fabian of Rome or Cyprian of Carthage). In fact, the bishop had an expected social role within the church. His responsibility for hospitality was considerable, including attending to traveling missionaries and the poor of the city. The bishop's share (normally a quarter of the congregational offerings) from the church's treasury was also the resource on which he relied for sustaining the poor, the protection of whom was one of his primary responsibilities.[24] In the fifties of the third century, the Roman church is known to have fully supported one bishop, 46 presbyters, 7 deacons, 7 sub-deacons, 42 acolytes, 52 exorcists, readers and doorkeepers,

23. Cf. Neil McLynn, *Ambrose of Milan: Church and Court in a Christian Capital* (Berkeley: University of California Press, 1994).

24. Henry Chadwick, "The Role of the Christian Bishop in Ancient Society," in *The Center for Hermeneutical Studies in Hellenistic and Modern Culture. Protocol of the 35th Colloquy* (Berkeley: University of California Press, 1979), 5. Augustine tells us that on the anniversary of the bishop's ordination, he was expected to give a general dinner for the poor on the church roll.

and more than 1500 widows and needy persons, "all of whom were fed by the grace and kindness of the Lord."[25] By the fourth century the bishop's role in this regard had increased. It was understood that the church's bishop was "a lover of the poor" (whether they be Christian or not) which was, ironically perhaps, a source of his authority and political recognition in Mediterranean communities. A canonical regulation states, "A bishop that loves the poor, the same is rich, and the city and its district shall honor him."[26] The indiscriminate charity of the church is confirmed by Julian, the so-called "apostate" emperor whose reign (361-63) was motivated by an attempt to encourage a revival of paganism. He grudgingly acknowledged that Christians did not confine their help to fellow Christians: "These godless Galileans [his word for Christians] feed not only their own poor, but others, while we neglect our own."[27]

The bishop would also be entrusted with young children made wards of the church. Orphans or children otherwise abandoned would be taken into the bishop's household as part of the pastoral obligation to fulfill the evangelical precept of James 1:27. Henry Chadwick reports that this special care for the poor, for waifs and strays, is often mentioned in the epitaphs of bishops in addition to the excellence of their instruction. One bishop was praised, as the inscription put it, for "teaching apostolic doctrine so as to make all his congregation weep for their sins."[28]

The apostle Paul instructed the Corinthians that they must not take their grievances against one another to the secular law courts but settle their disagreements within the body of Christ (1 Cor. 6). Application of this injunction meant that the arbitration of disputes over various personal interests and property between Christians became a major, and often irksome, preoccupation of the bishop. After Constantine,[29] the bishop's involvement could extend to concerns beyond that of church members, since it was felt that the insightful gifts of the Spirit enabled bishops as holy men capable of discerning the human heart. No less binding upon the episcopal

25. Eusebius, *Ecclesiastical History* VI.43.11.

26. Canon 14 in *Pseudo-Athanasius*. Quoted in Peter Brown, *Power and Persuasion in Late Antiquity: Towards a Christian Empire* (Madison: University of Wisconsin Press, 1992), 91.

27. Julian, *Epistle* 84a.

28. Chadwick, "The Role of the Christian Bishop," 6.

29. Constantine allowed a civil case to be transferred, at the request of either party, to the bishop provided that there should be no appeal of the decision (*Codex Theodosianus* I.27.1).

task was interceding for members of the flock when they were in trouble with the courts or the imperial government. Augustine, for example, found this duty especially time-consuming and irritating, although it was the only way to insure justice for the oppressed.

The redemption of prisoners of war was another task that fell to the bishop, and one for which bishops thought it morally right, if need be, to sell the church's sacred vessels for serving communion (eucharist) in order to procure ransom money.[30] In one instance, the bishop of the town of Amida, named Acacius, sought to rescue seven thousand Persian prisoners of war who were starving in Roman compounds. Despite the fact that his church was within Roman territory, and that the Roman and Persian Empires had been deadly enemies for over a century, the bishop successfully pleaded with his congregation to melt down the church's silver vessels ("Our God, my brethren, needs neither dishes nor cups") and use the money to buy off the Roman captors. After doing so, the church fed and sheltered the foreigners until they could return across the border.[31]

Those seeking asylum from the authorities or imprisoned awaiting capital punishment counted on the social power of the bishop. A certain bishop named Paul, who assumed a pastorate in 419, became renowned for his exceptionally frugal lifestyle in order to acquire a deeper spirituality. He was furthermore said to be "solicitous about the needs of the poor to as great extent as any man; he untiringly visited those in prison, and on behalf of many criminals interceded with the judges, who readily attended to him on account of his piety."[32]

Most of all, bishops were entrusted with the "handing over" of the apostolic Tradition to new Christians and with the preaching of the gospel. Administration of the word and the sacraments (or ordinances) of the eucharist and baptism were central. So Athanasius writes in a letter to a fellow bishop who was not fulfilling his pastoral duties, "[B]efore your election, you lived to yourself, after it, you live for your flock . . . the laity expect

---

30. When the church had insufficient funds to cover expenses, Augustine is said to have ordered the melting down of the "holy vessels" for distribution among the poor and for the benefit of captives (*Life of St. Augustine* c. 24). Ambrose of Milan was sorely harassed by "Arian" members of the his congregation for breaking up the church's silverplate in order to ransom captives from the Goths. *On Offices* II.28.136.

31. Socrates, *Ecclesiastical History* VII.21. This is all the more remarkable when we learn how the Persians often persecuted Christians in their territories.

32. Socrates, *Ecclesiastical History* VII.17.

you to bring them food, namely, instruction from the Scriptures."[33] This was an injunction the majority of bishops took to heart.

Zeno of Verona

A good case study on the role of bishops is the 93 authentic sermons — the oldest surviving Latin collection — delivered in the 360s by a little-known bishop named Zeno. One translator correctly observes that Zeno was not as important intellectually or historically as an Ambrose, Jerome or Augustine — "he was no giant on the stage."[34] And yet I suggest that this bishop was more representative of the majority of bishops in the mid-fourth century, just as the less celebrated pastors in our society are a better barometer for measuring the true condition and challenges of ministry.

After Zeno's death, it appears that a later editor took the trouble of editing and publishing the written drafts of his sermons, presumably as a way of preserving the pastor's faithful teaching within the life of the community. Two-thirds of these sermons, delivered over a period of eight years, pertain to Eastertide, and it may have been during these holy days when the former bishop's works were read in his memory.

Influences on Zeno's thought can be traced back to Tertullian, Cyprian, Lactantius and Hippolytus's *Apostolic Tradition,* and as such, show that the Tradition from the second and third centuries was still flourishing and informing the theology of the post-Nicene era. At the same time, Zeno shows concern with the "Arianism" and modalism of his own era, responding with the Nicene concept of consubstantiality regarding the Father and Son, which he has probably learned from other Western writers rather than from the creed itself.

Besides sermons on the preparation for Easter, various other themes are treated, most of them having an exegetical nature, concerning such topics on moral character as greed, patience, humility, justice and fear. Doctrinal themes are announced by titles like "On the Resurrection," "Sermon on Faith, Hope and Love," "Sermon on Jacob's Dream," "On the Birth of Our Lord," or on certain Old Testament figures and books of the Bible. One sermon given to newly baptized Christians, urges them to put away their "old life" in which they consulted the signs of the zodiac for the fu-

33. Athanasius, *Epistle to Dracontius* 2.
34. Gordon Jeanes, trans., *The Day Has Come!* (Collegeville, Minn.: The Liturgical Press, 1997), 3.

ture: "Brothers, your birth is of the following kind. First it was not Aries but the Lamb who received you; he rejects no one who believes in him . . ." (I.38.3). Elsewhere, Zeno admonishes his flock with pastoral zeal: "Guard carefully, strictly, and faithfully the royal favor of mercy which you have received from God. . . . Rejoice freely! Now you owe nothing to the world" (I.42.1). Here we have a "post-Constantinian" bishop, some thirty years after Nicaea, whose views and pastoral agenda were shaped by Scripture and the early Tradition and, to a lesser extent, the theology of the Nicene faith. Imperial ideology is certainly not governing the Christianity presented in these pages.

Because the season before Easter is the period of baptismal preparation, many of Zeno's extant sermons have to do with the necessity of repentance and commitment, particularly endurance in the Christian life. Sounding like an old-time gospel preacher, Zeno explains to his congregation that the Christian message both harms and heals, hating sin, yet loving the sinner.

> Oh what goodness of our God! What pure love of our good mother [the church]! She has taken people different in race, sex, age and rank; like an evil stepmother she kills them out of hatred of their crimes, like a loving mother she keeps them safe and does not bring back the dead to life before she has extinguished all the old poison. (II.29.2)

As God is holy, so the church is deemed holy, according to the expectation of every one of its members. This holiness extends also to what a Christian should believe, especially as it concerns faithful teaching about Christ. That the divine Word was born, lived as a man, suffered, died and rose again in no way insinuates the inferiority of the Son's being or, consequentially, his ability to save. Zeno presents a pro-Nicene Christ in his usual language of rich imagery.

> This is our God, the co-eternal Son of the eternal God. This is both a human being and God because he stood as mediator between the Father and humanity to prove flesh with its weakness and majesty with its power. This is our sun, the true sun, which with the abundance of its brightness lights the dazzling fires of the world and their sisters, the fires of the shining stars of heaven. This is the one which set once for all and rose again, never to repeat its setting. (II.12.4)

Between Bishops and Emperors

Most bishops were not looking for ways to extend their ecclesiastical dominion, either in collusion with other bishops or by accessing political power from the state. The fear of "hierachicalism" that allegedly superimposed itself on unwitting congregations after Constantine is a complete fabrication. On the contrary, there often existed tensions between the clergy and Christian emperors throughout the fourth century, usually over the issue of right doctrine. These tensions sometimes led to the bishop's outright rejection of the emperor's claim to rulership or to the banishment of the bishop by the emperor. Politics and religion did indeed coincide within the Roman Empire, but not always in the manner we may think.

Athanasius, bishop of Alexandria for nearly forty-five years, seems never to have had an easy relationship with any Christian emperor, including Constantine. Despite (or because of) his pro-Nicene position, Athanasius had to leave Alexandria for temporary refuge or exile on five occasions.[35] Most problematic was Constantius II (337-361) who, like his father, sought to restore unity in the church after the outbreak of the so-called "Arian controversy," but he favored credal solutions toward achieving this unity which were less contentious than the Nicene Creed. Initially, Athanasius blamed anti-Nicene bishops for influencing the emperor with bad ideas. By the time he writes the *History of the Arians* (c. 357), however, Athanasius (again in exile) openly denounces Constantius for promoting the suppression of orthodoxy and disrupting the internal affairs of the church so that he is revealed for what he truly is — an Antichrist and a ruler more bitter that Pontius Pilate.[36] Athanasius then states in idealistic terms how the church does not find its authorization from the edicts of the emperor:

> For if a judgment had been passed by bishops, what concern had the emperor with it? . . . When did a judgment of the Church receive its validity from the emperor? Or rather when was his decree ever recognized by the Church? There have been many councils held heretofore, and

35. The first instance was when he absolutely refused to admit the presbyter Arius back to the communion of the Alexandrian church and on account of other charges lodged against him by his enemies. Constantine demanded that Athanasius leave the city for his intransigence and until the truth of the charges against him could be sorted out. The bishop remained in exile until the emperor's death in 337.

36. Athanasius, *History of the Arians* 67; 68. Cf. 76-78.

many judgments passed by the Church; but the Fathers never sought the consent of the emperor thereto. . . .[37]

While we can attribute the zeal of Athanasius's words to exaggeration in order to distance himself from an anti-Nicene emperor, they should not be chalked up to pure fantasy. The majority of bishops like Zeno or his contemporary from Gaul, Hilary of Poitiers, could have easily endorsed such a perspective. No action of bishops in council should be overturned by imperial edict — a rule Constantine himself laid down. As Hilary declared, it was not the decrees of the emperor but "apostolic-minded men, by continual public proclamation of the faith in its completeness to supress the attempted yelps of heresy and, by setting forth the truth of the gospels, to extinguish the frowardness of erroneous doctrine."[38]

Like Athanasius, Hilary of Poitiers thought of Constantius as intentionally orthodox though deceived by unscrupulous counselors. But after his own exile for reasons never stated, the forced exile of other pro-Nicene bishops, and the culmination of a gathering of bishops held in Constantinople (January 360) at which an "Arian" type of creed was ratified as the catholic faith,[39] his attitude dramatically changed. Against the emperor's attempt to mandate religious unanimity on the basis of this creed, Hilary prepared a protest statement in the form of a manifesto: "We fight against a deceiving persecutor, against a flattering enemy, against Constantius, the antichrist."[40] As an enemy of the true church of Christ, Constantius is said to take his place along with the other imperial persecutors. Hilary had tact, but not when it came to unjustifiable imperial interference with the affairs of the church. So he expresses his desire to stand boldly as a "confessor" before Constantius just as he would before Nero or Decius, for this is what Constantius has become. "I declare to you, Constantius, what I would say to Nero, what Decius and Maximianus would hear from me, namely, you fight against God, you rage against his church, you persecute the saints,

37. Athanasius, *History of the Arians* 52 (Nicene Post-Nicene Fathers, IV.289). As meritorious as Athanasius's words sound and were undoubtedly true for many bishops, he is omitting several occasions where he sought to win approbation from other emperors for his side.

38. Hilary of Poitiers, *Against Valens and Ursacius* I.viii.5.

39. This was the Ariminum creed which was ratified at Constantinople (360). Any bishop who did not subscribe to the statement was exiled, and a new bishop would be elected in their place. It was this event about which Jerome later opined, "The entire world groaned and was amazed to find itself Arian" (*Dialogue against Luciferians*, 19).

40. *Against Constantius* 5.1-3.

you hate the preachers of Christ, you annihilate religion; [you are] a tyrant not only of human affairs but of divine."[41]

Hilary's words are not mere rhetoric. He seems prepared to suffer martyrdom for his protest, making it clear that he will no longer remain silent about the anti-Christian (viz., anti-Nicene) persecution which has been reincarnated under Constantius. The manifesto is devoted to establishing the illegitimacy of Constantius's rule as a *tyrannus,* not a Christian emperor, thus justifying a case for Christian civil disobedience. The point had immediate relevance for Hilary, who returned to his church in Gaul by the spring of 360 in blatant disregard of the strictures of his exile.[42] There he would remain, preaching and writing biblical commentaries, until his death in approximately 367.

That Constantius would be the recipient of such ire from pro-Nicene bishops is not at all surprising, though both episodes (and these were not isolated cases) demonstrate the lack of concerted action that supposedly existed between bishops and the state after Constantine. In other words, faithful Christian doctrine was not sacrificed on the altar of political opportunism.

The situation of Gregory of Nazianzus is somewhat different from Hilary's or Athanasius's experience. For most of Gregory's episcopal career, the emperor Theodosius (379–395) was a staunch advocate of the Nicene faith and supported him in his undertakings.

Known in Greek Orthodoxy as "the Theologian" for his contributions to trinitarian thought, along with those of his fellow Cappadocians, Basil and his brother Gregory (of Nyssa), this Gregory produced some forty-five addresses called the *Theological Orations* (five of which were first preached in the church of Anastasia in Constantinople),[43] moral discourses, sermons for holy days (Easter, Christmas, Pentecost), funeral eulogies, over one hundred poems, and well over two hundred letters which survive.

Although he was invited by the Nicene congregation[44] to become

---

41. *Ibid.,* 7.1-5.

42. See D. H. Williams, "The Anti-Arian Campaigns of Hilary of Poitiers and the *Liber Contra Auxentium,*" *Church History* 61 (1992): 7-22; *idem, Ambrose of Milan and the End of the Nicene-Arian Conflicts* (Oxford: Oxford University Press, 1995), 43-45.

43. These *Orations,* probably a selection made after his death, constitute Gregory's principal claim to fame in the Eastern church.

44. Pro-Nicene sympathy was in the minority since Demophilus, an "Arian" bishop, had held leadership in Constantinople. In his poem entitled *Concerning Himself and the Bishops,* Gregory describes the Nicene congregation as "orthodox but limited as

bishop of Constantinople in 379, being second in the East only to Alexandria in prestige, Gregory had little interest in acquiring a power base, nor did he hunger after ecclesiastical intrigue, and he had little tolerance for hypocritical bishops who did so. More than lions, leopards or snakes, he says, one should beware of "bad bishops," bishops whose teachings are rendered null by a lifestyle of ease, absence of sacred learning, and a lack of cultivating the Christian virtues. They are ambivalent with regard to their faith, whose norm is opportunity, not the law of God.[45] Instead, a bishop should be, "let me say it openly, from among the very best!" In a narrative poem of his experiences in Constantinople, Gregory discusses the pastoral role of a bishop which, he insists, must be much more than eloquence. It is about fulfilling the [scriptural] commandments as perfectly as possible, ministering to the sick and poor, exercising hospitality, perservering in prayer, putting restraint of the senses, control of the tongue and curbing the flesh by the power of the Spirit.[46]

On 24 November 380 the emperor Theodosius entered Constantinople with royal splendor, ordering that "Arianism" should be ejected, along with its bishop, and pro-Nicenism installed as the premier faith.[47] Despite such a great victory over his opponents, Gregory's reaction to the use of imperial force is carefully worded in the negative. For while he admits Theodosius was wondrously devoted to the Trinity, "his zeal of spirit was not the kind to emulate," lacking vision in the propagation of the faith.

> I do not consider it good practice to coerce people instead of persuading them. Persuasion has more weight with me, and indeed with those very people I direct towards God. Whatever is done against one's will, under the threat of force, is like an arrow artificially tied back, or a river dammed in on evert side of its channel. Given the opportunity it rejects the restraining force. What is done willingly, on the other hand, is steadfast for all time. It is made fast by the unbreakable bonds of love.[48]

---

yet" (lines 82-83) and that his work there was as "in the midst of wolves I built up a congregation. . . . I lit the lamp of the Trinity for people hitherto in darkness" (ll. 116-19).

45. *Ibid.,* ll. 335-37.

46. *Concerning His Own Life,* ll. 1218-24.

47. Socrates, *Ecclesiastical History* V.6; *Codex Theodosianus* XVI.5, 6; Williams, *Ambrose of Milan and the End of the Nicene-Arian Conflicts,* 164-66.

48. *Concerning His Own Life,* ll. 1293-1302. This is the same Theodosius whom Ambrose of Milan challenged for ordering the massacre of seven thousand civilians in Thessalonica when a mob attacked and murdered several officers of the city garrison. Ambrose refused to meet with the emperor in Milan, sending him a letter instead

Gregory was all too aware that imperial compulsion could work both ways. He had lived through the hazardous eighteen-month reign of the emperor Julian (361–363), who had converted to paganism and tried to make it the religious standard empire-wide. Nor did the reign of Valens (364–378) in the eastern half of the empire offer much relief for Christians committed to Nicene orthodoxy who were subject to persecution.[49] Imperial power was inherently risky business for the church, and Gregory knew it. To his philosophical mind, truth that impacts the soul cannot simply be legislated for lasting effect. Whatever political-ecclesial possibilities were now before him as the Nicene-Constantinopolitan faith swept the field held no attraction. Midway through the Council of Constantinople (381), Gregory's penchant for a quieter life and revulsion of theological discord got the better of him. He resigned his episcopate and returned to his family home in Nazianzus, where, in theological and spiritual contemplation, he directed himself "toward the unshaken seat . . . where is my Trinity, and that united brightness by the faint reflections of which we are now upraised."[50]

To sum up this first section, we fail to do justice to the evidence by characterizing patristic bishops as parties interested in capitalizing on imperial favor of the church through hatching schemes and political maneuvers with little concern for the integrity of truth or fulfilling the Beatitudes of Jesus. To be sure, the christianization of the Roman Empire meant the emergence of a new type of leader within the community, which the emperors tried to harness to their social purposes by assimilating them to magistrates, and fostering their charitable welfare, and in times of war or political crisis, by using their independence and "neutrality" for complex negotiations.[51] And yet these bishops no less represented the unity and continuity of Christian society guided by rules formulated within the Tradition which they had received and sought to uphold.

(Epistle 51), until the emperor performed public penance as a display of his guilt and need of forgiveness.

49. "He [Valens] was a persecutor following a persecutor [Julian] . . . although he was not an apostate, he was certainly no better to the Christians." On St. Basil 30.

50. Gregory of Nyssa, Concerning His Own Life, ll. 1947-49.

51. Chadwick, "The Role of the Christian Bishop," 14.

2. LATE PATRISTIC THEOLOGY AND PRACTICE, ESPECIALLY CONCILIAR CONFESSIONS, WERE DERIVED FROM EPISCOPAL AND IMPERIAL AUTHORITY RATHER THAN FROM THE LIFE OF THE CONGREGATION.

Besides the concerns with an episcopal "hierarchy," Free Church historiography has also been suspicious of whatever is produced by the hierarchical institution, namely, creeds. The Nicene Creed, with its connection to Constantine, is seen as the exemplar by which subsequent credal development is measured. Its formulation represented a watershed in church history, as Eduardo Hooernaert maintains: "Nicaea is situated in a movement that has substituted for the pluriform, communitarian, and largely democratic model of the origins of Christianity a uniform and 'catholic,' hierarchical and clerical model."[52] Similar to Weaver's arguments (above), Nicaea as a political and theological extension of Constantinianism is based upon the supposition of its imperial character and thus its disjunctive character for introducing a uniformity of doctrine: "one church, empire, one faith, one truth."[53]

The problem with this view is its need to simplify credal formulation and development to the point of distortion. To assume that the production of fourth-century creeds was the result of the imperialization of the church is to miss the less flamboyant truth that the foundation of these formulas was derived from a congregation's devotional life and practice. What the people of God confessed in worship was the basis for the structure, concepts, and the very language itself of the creeds. The step from local confession to ecumenical creed was a small one, a matter of context, both beginning with the word of faith, *credo* — I believe.

Fred Norris usefully remarks that "Schemes of organization do not determine the nature of the Church."[54] A mere collective of bishops do not make for (sound) Christian doctrine, nor does episcopal opinion on its own merits. Credal statements had to represent the common mind of the church or else they would not be accepted and employed by the larger

---

52. Eduardo Hoornaert, "The Nicene Creed and the Unity of Christians," in *Faith to Creed: Ecumenical Perspectives on the Affirmation of the Apostolic Faith in the Fourth Century*, ed. M. Heim (Grand Rapids: Eerdmans Publishing Company, 1991), 112.

53. *Ibid.*, 113. "The unity and even uniformity of the faith proclaimed symbolizes, and in a very concrete way realizes, the unity of the empire."

54. Frederick Norris, *The Apostolic Faith: Protestants and Roman Catholics* (Collegeville, Minn.: Liturgical Press, 1992), 113.

body of believing Christians. One early fifth-century definition of the original (Greek) word for creed, *symbolum,* was to take the term "symbol" literally as "token" or "sign."[55] In other words, the creed is a designated symbol for a fuller and wider description of the church's faith from which it stems. Interestingly, the term *symbolum* had already been used by Cyprian in the third century to refer not to a declaratory statement, but to the *interrogatio* or set of questions put to baptismal candidates intended to flesh out their beliefs. In either case, the *symbolum* signaled the *consensus fidelium* (a consensus of the faithful), a kind of verbal extension of the believing communities. It may be expressed through a council of bishops, or in a manual of discipleship, or a baptismal confession, but it was not something hoisted upon the churches as an object foreign to the congregation. Thus, the Nicene Creed was not the result of authoritarian movements of an episcopal bureaucracy. It had its theological and historical precursors in earlier church Tradition and Scripture, and its veracity was validated by upholding them.

Councils before Constantine

The convening of councils and promotion of their decisions was hardly new to the fourth century. Councils, which we may broadly define as meetings attended by representatives of a number of individual churches to resolve problems in common, set policy, or ordain new bishops,[56] appear in our sources from the beginning of the second century. Three times does Ignatius, bishop of Antioch, refer in his letters to the "peace" (cessation from persecution) that has come to the church at Antioch since his arrest (c. 115), enjoining his readers to elect a delegate as representative and go to the church as an encouragement and, presumably, to help with the appointment of a new bishop.[57] Ignatius's words reveal the deep solidarity and reciprocity that bound together widely scattered congregations. Along with the model furnished in Acts 15 of the so-called "Jerusalem council," we can see the precedent which such gatherings provided for a similar system of representation in the development of councils. "Councils thus be-

55. Rufinus, *A Commentary on the Apostles' Creed,* 2.

56. James Alexander, "Church Councils and Synods," in *Early Christianity: Origins and Evolution to A.D. 600,* ed. Ian Hazlett (Nashville: Abingdon Press, 1991), 124.

57. Ignatius, *To the Philadelphians* 10.1-2; *To the Smyrneans* 11.2; *To Polycarp* 7.1-2.

gan as congregational meetings expanded by the inclusion of visiting members, usually bishops or other clergy, from churches round about."[58] How broadly represented churches were at such councils depended in part on the geographical groupings of churches in a given area as well as the severity of the problem which had to be confronted. Conciliar decisions were regarded as binding on all the participants, though these decisions were often circulated more generally by way of a letter produced in the name of the council in order to garner further adhesion.

Such letters have been preserved from enclaves of bishops meeting throughout Asia Minor in the later second century over the issue of ecstatic prophesying.[59] A Christian group calling itself the "New Prophecy" agitated not a few churches because of its claims to special gifts of prophecy from the Holy Spirit which were manifest through trance-like seizures and frenzied speech. Bishops and representatives from various churches were convened and, after examining the sayings carefully, rejected them as spurious, excluding the adherents from fellowship. The correct date of celebrating Easter caused even wider dissension, affecting both eastern and western parts of the empire, and prompted the need for numerous councils of church leaders with the aim of coming to some agreement.[60]

By the third century we hear of councils meeting on a regular basis, either annually or twice-yearly. Conciliar activity, it seems, was becoming an essential feature of the way the church governed itself on a scale larger than the local congregation. This pattern did not exclude the calling of special councils to deal with immediate crises, such as the (sixth) Council of Carthage, which was convened by Cyprian in 256 and unanimously decided to not recognize the efficacy of heretical baptisms.[61]

The earliest lists of conciliar decisions to survive come from the first part of the fourth century. As might be expected, recovery of the church after enduring the horrific persecutions of Diocletian and Galerius was the focus of the Council of Ancyra (which met sometime between 314 and 319) on how to reconcile those who lapsed during persecution.[62] There were many such cases among clergy and laity and the problem was how to deal justly with them without arresting the healing process needed for the

58. Alexander, "Church Councils and Synods," 125.
59. See Eusebius, *Ecclesiastical History* V.16, 10; 19.3-4.
60. *Ibid.*, V.23-25.
61. Cyprian, *Epistle* 73.1. Seventy-one bishops are said to have attended.
62. That is, those who ran away, renounced their Christian faith, offered sacrifice to the gods, or bribed officials to look the other way.

church overall. In the west, the Council of Elvira (c. 305) in southern Spain was attended by nineteen bishops and twenty-six presbyters. The persecution had ended earlier in the west than in the east, so we hear little about issues of restoration. Instead, their concern was with a host of practical problems similar to those one might find among a meeting of the clergy today, such as dealing with the legitimacy of second marriages, discipline for immorality among clergy, financial management and abuse, and admission to communion after falling into heresy, in addition to those matters peculiar to the times.[63]

Nicaea and After

If a creed was formulated and promulgated by a council before the fourth century, evidence for it does not survive. Prior to this time, creeds and summaries of faith had been local in character and derived their authority from the practice of the local church from which they emerged. To our knowledge Nicaea was the first instance that bishops collectively framed a credal statement as an intended norm for teaching orthodox doctrine. The creed produced by the council, not to be confused with the Nicene-Constantinopolitan Creed used much later in liturgical affirmations of faith, is typically divided into three parts (in keeping with the trinitarian structure of confessions), closing with an anathema at the end which was expressly written against Arius and his episcopal supporters:

> We believe in one **God, the Father, Almighty**, maker of all things visible and invisible;
>
> And in one **Lord Jesus Christ, the son of God**, begotten from the Father, only-begotten, that is, from the substance of the Father, God from God, light from light, true God from true God, begotten not made, of one substance from the Father, through Whom all things came into being, things in heaven and things on earth, who because of us men and be-

---

63. "The Canons of the Council of Elvira," in *A New Eusebius: Documents Illustrating the History of the Church to* AD *337*, ed. J. Stevenson (London: SPCK, 1987), 290-93. Other canons discuss the treatment of pagan priests who converted to Christianity but continued to sacrifice, dealing with those who beat their slaves to death, and an interesting though not entirely explained precept: "There shall be no pictures in church, lest what is reverenced and adored be depicted on the walls."

cause of our salvation came down and became incarnate, becoming man, suffered and rose again on the third day, ascended to the heavens, will come to judge the living and the dead;

And in the Holy Spirit.

But as for those who say, there was when he was not, and, before being born he was not, and he came into existence out of nothing, or who assert that the son of God is a different hypostasis or substance, or is subject to change or alteration — these the Catholic and Apostolic Church anathematizes.

This conciliar creed and those to follow were meant to have more than a local authority, acting as a voice for the general consensus of the faith. But this new era of creeds should not be interpreted as a move on the part of the councils to supercede existing local baptismal confessions. Such a thing was not in the minds of those who formulated them, as I will discuss below. It is nonetheless easy to overemphasize the differences between the two kinds of creeds. In this regard J. N. D. Kelly makes an important statement in his classic study on ancient creeds: "The early fourth century is acclaimed as having inaugurated the transition to this new type of formulary, but like most other historical transitions it was not in fact quite so abrupt as it has seemed."[64]

Just as the motive of obtaining assurance about the soundness of one's belief was implicit in baptismal confessions and the rule of faith, so conciliar creeds were deliberately framed with this point in view. Both local and conciliar standards of faith commonly carried with them the idea of excluding error as a means of maintaining theological purity within the church. While it is true that the Nicene Creed as a conciliar document broke new ground, its conception and wording did not originate from Constantine,[65] nor was using a credal format as a test for orthodoxy some-

64. *Early Christian Creeds,* 3rd ed. (London: Longman, 1972), 205.
65. A commonly held view was that Constantine suggested *homoousios* as a sufficiently ambiguous term to be included in the Creed of Nicaea in order unify the churches. The term was anything but ambiguous for most bishops present at the council, which was evident in the years afterwards. Nor did Constantine convoke the council singlehandedly, despite Eusebius's oft-cited narrative to the contrary. A more likely course of events is suggested by Rufinus's *Ecclesiastical History* I.1 who says the emperor summoned the council at the suggestion of the bishops (*ex sacerdotum sententia*). The council may have already been in the planning before the emperor's involvement since it was originally slated to be held in Ancyra. We know only that

thing unfamiliar to the early church.[66] Quite to the contrary, the Nicene formulation was the sensible development of a practice that had been gaining ground over the previous century or more.

There is no doubt among patristic scholars that the Nicene Creed was worded in accordance with formulas of faith already utilized in churches prior to 325, with the exception of the phrases "true God from true God," "from the substance of the Father," and "of same substance of the Father" *(homoousios)*. The problem is whether we can determine what church confessions or previous statements of faith were being consciously used as a working model for the council. For a long time it was held among scholars that the baptismal creed of Caesarea, as quoted by its bishop Eusebius in a letter in order to exculpate himself from any suspicion of "Arianism," was that model because of similarities in wording.[67] The fact that Eusebius makes no attempt to insinuate that his church's baptismal formula was the one utilized by the Nicene Fathers — a connection he would have made as a sure means to clear himself — undermines this possibility. It seems more likely that the council utilized an eastern creed from the church(es) in the Syrian or Palestine area. There are resemblances between the Nicene Creed and the one used by Cyril of Jerusalem in his catechetical lectures written c. 350,[68] besides the one presented by

---

Constantine convinced the bishops to move it to Nicaea for the expediency of bishops coming from the west.

66. The use of credal formulae as a test for ascertaining orthodoxy had happened at least twice before Nicaea. At Antioch in 268 for the examination of Paul of Samosata (who denied Christ's pre-existence as a separate person from the Father), and in the same city in early 325, an anti-Arian council met just several months before the convening at Nicaea and without any participation by or influence of Constantine. R. P. C. Hanson, *The Search for the Christian Doctrine of God: The Arian Controversy 318–381* (Edinburgh: T. &T. Clark, 1988), 146-51. In both cases, a bishop(s) suspected of heretical views was examined by his peers and asked to subscribe to a statement of faith.

67. Further, in the beginning of the letter written to his congregation, Eusebius says he is sending them a copy of the Caesarean baptismal document he confessed at Nicaea, and secondly the statement of faith issued by the Nicene council which "made some additions to our phrases." A good translation of the letter can be found in E. Hardy, ed., *Christology of the Later Fathers* (Philadelphia: Westminster Press, 1954), 335-40.

68. The eighteen catechetical lectures were delivered to baptismal candidates in explanation of the creed which Cyril asserts to be "the holy and apostolic faith" of Jerusalem dating back before Nicaea (*Cat.* XVIII.32). It is noteworthy that the bishop of Jerusalem at the actual time of the council was Macarius, a staunch supporter of opposi-

Eusebius.[69] Kelly suggests an eastern creed cited by Epiphanius in c. 374 may also have been a candidate, but it is too heavily interpolated with post-Nicene language to be of any assistance in making a comparison. It is doubtful whether the Fathers at Nicaea actually revised one of these confessions; more probably, the council drew upon one from the region that has been lost. In either case, it is clear that the faith articulated at Nicaea was not forged in isolation from the faith professed by the churches. And the bishops present as delegates from their churches sought to endorse a doctrinal statement which did the most justice to the traditional faith as they and their churches understood it.

Exactly whose idea it was to add the language of consubstantiality is still debated, perhaps Ossius of Cordoba (one of the very few of western bishops present and a confidant of Constantine), or, more likely, Marcellus of Ancyra (a strong proponent of "one substance" vocabulary). It seems the phrases were included deliberately to rule out any accommodation to Arius's views. Ambiguity was not the goal here. Ironically, the final version of the creed may have seemed like a good compromise statement to the emperor, but it did not appear that way to anyone else, as we will see.

---

tion against Arius and his episcopal colleagues. The following formula has been culled from Cyril's exposition:

> We believe in one God, the Father Almighty, maker of heaven and earth, of all things visible and invisible;
> And in one Lord Jesus Christ, the only-begotten Son of God, who was begotten of the Father as true God, only-begotten before all ages, by whom all things were made; who appeared in the flesh, and became man; who was crucified and buried and rose again from the dead on the third day, and ascended to heaven, and sat down on the right hand of the Father, and will come again in glory to judge the living and the dead, of whose kingdom there will be no end;
> And in one Holy Spirit, the Paraclete, who spoke in the prophets, and in one baptism of repentance for the remission of sins; and in one holy catholic church, and in the resurrection of the flesh, and in the life everlasting.

69. The following was presented by Eusebius, originating from Caesarea:

> We believe in one God, the Father Almighty, maker of all things visible and invisible;
> And in one Lord Jesus Christ, the Word of God, God from God, light from light, life from life, Son only-begotten, first-begotten of all creation, begotten before all ages from the Father, through whom all things came into being. . . .
> And also in one Holy Spirit.

3. CONCILIAR CREEDS WERE MEANT TO SUCCEED THE CONFESSIONS AND FORMULARIES OF THE LOCAL CHURCHES.

Our primary difficulty in making judgments about the motivations behind the construction of the Nicene Creed is that official minutes, or *acta*, were either not taken or have not come down to us for some reason. The case for their nonexistence has greater support from the fact that there are no overt or recognizable references to such *acta* by those who were contemporaries of the council. One would think that a council of tremendous importance, theologically and historically, would have been recorded until we remember that the preeminence attributed to the council and its creed was not acknowledged until much later. Even the epithet "ecumenical" was assigned to the Council of Nicaea, in the sense of being a special and definitive category of synod, only gradually. The problem with the "fall" paradigm with regard to Nicaea is that it exaggerates the centrality of the council's position in history, even though little acknowledgement was made of its creed for roughly thirty years. Evidently, it was not at all clear to the majority of bishops after the council that the Nicene Creed was the best articulation of the Christian doctrine of God.

According to Hoornaert, Nicaea was the establishment of a "new memory of the Christian people," a post-Constantinian memory, eradicating the old.[70] But if Nicaea was the beginning of a "new memory," why is it practically ignored as a unique vehicle for defining Christianity until the late 350s, while other creeds are put forward instead? It is commonly recognized among patristic scholars that the Nicene Creed and its controversial term *homoousios* registered almost no notice at all in the theological disputations for over a quarter of a century after the council. This is largely because the creed did not solve the trinitarian or christological disputes which were dividing eastern bishops at the time, both because its "substance" terminology was controversial and because for many, it seemed to endorse a form of modalism.[71] Athanasius, who is usually credited with being Nicaea's most vociferous proponent, in fact exhibits no inclination to push *homoousios* until about 352-53 when he defended its validity as scriptural in principle.[72] Whatever ecclesial unity Nicaea was supposed to

70. Hoornaert, "The Nicene Creed and the Unity of Christians," 113.

71. A strong advocate of *homoousios* language at Nicaea, Marcellus of Anycra had been accused of teaching that the "same substance" of the Father and the Son meant that there was no real distinction between the Father and the pre-incarnate Word.

72. In Athanasius, *On the Definition of the Nicene Creed*. See chapter 1 above.

achieve had not been working. This is dramatically underscored by Constantine himself, who was present at a small synod in Nicomedia (327-28) and agreed with the decision to grant the presbyter Arius readmission to the Alexandrian clergy on the basis of a formula that made no allusion to Nicaea.[73]

In the west it was no different. Not until the mid 350s do we begin to see the Nicene Creed mentioned in local synods as the sole standard of orthodoxy. In 356, we know of one bishop who claims never to have heard the creed recited.[74] Such agnosticism in all likelihood was the norm among western church leaders. At later councils of bishops in Arles (353), Milan (355) and Ariminum (359), which was the largest attended council in the west, the Nicene Creed was put forward only to be rejected by a vocal minority who substituted another creed and cowed the majority of western bishops into endorsing their opinion. While Nicaea was acknowledged as an authoritative statement by 359, this acknowledgement seems to have just begun to enter the ecclesial consciousness of the west. André De Halleux makes the plausible argument that the Nicene Creed did not become a part of the church's overall "web of Tradition" until the Alexandrian Synod (362). It was there that eastern and a few western bishops jointly confessed the Nicene faith as an exclusive canon of orthodoxy by which every confession should conform.[75]

The ensuing "neo-Nicene" era, as we might now call it, in which there was a widespread identification of bishops and churches with one theology, was not propelled by the conviction that the creed acted as a symbol of the unity of the empire, or that it provided an avenue for domination over one's opponents. The ecclesiastical-political theory of "one church, one empire, one faith" is indebted to subsequent church historical reconstructions rather than the actual experience of fourth-century Christianity.

Unity was hard to come by, and conciliar creeds, no less the Nicene Creed, came to be accepted by the faithful only in slow stages. Conciliar formulas had to be proven and internalized by the life experience of the churches before they gained wide approval. Thus Maurice Wiles contends that it was the practice of Christians praying to Christ as God that influ-

---

73. Athanasius, *To the Bishops of Egypt* 18; *To Serapion* 2.

74. Hilary of Poitiers, *On the Synods* 91.

75. Andre De Halleux, "Toward a Common Confession of the Faith according to the Spirit of the Fathers," in *Faith to Creed*, 29.

enced the course of the "Arian controversy," leading to an acknowledgment of the full divinity of Christ.[76] An inferior Son failed to do justice to Christian apprehension of Christ as a fitting object of worship and adoration. What would be the point of prayer to Christ if he were a secondary figure? Witness the prayer of worship, for example, offered by the congregation in fourth century Milan:

> We beseech Christ and the Father,
> and the Spirit of Christ and the Father,
> who are one and omnipotent.
> O Trinity, assist us who pray to you!

Similarly, the appeal to the use of baptismal formulas played the largest part in winning general acceptance for the divinity of the Holy Spirit. Why does the church baptize in the name (not names) of the Father and of the Son and of the Holy Spirit if they do not share a common divinity? Christian piety not only affected the making of creeds, it significantly determined their outcome.

The Tenacity of Local Confessions

The most damaging criticism that opponents of "Constantinianism" have sounded before Free Church ears is the one that asserts that the conciliar production of creeds, such as Nicaea, replaced the voice of the worshiping communities in the definition and preservation of faithful doctrine.[77] It was a further indication that imperial jurisdiction, in its bid to create ecclesial uniformity, was holding sway over the life of the church.

As mentioned above, there survives a collection of instructional lectures on the "creed" delivered to baptismal candidates in Jerusalem by Cyril of Jerusalem. The reader will notice again that the creed which is explained is not the Nicene Creed, though the lectures were composed some twenty-five years after Nicaea. In fact, nowhere does Cyril make mention of Nicaea as a touchstone of faith. The confession of Jerusalem represents the faith "of the catholic church" (*Cat.* XVII.3), meaning that the the apos-

---

76. Maurice Wiles, *The Making of Christian Doctrine* (London: Cambridge University Press, 1967), 56ff.

77. See D. H. Williams, "Constantine, Nicaea and the 'Fall' of the Church," in *Studies in Christian Origins,* ed. L. Ayres and G. Jones (London: Routledge, 1998), 117-36.

tolic teaching is wholly vindicated by the faith (creed) of the Jerusalem church on account of its antiquity and agreement with Scripture from which it is drawn.

About the same time that Cyril was writing his lectures, far away in northern Italy Fortunantianus of Aquileia was busy composing a commentary on the Gospels. Only fragments of his commentary have come down to us,[78] but enough of it survives to demonstrate that by the late 340s or early 350s the faith was continuing to be defined by the standards of the local church. Repeatedly Fortunantianus stresses that the faith has been preserved because it has been handed down from the apostles — what he calls the *apostolic doctrina* (the apostolic teaching) as "the wings of the church" — though there is no specific mention of his church's confession. Nor is appeal made to a conciliar creed, much less Nicaea. The bishop certainly knew of the Nicene Creed, since he gave it implicit support at the Council of Serdica in 343, and subsequently denied it at the Council of Milan (355). It would seem that the Nicene Creed had only minimal standing in his mind, just as it probably stood in the minds of most western bishops.

Half a century later in the same church of Aquileia, Rufinus responded to a certain bishop's request that he write "an essay on the faith *(de fide)* based on the contents and rationale of the Creed *(symbolum)*." What he commented upon was not the Nicene Creed but the creed to which he pledged himself in baptism at the church of Aquileia.[79] His *Commentary of the Apostles' Creed* provides the most extensive credal exposition in patristic literature, and it supplied the chief testimony for the confessions of the churches at Rome and Aquileia. These church confessions were, per Rufinus, important witnesses to the Apostles' Creed from which they descended, investing these local creeds with a unique authority for the preservation of Christian doctrine.

The problem, however, was that recent heretics, such as Photinus of Sirmium (a modalist), had so twisted straightforward orthodox statements so as to support their contentions that Rufinus is obliged in his exposition "to restore and emphasize the plain, simple meaning of the Apostles' words, and at the same time, to fill in the gaps left by my pre-

---

78. *Commentarii in evangelia* (in *Corpus Christianorum, Series Latina* IX.367-70). The three fragments consist of commentary on two passages from Matthew (21:1-9 and 23:34-38) and a prologue, perhaps intended for the whole commentary.

79. *Commentarius in symbolum apostolorum* 1.3.

decessors."[80] In other words, the traditional wording, susceptible to false interpretation, must be translated in terms of orthodox thought which, for Rufinus, is also found in Nicene-Constantinopolitan theology. The reader will recall (in chapter 3) that the rule of faith had to fulfill the same clarifying role for baptismal creeds. Rufinus makes no citations or specific allusions to a conciliar creed, but he recognizes that the doctrinal extremes of modalism or "Arianism" are refuted by explicating the proper meaning of the creed — namely, that the Son was begotten before the ages of the Father's very substance, and that the Holy Spirit is in no less a category of being than the Son.[81]

It is true that the Nicene "stamp" of substance terminology can be seen in the wording of a creed supposedly from Antioch mentioned by John Cassian in 430, or in the two cited by Epiphanius in the mid-370s. Yet these formulas seem to fit in the category of interpretive versions of Nicene theology, antiheretical in their intent, rather than longstanding confessions of the church.

To conclude, the authority attributed to local creeds was grounded on their venerable connection to the apostolic faith, and on the year after year practice of hearing and reciting them in worship and baptismal instruction. Symbols from Nicaea and Constantinople are clearly distinguished as having another origin which provided an interpretive mechanism for defining contemporary parameters of orthodoxy and heresy. They were not meant to replace the baptismal confessions, since the latter were still regarded as the sacramental *regulae* of the Christian faith. Undoubtedly this explains why Hilary of Poitiers comes to the end of his twelve-volume *On the Trinity* (c. 362), after providing a detailed defense of trinitarian theology based on the Nicene Creed, by concluding with the prayer: "Keep, I pray Thee, this my pious faith undefiled, and even until my spirit departs, grant that this may be the utterance of my convictions, so that I may ever hold fast that which I professed in the creed of my regeneration when I was baptized in the Father, and the Son, and the Holy Spirit."[82] The creed he is alluding to is not from Nicaea.

---

80. Rufinus, *Commentary on the Apostles' Creed* 1, trans. in J. N. D. Kelly, *Rufinus: A Commentary on the Apostles' Creed*, Ancient Christian Writers no. 20 (Westminster, Md.: Newman Press, 1955), 29.

81. Rufinus, *Commentary on the Apostles' Creed* 37.

82. *On the Trinity* XII.57. Cf. *Epistle to Constantius* 7 (so-called *Liber II ad Constantium*): "the safest thing for us to do is to keep hold of the first and only gospel faith confessed and understood at baptism."

4. SCRIPTURE LOST ITS UNIQUE AUTHORITY IN THE CHURCH WITH THE CONSTRUCTION AND PROLIFERATION OF THE UNIVERSAL CREEDS.

More than one analyst of the trinitarian and christological conflicts of the fourth century has said that their chief point of contention was primarily about the right interpretation of the Bible. This is of course absolutely true. The vast majority of polemical documents of the era defending the theology associated with the Nicene Creed and its endorsement at Constantinople in 381 were busy contesting the meaning of Scripture with their opponents, as were those who attacked them.

One of the lessons that Ambrose had to learn when he became the new bishop of Milan in 374 was that his anti-Nicene antagonists knew their Bibles and were prepared to use them in order to defend their understanding of Christ. He found himself four years later writing a work of self-defense against accusations that his faith in God as Father, Son and Spirit as three equals in substance was really the same thing as declaring three gods. In his first pro-Nicene polemic, *On the Faith*, Ambrose arraigned the "Arian" view of God in two volumes with all the classical theological arguments he could muster only to discover that it was not enough. His chief adversary, Palladius of Ratiaria, threw at him in response a host of scriptural passages which would have to be answered, passage by passage, if he were to make a sufficient case for full divinity of the Son. Not until almost three years had passed did Ambrose release a kind of sequel in three more volumes,[83] this time giving detailed attention to the passages in the gospels that speak of the Son's incarnation, which Ambrose now realized was absolutely central to the preservation, or dissolution, of the essential unity of the Father and the Son. How does one rightly construe the figure of Jesus Christ who is worshiped as "my Lord and God" and feared by demons, who raised others from the dead and in the end was himself resurrected, and yet who also truly suffered human weaknesses graphically illustrated in his moments of ignorance (Matt. 24:36), admitting that the "Father is greater than I" (John 14:28), and experienced fear and anxiety (Matt. 26:38)? Does the very fact that the Son was "begotten" by the unbegotten Father indicate a difference of substance between the two, just as the Son is the one who is "sent" or originated from the divine being of

---

83. D. H. Williams, "Polemics and Politics in Ambrose of Milan's *De fide*," *Journal of Theological Studies* 46 (1995): 519-31.

the Father? It was not sufficient merely to cite alternative passages such as John 1:1, which insinuates the eternality of the Word, "who was with God and was God," or John 10:30, "the Father and I are One," without asking how all (or most) of the Gospel images could be integrated in a single picture of Christ without violating his humanity or mitigating his divinity.

Ambrose's experience demonstrated his expanding understanding of just how much the Bible was the true battleground of the fourth century. Pro-Nicenes often remarked on the invariable demand of the "Arians" for scriptural proof, and on how they accused advocates of Nicaea of introducing the nonscriptural term *homoousios* into the creed. The "Arian" bishop Maximinus denounced Augustine in a debate around 427, claiming that the latter did not stick to the Bible for the "facts" of the faith.[84] But Maximinus, as other anti-Nicenes, exaggerated his own literal approach to the language and meaning of Scripture while devaluing his opponents' commitment to scriptural truth. The facts are that both groups relied upon confessional presuppositions for their exegesis and that orthodox writers were no less insistent on the use of Scripture as a unique norm for the faith. We can almost hear Cyril of Jerusalem admonishing his people with the words, "Do not simply believe me, when I tell you these things, unless you get proof from the Holy Scriptures."[85]

Creed and Scripture

As we have seen with Zeno or with Gregory, theological exegesis through exposition of Scripture was important for the church. Sacred writ, both Old and New Testaments, was the means by which God spoke to the faithful in clarity and in mystery. But the reading of the Bible was not a private affair. It was impossible to interpret Scripture rightly without the consensual (pro-Nicene) Tradition of the church. More than the church histories ever indicate, worship and Scripture formed those positions, hammered out by the Fathers, which we now consider orthodox and catholic. It is this "reading" of Scripture that lies behind the origin of the great creeds of the fourth and fifth centuries, the credal statement being a sort of symbiotic rendering of the church's practice, faith confession, and sacred text in condensed form.

---

84. *Debate with Maximinus* 15.20.
85. Cyril of Jerusalem, *Catechetical Lectures* IV.17.

Let us return one last time to Athanasius and his work on defending the scriptural veracity of Nicene theology. Probably in answer to the query of a western bishop, Athanasius undertook for the first time (c. 352) a sustained response to the criticisms which had dogged the Nicene Creed since its publication, namely, that it could not be a faithful exposition of Scripture because it used nonbiblical terminology. In *On the Defense of the Nicene Definition*, Athanasius does not try to dispute the assertion that the expressions "from the essence" or "of the same substance" *(homoousios)* are not found in Scripture and are peculiar to the council's wording. His "Arian" opponents, he says, have done the same thing when they describe Christ as "out of nothing" or the Father as "the Unoriginate" (as opposed to Christ who was "begotten" or originated).

The problem the council faced, according to Athanasius, was how to interpret certain passages in Scripture pertaining to Christ's identity in light of the full scope of scriptural teaching. Everyone agreed that the Son was "from God" (2 Cor. 5:17), but in what way should this be proclaimed without insinuating that the Son comes "from God" just as all created things do? It was too easy to equivocate the apostles' meaning as the "Arians" seemed to do. If the Son was "begotten," was he not "made," and in this sense "from God"? The council was compelled therefore to exercise greater specificity by defining just how the Son of God and eternal Word is "from God." Athanasius explains,

> Accordingly they wrote "from the substance of God" in order that "from God" might not be considered common and equal in the Son and in things created. . . . For though all things are said to be from God, yet this is not the sense in which the Son is from Him" (c. 19).

As the Word of God, the Son is not a creature, and is rather, as Paul says (1 Cor. 8:6), the one through whom all things were made. For neither are "all things" as the Son, nor is the Word one among others, since he is the Lord and Framer of all: "And on this account did the Holy council declare expressly that he was of the substance of the Father, that we might believe the Word to be other than the nature of things originate, being alone truly from God." Without apology the creed employed the use of *homoousios*, a nonbiblical word, as the logical outcome of the "sense of the Scriptures" and of what the church has generally understood, regarding Christ's identity as the Son who is "from God" (c. 20).

C. S. Lewis, who was a strong proponent of Athanasius's incarnational theology and of the indispensable role of the Nicene Creed as a "map" for contemporary theology, emphasizes the same point:

> Now that is the first thing to get clear. What God begets is God; just as what man begets is man. What God creates is not God; just as what man makes is not man. That is why men are not Sons of God in the sense that Christ is. They may be like God in certain ways, but they are not things of the same kind. They are more like statues or pictures of God.[86]

For the early Fathers, the great creeds which maintained three persons in one nature (Trinity) and two natures in one person (Christ) were not merely drawn from the Bible; they were a definitive and legitimate extension of scriptural teaching. Credal statements were not proposed as antitheses to Scripture or as alternative norms of the faith. They were meant as fitting representations of biblical truth, drawn from scriptural precepts and designed by scriptural language as much as possible. As Augustine reiterated, credal language proves the authority of the "divine books" and is an extraction of its truth.[87] The late patristic writers, knowing the Bible as well as they did, realized that some unifying interpretative principles were necessary for scriptural exegesis. Thus, confessional statements emerged through the cooperative effort of churches, and their leaders intended them to serve as hermeneutical models for understanding God as Trinity and Incarnate in Christ. Rightly it has been said that if the creeds and work of the early theologians were not available, we would have to invent them. "At the very least," says Frederick Norris, "the creeds will remain both handy statements of the problems faced in interpreting Scripture and short descriptions of the ways in which early theologians faced those issues, and tried to state the center of Christian faith within their churches and to their cultures."[88]

To say that the formulators and defenders of the Nicene (and Constantinopolitan and Chalcedonian) Creed were fighting to preserve the Tradition of the church is true, though in the sense that they were

---

86. C. S. Lewis, *Mere Christianity* (New York: Macmillan Publishing, 1943), 138. Lewis also wrote an introduction to Athanasius's *On the Incarnation of the Word:* see St. Athanasius, *On the Incarnation,* repr. of 3rd ed. (Crestwood, N.Y.: St. Vladimir's Theological Seminary, 1993).

87. Augustine, *Epistle* 238 ("To Pascentius," an Arian official of the imperial service).

88. Frederick Norris, "Wonder, Worship and Writ: Patristic Christology," *Ex Auditu* 7 (1991): 60.

drawing on the Tradition as they engaged in the task of constructing Christian doctrine. Through this process they worked out a form of some of the most crucial doctrines, not only of the Bible, but of the very spirit and genius of Christianity itself. And it was only very slowly that post-Nicene pastors recognized that in forming their doctrine of God they could not possibly confine themselves to the words of Scripture. As we have seen, the development and function of conciliar creeds, as well as the production of theological treatises, commentaries, and catechisms, had to do with the debate about the meaning of the Bible. Any attempt to answer the problem of interpretation in purely scriptural terms inevitably leaves unanswered the question, "But what does the Bible mean?"[89] There was still need, as there had been since the second or third generation of Christians, for a stated standard of faith to act as guide, but at a more universal level, given the size and diffusion of the post-Nicene church.

We have reviewed sufficient evidence to controvert the notion that conciliar creeds in the post-Constantinian era are best understood as a by-product of imperial politics which demanded ecclesial uniformity, or as the maneuvers of an episcopal hierarchy to control congregations, a drastic departure from the Christianity of earlier centuries. The formal and local confessions of theological faithfulness evolved in a dynamic relationship of complementarity which was not circumvented by the political and social benefits provided by Constantine and his successors for the church. Rowan Williams, I think, has put it best:

> What the church discovered in the painful years after Nicaea was that its own inner tensions could not after all be solved by a *deus ex machina* on the imperial throne; and that its relationship with the empire intensified rather than solved the question of its own distinctive identity and mission. It was unable to avoid reflection on its defining conditions, unable to avoid a conscious and critical reworking of its heritage, unable, in short, to avoid theology.[90]

To not see the normative value of the truths housed in great confessions of the late patristic era is to turn a blind eye to the assertion that every evangelical would accept: the sovereignty of God in each era of the church's life

89. Hanson, *The Search for the Christian Doctrine of God*, 848.
90. Rowan Williams, *Arius: Heresy and Tradition* (London: Darton, Longman & Todd, 1987), 236-37.

in history, based on Jesus' promise to build his church with the assurance that the gates of hell will not prevail against it. My argument should not be construed to mean that we ought to accept the great creeds as infallible. The patristic view of councils and creeds made no such claim. Councils, no matter how many bishops attended, were not deemed oracles of divine revelation.[91] General creeds of the fourth and fifth centuries were deemed authoritative by the churches who received them because they were viewed as faithful conductors of the Christian doctrine of God found in Scripture and the Tradition. In an age when the doctrinal details consumed the attention of pastor and parishioner alike, any credal statement for general subscription was subject to careful scrutiny. We should not, therefore, take lightly the ancient church's acceptance of its creeds. Much more time and judicious hesitancy were involved in the process of their reception than the telescoping tendency of our later histories would indicate. Like guideposts along a precipitous mountain pass, the consensual creeds and theological writings of patristic Christianity were meant to mark the path of doctrinal trustworthiness and theological constancy, as they still do, for every subsequent generation of pilgrims.

91. In distinction from the position of Vatican II which declared that bishops of the church can "proclaim Christ's doctrine infallibility," especially in councils, the early church had no such view of authority for itself.

CHAPTER 6

Scripture and Tradition in the Reformation

The Protestant Reformation began when a Catholic monk rediscovered a Catholic doctrine in a Catholic book.

Peter Kreeft, *Fundamentals of the Faith*

There is reliable proof only of what has received the assent of the church universal, and not merely that of Rome.

Martin Luther, *The Pagan Servitude of the Church*

The term "Protestant" is commonly used with a negative connotation. Everyone knows that Protestants are those who "protest" and dissent from Roman Catholicism. While historic Protestantism did indeed register a series of objections to Roman Catholic dogma and practice, such a definition is nonetheless unfortunate and even imbalanced for the reason that the Reformation was at heart an affirmation, a vigorous protestation of positive principles. A Protestant was, as the primary meaning of the Latin verb *protestare* indicates, one who seeks "to bear witness," or "to declare openly." Historically, Protestants are those who have sought to affirm certain tenets of their faith which bear witness to the apostolic message. John

173

Wesley's letter to a Roman Catholic acquaintance on 18 July 1749 offers a prime example of this when he defined "a true Protestant" in accordance with a series of doctrinal professions, each beginning with the ancient words, "I believe." Wesley obviously felt it was more important to describe what Protestantism stood for rather than what it stood against. Not once did he tell his reader what Protestants rejected and opposed.

Today's Protestants should take a lesson from their ancestors. To be Protestant does not imply detachment from doctrinal theology, liberation from ecclesiastical authority, or discarding the tradition(s) of the past. Being Protestant is not synonymous with being anticatholic in the sense of rejecting the faith as it developed prior to the Reformation. For that matter, being Protestant is not the antithesis of being Roman Catholic, though certainly it is in distinction to Roman Catholicism. In the twentieth century, the original notion of Protestantism resurfaced in the "confessing church" of the Barmen Declaration (1933). In this document Christian pastors and theologians testified to or bore witness to the evangelical principles of the Christian faith in their resistance to the co-opting of churches in Germany by the Third Reich.

What general attitude did the Reformers harbor toward the early Fathers and, particularly, toward the consensual Tradition of the early church? Baptist theologian Bernard Ramm erroneously claims the Reformers rejected the concept of tradition on three grounds: (1) all that God intended the church to have was in the New Testament; (2) certain doctrine and practices of Roman Catholicism are at variance with the New Testament; and (3) "It is impossible actually to specify the borders of this tradition or its precise contents." Such a suspicion, he says, is vindicated by the fact that much of the tradition is embodied in New Testament apocrypha. In other words, the majority of Catholic "tradition" comes from the documents of the second century that were falsely attributed to certain apostles, often teaching doctrines and portraying practices at variance with the canonical texts.[1]

Noteworthy is Ramm's not uncommon confusion that "tradition" is a (human) product of Roman Catholicism, imposing its authority through the ages and that it is, therefore, an alternative source of authority incongruous with Scripture. We have already found that neither of these propositions are historically accurate, nor is Ramm's contention that it was

---

1. See the collection of such texts in M. R. James, *The Apocrypha of the New Testament* (Oxford: Clarendon Press, 1953).

in rejection of Tradition that led the Reformers to the doctrine of *sola scriptura.*[2] The gospels, acts, and apocalypses that are called apocryphal do mirror what might be called "popular Christianity" of the second and early third centuries and for this reason exhibit some of the theological characteristics of the church's Tradition. But it is quite erroneous to imagine that apocryphal texts were the primary source of that Tradition.

The early Tradition was certainly catholic, not Roman Catholic, and it formed the basis upon which Scripture was first written and later judged to be canonical. The sixteenth-century Reformers were cognizant of this distinction and highly valued the Tradition located in the Fathers as a means of interpreting biblical truth. One might expect that because the Reformers dismissed "human institutions," which they associated with the Roman church, they would have discounted the patristic writings as human superstition. This was far from the case, however. The Protestant assault on some of the scholastic theologians of the Middle Ages and most decrees of medieval popes was not understood as an attack on or break with the catholic nature or wholeness of the Christian faith, as exhibited in Scripture, epitomized in the ecumenical creeds, and expounded by the early Fathers. On the contrary, the writings and confessions of the Fathers, especially Augustine, served as critical links to their own theology and reforming efforts. In large part this dependency had to do with the belief that the Fathers were attempting to develop a truly biblical theology — which was precisely what the Reformers wanted to develop. Augustine's statement that "The student who fears God earnestly seeks his will in the holy scriptures"[3] had an effect on people like Luther or Melanchthon of looking into a mirror. They understood themselves as trying to do the very thing Augustine had done.

The problem with understanding the Reformation as primarily a negatively charged reaction to the institutional church is that we will fail to appreciate the organic connection that existed in the minds of the first Protestants between their time and what came before, and between Scripture and the broad base of the church's teaching. For the magisterial Reformers especially, any attempt to juxtapose the joint role these played in light of a renewed emphasis on the Bible erroneously construes the period as a "simple classification in terms of priority of church over Scripture, or

---

2. Bernard Ramm, *The Evangelical Heritage* (Grand Rapids: Baker, 1973), 29-30.

3. Augustine, *On the Christian Teaching* III.1. Trans. from R. P. H. Green, *Augustine: De doctrina Christiana* (Oxford: Oxford University Press, 1995), 132.

Scripture over church."[4] Their point was not to make Scripture autonomous, liberated from its ecclesiastical shackles, in a gnostic-like fashion
which allows the individual reader to entertain any spiritual or theological
"truth" whatever. Rather, Scripture was supposed to be free in order to
stand in judgment of all traditions and practices. Reclaiming Scripture for
the church was to lay claim to rediscovering and reappropriating the roots
of catholicism without Romanism. It was to bring the interpretation of
Scripture back to its rightful "home."

Ramm's assertion that the Reformers rejected the concept of tradition and the authority of the Fathers and councils in their bid for Scripture
alone demonstrates a blind spot common to evangelicals which wrongly
construes the sixteenth-century conflict as one of Scripture versus tradition. Scripture was not something that could be properly understood apart
from the foundational Tradition of the church, even when certain institutions of the church were being opposed. In what follows, I want to argue
that the Reformation was not about Scripture versus tradition but about
reclaiming the ancient Tradition against distortions of that Tradition, or
what eventually became a conflict of Tradition versus traditions. To put
this another way, the insight which we received from the Protestant Reformation is that every church's "traditions" are subordinate to Holy Scripture and under the judgment of the Tradition, Christ being the Lord of
both.

In many ways the basis of reform in the sixteenth century was over
the rightful authority to claim the early church as its legitimate heir. Both
Protestants and Roman Catholics contested with each other over this prerogative. It was generally agreed that reform should take place in accordance with the model provided by the patristic sources. The discord between Protestants and Roman Catholics and between Protestants and
Protestants was over how these sources were to be used for the church's reform and how extensive these reforms needed to be.

Where the Reformers did have a problem with the Fathers was not
with the Fathers per se, but with how they were haphazardly cited as authorities in support of almost any teaching, with no cognizance of the
teaching's intent. Of course, all writers of this period still subscribed to the
medieval practice that utilized passages from ancient texts with little or no

4. Alister McGrath, "Reclaiming Our Roots and Vision," in *Reclaiming the Bible
for the Church*, ed. Carl E. Braaten and Robert W. Jenson (Grand Rapids: Eerdmans
Publishing Company, 1995), 68.

regard to their historical context. But the key difference for the Reformers was a consciousness that the patristic sources, as important as they were, should not be cited arbitrarily as "authorities" for the maintainence of any doctrine or practice (as theologians throughout the Middle Ages did), except as they were in congruence with Scripture. This was a more or less selective view of the Fathers' teachings that opposed the *method*, if that is an accurate word, of using the Fathers as justification for almost every "tradition" found in the church, whether it was based in Scripture or not. Reflected here are the effects of the more discriminating view of the ancients taken by Renaissance scholars in their revival of the patristic sources. With disparaging tones Erasmus compared the spiritual dearth of his own day with "those theologians of old, Origen, Basil, Chrysostom, Jerome" wherein one finds "a kind of golden stream is flowing . . . [and] the oracles of eternal truth are thundering."[5] And yet not all the Fathers come in for unreserved praise by Erasmus, who considers them fallible and some self-contradictory. On their part, the Reformers had no desire to overturn patristic authority in the church, but nor did they assume its value unequivocally, as they challenged the ways in which the Roman church had come to use that authority, as well as subordinating patristic writers to the papal office. Thus, interest in the early church did increase with the Reformation because of the growing need to evaluate the relationship between patristic testimony and that of Scripture.

A strong but discerning view of patristic authority also prompted the early creeds to assume a new importance. The Nicene and Apostles' Creeds foremost became documents that linked Scripture to the early church. This was partly due to the fact that it was believed, erroneously based on Rufinus's fifth-century work, *A Commentary on the Apostles' Creed*, that the Apostles' Creed should be divided into twelve articles, because each was contributed by one of the twelve apostles. It also had to do with a polemical necessity of refuting the accusation by the Roman church that Protestants were preaching a new and different Christianity. At the Baden Disputation of 1526, the reformer John Oecolampadius could not argue from Scripture without exposing himself to the charge of spiritualism or subjectivism.[6] He dealt with the criticism of his opponents by having re-

5. Quoted in Jan Den Boeft, "Erasmus and the Church Fathers," in *The Reception of the Church Fathers in the West: From the Carolingians to the Maurists*, vol. 2, ed. I. Backus (Leiden: E. J. Brill, 1997), 549.
6. I. Backus, "The Disputations of Baden, 1526 and Berne, 1528: Neutralizing the Early Church," *Studies in Reformed Theology and History* 1 (1993).

course to the writings and formulas of the early church as a means of demonstrating his continuity with the message of the ancient Tradition. In Martin Bucer's *Gospel Commentaries* (1527-28), patristic writers served as direct sources of his theology, though they are rarely mentioned by name. By the time Bucer penned his *Romans Commentary* (1536), the Fathers are overtly cited and their exegesis is seen as even more central to the interpretation of Scripture. Incumbent upon the Reformers, therefore, was the task of defining themselves as truly catholic in the light of patristic testimony against charges of novelty.

The position of the Reformers, however, was not purely a defensive one; there was a general impression that the teachings found in the great creeds were essentially expositions of Scripture. The reformer Urbanus Rhegius (d. 1541), for example, was committed to the idea that Scripture should always be interpreted in accord with the received teaching of the universal church, and maintained that preachers should be ready to cite opinions of the Fathers in support of their points. Indeed, Rhegius argued that that no true understanding of Scripture could exist apart from the fundamental articles of the faith because these were forged during the earliest centuries of the church. Not just any opinion of a church father could be used, but only those which agreed with the consensus of the ancient faith as required by the principle of catholicity and Scripture.[7] This approach was at the heart of the Reformers' rebuttal of the Roman church's claim to authorize ecclesiastical and doctrinal traditions alike. As the Reformation became increasingly associated with the recovery and reestablishment of the original Tradition in the church, using the same patristic sources of their opponents, the issue also became how one could discern which of the traditions truly reflected the ancient Tradition.

The First Protestants

What some readers may find surprising is that the term "Protestant" was not used until much later in the Reformation as a reference for marking religious affiliation. The term originally referred to the "protestation" of the

7. Scott Hendrix, "The Use of Scripture in Establishing Protestantism: The Case of Urbanus Rhegius," in *The Bible in the Sixteenth Century*, ed. D. C. Steinmetz (Durham: Duke University Press, 1990), 44-47.

six princes and fourteen south German cities at the second Diet of Speyer (1529) against the rescinding of the religious freedom guaranteed by the first Diet of Speyer three years earlier. Despite the popular mythology surrounding the term, the "protest" was not against Rome directly nor against its traditions, but against any imposition of controlling policies over independent estates in southern Germany.[8] In fact, the very words "Protestant" and "Protestantism" do not appear in the writings of Luther (apart from a political reference to "protesting estates"), nor in the Lutheran *Book on Concord* (1580), nor in any edition of the Anglican *Book of Common Prayer* (first edition, 1549), nor in Calvin's *Institutes of the Christian Religion* (first edition, 1536), nor in the two most widely used Reformed confessions of the sixteenth century, the Heidelberg Catechism (1563) and the Second Helvetic Confession (1566).[9] In like manner, these texts did not identify their opponents as "Catholics," but rather as "Romanists," "Papists" and so on. One could describe the prevailing attitude at this time, as a modern writer once said in a little-known book, that "Catholic" represented something too big for Romanism.[10] The Reformers perceived themselves as sharing in the continuing communion with the "holy and catholic and apostolic church" as true catholics, and that catholicity did not depend on allegiance to the bishop of Rome. By the late seventeenth century the term "Protestant" had made a transition from a legal understanding to a confessional one in the sense of being "anti-Catholic," gradually displacing the older term "evangelical," which was the descriptive term first used in 1520s.

Despite complaints which some Protestants have often lodged against the post-Constantinian setting of patristic creeds and councils, it must be admitted that the beginning of the Protestant Reformation was a highly political affair. German nationalism, anti-papalism, the peasants' rebellion, and economic crises all came together to weave a complex web of factors around the rejection of the sale of indulgences. Anti-Roman sentiment ran strong in Luther's time among princes and commoners alike, and it had no necessary connection with theological reform. Steven Ozment comments that

---

8. Alister McGrath, *Evangelicalism and the Future of Christianity* (Downers Grove, Ill.: InterVarsity Press, 1995), 21.

9. David Lotz, "Protestantism," in *The Oxford Encyclopedia of the Reformation*, ed. Hans J. Hillerbrand (Oxford: Oxford University Press, 1996), 356-57.

10. J. H. Nichols, *Primer for Protestants* (New York: Association Press, 1947), 9.

the Reformation came to be closely identified in the minds of contemporaries with what we today might call states' rights or local control. To many townspeople and villagers, Luther seemed a godsend for their struggle to remain politically free and independent. . . . Certain groups favored the Reformation more than others, and for reasons that had as much to do with money and power as with faith and piety.[11]

The Reformers themselves realized how mixed the motives were and understood that they needed to woo magistrates and princes if they were to succeed in the public domain. Even the radical spiritualist reformer Thomas Müntzer and the Anabaptist Balthasar Hubmaier were not opposed to cultivating local authorities for their own ends. Ozment puts it more strongly when he claims that the Reformers were prepared to serve any ruler willing to defend their doctrine, expose the machinations of the pope, and depose papist clergy.[12] The magistrates felt the same way about the practical usefulness of the Reformers.

All this is not to lay an accusation of religious hucksterism before the Reformers, who were aware, very much like the late patristic bishops, that to establish and maintain the doctrine they knew to be true, sufficient political support would have to be gained. We would hardly be justified in reducing their motives to a reaction against deeper political, social or economic issues as some interpreters are wont to do. In sum, the theological and spiritual birth of the Reformation cannot be singled out or closeted from the civil and political struggles which must surely be counted as its midwife. Luther or Zwingli and their fellow Reformers were just as ready as any early Father to take refuge in a favorable government when it suited their theological goals, but neither would they stand to have their preaching dictated by the secular authorities.

The Reformation and Patristics

An important part of the new intellectual climate that developed in Europe during the fifteenth and sixteenth centuries was a new industry of publishing editions of the early Fathers. Separate volumes of the Fathers' works or citations from them were available throughout the Middle Ages,

11. Steven Ozment, *Protestants: The Birth of a Revolution* (New York: Doubleday, 1991), 19.
12. *Ibid.*, 23.

such as commentaries on Lombard's *Sentences* and the *Milleloquium Sancti Augustini*.[13] The first edition of the *Opera Omnia Augustini* published in Basel by Johannes Amerbach (c. 1506) was the high point of the late medieval Augustinian revival. It is no accident that Luther, Staupitz, and the other Reformers knew Augustine more intimately than any of the other patristic writers. Erasmus produced his own edition of Augustine's works (1528-29) as well as new versions of many of the Fathers,[14] which came into general circulation and fueled both Protestant and Roman Catholic Reformations.

Also during this time, Latin translations of Greek works, varying in quality, were produced. By 1515 the first Latin edition of Basil of Caesarea's works appeared, as did subsequent translations of other Greek Fathers like Justin and John of Damascus. The Swiss reformer Johannes Oecolampadius was responsible for a considerable number of Latin translations and editions, including the newly discovered *Against Heresies* by Irenaeus. Even so, accessibility to the early Fathers for the Middle Ages was mostly through collections of excerpts from patristic sources on various topics known as *florilegia*. The best known and largest of these collections is the *Decree of Gratian* (compiled c. 1140 in Bologna) which amounted to nearly four thousand citations from the Fathers, as well as Aquinas's *Catena aurea in quattuor Evangelia (The Golden Chain on the Four Gospels)*, and the glossed (annotated) Bible.[15]

Roman Catholics and Protestants alike made use of these anthologies, endeavoring to show by citing different Fathers or different excerpts from the same Father how their doctrine represented the patristic and therefore true teaching of the church. A. N. S. Lane has devoted considerable time to tracing printed (as distinguished from manuscript form) pa-

---

13. Completed in 1345 by Bartholomew of Urbino, the *Milleloquium* consists of approximately 15,000 passages from Augustine's works, arranged alphabetically in 1,081 entries. For details, see E. L. Saak, "Augustine in the Later Middle Ages," in *The Reception of the Church Fathers in the West*, ed. I. Backus, vol. 1 (Leiden: Brill, 1997), 379-84.

14. Cyprian (1520), Arnobius (1522), Hilary of Poitiers (1523), Jerome (1524-26), Irenaeus (1526), and Ambrose (1527). Erasmus subsequently produced revisions of Jerome who, for all his own translations of biblical and patristic texts, became "the embodiment of the Renaissance ideal." H. A. Oberman, *Masters of the Reformation*, trans. D. Martin (Cambridge: Cambridge University Press, 1981), 72-73.

15. Irene Backus, "The Early Church in the Renaissance and Reformation," in *Early Christianity: Origins and Evolution to A.D. 600*, ed. I. Hazlett (Nashville: Abingdon Press, 1991), 295.

tristic anthologies in their different editions, and suggests in a preliminary report[16] that they can be placed in three broad categories. First, there was the practical medieval anthology designed to distill ancient wisdom for the busy man. Many scriptural devotionals today operate on this same principle of excerpting texts for Christians. A second category was the polemically oriented anthology, intended to muster theological support for one's position. Melanchthon's *Sententiae Veterum (Opinions of the Ancients)* had a decidedly pro-Lutheran cast and went through at least six editions. Finally, there were anthologies of scriptural commentary, drawing together citations from patristic commentaries on specific books of the Bible. We can be reasonably confident that various texts of the Fathers were available to the literate, albeit usually in piecemeal form. Like reading through a collection of newspaper clippings without headings or dates, sixteenth-century writers would sift through stacks of ancient authorities largely detached from their historical context and meaning. The rise of partial and complete editions of the Fathers was therefore crucial as an aid to their interpretation and abetted the claims of the Reformers to know the patristic mind.

Luther

As with all revered figures of church history, Martin Luther's life story and thought has been caricatured in ways that do and do not match up with his own statements, especially as it pertains to his earliest years. The standard Protestant way of reading the young Luther is to present him as one who could find no lasting peace within the edifice of the Catholic Church, organized as it was around sacramental practice, credal dogma and mystical aspiration. The exercise of these were, in the last analysis, only denials of our depraved condition, not adequate responses to it. In none of them could Luther find an answer to his burning question, "How can I find the graciousness of God?" Then in 1518, once the indulgence issue was underway, Luther suddenly found the assurance of God's gracious forgiveness through the study of Paul's Epistles and the Psalms, which became the basis of his "Reformation breakthrough." It was a kind of conversion experience tantamount to what had happened to Augustine when he was reading

16. A. N. S. Lane, "Early Printed Patristic Anthologies to 1566: A Progress Report," *Studia Patristica* 18 (1989): 365-70.

Paul' letter to the Romans in the garden near Milan. The problem with this scenario, as suggested by Luther scholar David Yeago, is that it makes Luther's "Reformation breakthrough" seem like a full-scale refounding of Christianity in the manner of another Pentecost. Twenty years later Luther would describe his early experiences as a "redisovery" of the gospel, but it would be a mistake to interpret this as implying that the gospel got lost somehow between Pentecost and the Reformation.

Most importantly, the caricature of this "breakthrough" stands in no significant relationship with the preceding Christian tradition. Rather, "it came about by way of a pure encounter of the naked human condition with the naked Pauline kerygma, mediated by no diachronic historical process. . . . The catholic tradition figures in the story only as that which Luther had to overcome, to 'breakthrough', on his way to 're-discovering the gospel.'"[17] It follows that those who are interested in the heritage of the Reformation have little reason for concerning themselves with that tradition. If Luther's "faith" was quite different in kind from Catholic Christianity, then the new faith obviously demanded a new church. And yet historians agree that a breach with the Roman church was not what Luther intended by his reformation.

While 1518 marked an important development in Luther's theology, Yeago proposes that it was not a "turn" away from Catholicism but toward it in the sense that the origin of his early insights anchored Luther more deeply than before within the framework of Catholic Christianity. Concepts of transformative grace, christological dogma and a sacramentality of grace — these were aspects of historic Catholic doctrine that were his focus. Indeed, it was Augustine who provided the theological ground upon which Luther constructed his own theory of justification. As he was only too well aware, Augustine's reading of Paul's epistles had provided the bishop with the driving force of his mature theology. The notion that the just shall live by faith was confirmed by "the strong authority of apostolic teaching."[18] It was not a novel use of Pauline theology. About a half-century before Augustine had propounded his version of the doctrine of original sin and the complete gratuitousness of grace, Hilary of Poitiers reveals an understanding about justification by faith in his *Commentary on Matthew*. Several times Hilary explicitly refers to God's act of graciously con-

17. David Yeago, "The Catholic Luther," in *The Catholicity of the Reformation*, ed. C. Braaten and R. Jenson (Grand Rapids: Eerdmans Publishing Company, 1996), 15.
18. Augustine, *On Faith and the Creed* i.1.

ferring grace that comes, not by meritorious works, but through the justification of faith.[19]

Luther himself characterized the emergence of his theology between 1513 and 1518 as an impassioned effort that "the pure study of the Bible and of the Holy Fathers might be returned to honor."[20] The motive on which this retrospective statement was based is not hard to find. In November 1518 Leo X issued a bull (proclamation) which Luther understood to mean that the pope had arrogated to himself the power of defining church teaching without accountability to Scripture, the Fathers, or ancient church canons. Not suprisingly, when the same pope formally condemned Luther's views two years later in another bull, *Exsurge domine,* it was stated that the latter taught a doctrine of repentance and salvation that was "not founded on Holy Scripture nor on the holy ancient Christian doctors." Luther's offense was also his defense against such charges.

Luther's program for reform was both radical and conventional. It was radical in the sense that a great deal of medieval accretions that reconfigured sacamental life had to be sloughed off: "It is impossible to reform the church unless one uproots radically the canons, the decretals, scholastic theology, philosophy, logic, as they are taught today." In effect, ecclesiastical office alone was not a sufficient guarantee for securing an authoritative interpretation of the faith. In a way similar to Tertullian's insistence that no bishop or martyr was above the rule of faith, Luther declared that he would not recognize the dictates of any pope or monk unless their views were fortified by Scripture. Hilary and Augustine are cited in confirmation, as well as scriptural texts, in support of the sufficiency of Scripture.

But Luther's goals of reform were also along the lines of an internal reform of the Catholic Church, not a breach or division from it. Although he eventually rejected the authority of the pope, the magisterium and most church councils, yet the Tradition of the church was not discarded. By advocating the sufficiency of Scripture Luther did not intend to reject all that the church had held and used for the past 1500 years. Nor did he share the same idea about the church's "fall" with the Anabaptists.[21] His attitude to-

19. See his *Commentary on Matthew* 5.7, 20.7, 24.5, 27.7, and 33.5. It is entirely possible that Hilary's commentary may have contributed to the revival of Pauline studies in the West after the middle of the fourth century, as suggested by P. Smulders, "Hilary of Poitiers as an Exegete of St. Matthew," *Bijdragen* 44 (1983): 82.

20. *Luther's Works* (St. Louis: Concordia), 1.170. (Hereafter cited as *LW.*)

21. For Luther, sacred history was marked by repeated apostasies beginning in Genesis and continuing until the present time. The fact of apostasy is an integral part

ward the dogmas established by the early church revealed the more conservative and constructive aspects of his principle of authority.[22] As part of his larger catechism, Luther reasserted the Apostles' Creed, which he says was written by the Holy Spirit and was the perfect expression of his own religious understanding. Typically the creed is explained in three sections according to a trinitarian pattern — the Ten Commandments, the Apostles' Creed and the Lord's Prayer — which is the very structure Luther used to contruct his catechism. His commentary on the creed concludes with the words,

> Here you find the whole essence of God, his will and his work beautifully portrayed in few but comprehensive words. In them all our wisdom consists — a wisdom which transcends all human wisdom. . . . The law of the commandments does not make us Christians, for God's wrath and displeasure abides upon us because we cannot fulfill his demands. But the Creed brings us full mercy, sanctified us and makes us acceptable to God.[23]

The same attitude is espoused with the regard to the Nicene Creed, to which believers are urged to adhere as the best explanation of the doctrine of the Trinity. Nicaea was a pivotal conciliar moment in church history, since it not only demonstrated that the primacy of Rome had not existed in the early church, but it also set forth a theological measuring stick. Of the four great councils (Nicene, Constantinople, Ephesus and Chalcedon) and their creeds, Luther asserted, they established no new articles of faith but merely defended what had been given by the Holy Spirit to the apostles at Pentecost.[24] This understanding of continuity is a very patristic one, reminiscent of the approach taken by Vincent of Lérins.

---

of church history. There was, however, no sudden break in the church's history that radically altered its character, since Christ has always remained with his church until the consummation of the world.

22. John Headley, *Luther's View of Church History* (New Haven: Yale University Press, 1963), 86.

23. J. N. Lenker, trans., *Luther's Large Catechism* (Minneapolis: Augsburg Publishing House, 1967), chaps. 165, 167. In a sermon Luther preached on the catechism in 1528 he makes the same distinction: "This teaching [the Apostles' Creed] is different from that of the commandments. The commandments teach what we should do, but the Creed teaches what we have received from God. The Creed, therefore, gives you what you need. This is the Christian faith."

24. *LW,* 50.551, 607; Headley, *Luther's View,* 87.

The path to theological and ecclesiological renewal lay in a radical reappropriation of Scripture and the message of the Fathers. After the condemnation of his writings by the pope, Luther realized that the Roman church was not going to undertake a reformation of itself. In that same year he wrote an *Appeal to the Ruling Class* (1520), calling upon the German nobility to take the initiative of addressing abuses in the church according to the guidelines he laid down. The ultimate goal ought to be the convocation of a general or "free" council (i.e., not a papal council) to deal with the issues. Luther repeatedly insists that if the pope will not call such a council then it is up to the secular authorities to call one. Interestingly, Luther defends this appeal on the commonly believed notion that it was Constantine who called the Council of Nicaea, and not the pope as asserted in the *Donation of Constantine* and the *Decree of Gratian*.[25]

The purpose of the *Appeal* was to outline the topics of reform that an "ecumenical, free council" should address and the basis of authority on which its decisions should be grounded. Luther's attitude toward the early church is instructive in this context. Among his recommendations, Luther argues against the Roman practice of requiring the right to approve all ecclesiastical transactions by holding up the patristic model: "Christians used to choose their bishops and priests from their own members, and these were afterwards confirmed by other bishops without any of the pomp of present custom. St. Augustine, Ambrose and Cyprian each became bishops in this way" (I.i). Instead of having a bishop go to Rome for confirmation, the canons of Nicaea, "the holiest and most celebrated of all the councils," ought to be observed in which elected clergy are confirmed by two or more of the nearest bishops. If the pope wants to abolish this ancient statute and all other councils, Luther asks, what is the value of abiding by conciliar authority, which the Romanists held so dear? If the pope would defy Nicaea, what will prevent him from nullifying anything else with regard to the Christian faith?[26]

When it comes to the authoritative texts, Luther not surprisingly wants to jettison the accumulation of papal and conciliar decretals, proba-

---

25. Luther, *Appeal to the Ruling Class* I.iii, from the annotation of J. Dillenberger's translation: "After him [Constantine] many other emperors did the same, and these councils were the most Christian of all." Of course, the secular authorities acted as bulwark for his reform measures because of their own opposition to Rome. *Martin Luther: Selections from His Writings* (New York: Doubleday, 1958).

26. Luther, *Appeal* III.3. Cf. III.24 where Luther gives the same advice about "following the statutes of Nicaea" for choosing a bishop in Prague.

bly a reference to the *Decree of Gratian,* which also included scores of isolated statements of the Fathers. The problem was that these writings are carefully read and followed instead of Holy Scripture. Peter Lombard's *Sentences,* a topically arranged collection of opinions from the Fathers (the first edition being written in 1155), are specifically mentioned as among the most central texts studied by the theologians, whereas the Bible is left alone. This is completely backwards, Luther complains, arguing that the number of books on theology must be reduced and only the best be retained — a warning that modern writers and publishers of theology would do well to heed! More significantly, he claims the writings of the Fathers should be read not as an end in themselves but as precursors to the reading of biblical texts. This is in keeping with the original design of the Fathers: "The intention of the early Fathers in their writing was to introduce us to the Bible; but we use them only to find a way of avoiding it."[27] The point of tension was not between the Fathers and Scripture, rather how they were being used, or not being used. This is not to say that Luther put the Fathers and Scripture on an equal par, because he most certainly did not. There were several patristic writers, such as Origen and often Jerome (for their allegorical exegesis), whom Luther harshly criticized. Nevertheless, the Fathers, most of all Augustine, provided him with the starting points of his theology of the cross, of the wretchedness of the human condition, of justification by grace alone, and of loving God for his own sake. Just as importantly, the Fathers acted in an indispensable role as ancient witnesses against papal domination. In this sense, Luther bequeathed to Protestantism the mechanism of dividing the patristic legacy from the Roman tradition. The former was of the Spirit, the latter of human artifice. One could accept the authority of one without the other.

As Luther worked toward constructing an understanding of church history, he continued to value the importance of the early creeds and writings of the Fathers as vehicles for protecting the church from error. Not that the early period of the church provided him with an ideal age to which one must return. Its role operated rather like that of the Old Testament patriarchs for the church, revealing a permanent pattern which models faithfulness for all future believers. Luther had planned to deal extensively with the history of councils and creeds in the church, and in 1538 he published his own edited versions of the Apostles' and Athanasian Creeds, and the *Te Deum* — a hymn more than a confession — to which

27. Luther, *Appeal* III.25.

the Nicene Creed was appended. The work was entitled *The Three Symbols or Creeds of the Christian Faith,* and these statements are referred to in the preface as the "ground upon which the Christian faith is laid."

Luther would never change his view about the positive foundational role that patristic texts should play in shaping the church's identity, despite his pessimism about the possibility of ever seeing a general council realized which would act on these principles. Of course the early Fathers made mistakes and disagreed among themselves, but because all parties in his day ostensibly accepted the guidance of the Fathers, they provided the best platform upon which to hold a general council for reforming the church.

In *On the Councils and the Church* written a little later in his career (1539), the heart of Luther's argument does not regard the authoritative acceptance of the church's early creeds and doctors, but who has the right to claim them truly as authorities. Despite Rome's claim to the ancient tradition, "the present position of the church in the papacy is woefully at variance (as is evident) with the ways of the councils and the Fathers."[28] By "councils," Luther makes it clear that he means only the first four ecumenical assemblies, the "universal or principal" councils, against which all subsequent conciliar decisions must be judged.[29] Any true council, Luther declares (with some naïveté), is one that "confesses and defends the ancient faith and does not institute new articles of faith against the ancient faith, nor institute new good works against the old good works."[30] A true council, as demonstrated in the four principal councils, is one that is engaged in the exegesis of Holy Scripture.

Luther also blamed the papacy for playing the councils and Fathers against Scripture in order to legitimize its decisions founded on the claim of tradition.[31] Whereas the patristic writers knew that all their conclusions had to be submitted to the authority of the divine Scriptures, and indeed, their writing "directs us to Holy Scripture," he claims, Rome accuses him of not following the councils and Fathers but does not itself submit to Scripture. And in any case, if the papacy were to follow the precepts of the Nicene council it would have to burn all its bulls and decretals. Thus Luther was convinced that he and his reform movement were one with the ancient church, and that a recovery of the gospel from Scripture and the

28. *LW,* 41.14.
29. *LW,* 41.121-22.
30. *LW,* 41.135-36.
31. *LW,* 41.27-29.

credal tradition would restore the sense of true catholicity. Likewise, the confessional formulas of the ancient church — the Apostles' and Athanasian Creeds and the four ecumenical creeds — were trustworthy guardians of the truth of the incarnation of God in Christ.[32]

Calvin

This second-generation reformer also had to confront the problem of how often the "Romanists cite the ancient fathers against us" in order to support the superiority of their position. As his *Reply to Cardinal Sadoleto* (1539) shows, Calvin was convinced that the Reformation movement was in line with the doctrines of the early church.

> But here you bring a charge against us. For you teach that all which has been approved for fifteen hundred years or more, by the uniform consent of the faithful, is, by our headstrong rashness, torn up and destroyed. . . . You know, Sadoleto . . . that our agreement with antiquity is far closer than yours, but that all we have attempted has been to renew that ancient form of the church.

That true church which the apostles instituted is commensurate with the ancient form of the church exhibited by the writings of Chrysostom and Basil, among the Greek writers, and of Cyprian, Ambrose, and Augustine, among the Latins, which is in stark contrast to "the ruins of that church, as now surviving among yourselves." How can you accuse us of overthrowing the ministry and the church, Calvin asks, when our religion is embodied in the writings of the Holy Fathers and approved by the ancient councils?

The same issue is at stake in the preface which Calvin addressed to King Francis I in his first (1536) edition of the *Institutes of the Christian Religion*. Adversaries of the evangelical doctrine have raised up charges that it is "new" and of "recent birth," and "[t]hey inquire whether it is right for it to prevail against the agreement of so many holy fathers and against most ancient customs."[33] Realizing the seriousness with which these charges were regarded, Calvin counters the Romanist arguments with two

32. Eric Gritsch, "Martin Luther's View of Tradition," in *The Quadrilog: Tradition and the Future of Ecumenism*, ed. K. Hagen (Collegeville, Minn.: Liturgical Press, 1994), 71-72.

33. John Calvin, *Institutes of the Christian Religion*, praef. 3.

of his own: first, that their doctrines and practices are in fact contrary to the teaching of the early church, and second, that the message of the Reformers complies with that of the Fathers. To depict the Reformers as depisers and haters of the Fathers is ill-founded, he argues, because "[i]f the contest were to be determined by patristic authority, the tide of victory — to put it very modestly — would turn to our side."[34]

Unlike the Romanists who actually transgress the Father's teachings, Calvin says that he and his reforming contemporaries are so versed in the patristic writings "as to remember always that all things are ours to serve us, not to lord it over us." It was not an idle boast. To prove this contention, Calvin offers a long series of patristic testimonies denying the need of gold utensils for sacred rites, or affirming the eating of meat, or asserting that a monk ought to do labor with his hands, or disparaging anyone who claimed that marriage should be forbidden to the ministers of the church. Indeed, it was a church father who contended that the church should not set itself above Christ, who always judges truthfully, whereas ecclesiastical judges, "like other men," are often mistaken. Thus, Calvin concludes, it is his opponents who have diluted the clear message of the early church and Scripture with their hypocritical claims: "All the Fathers with one heart have abhorred and with one voice have detested the fact that God's Holy Word has been contaminated by the subtleties of sophists and involved in the squabbles of dialecticians."[35]

Throughout the *Institutes*, Calvin will never back away from asserting that it is the Reformers alone who may justly lay claim to the ancient authorities. In the process of this defense, he has shown a broad and sometimes intimate knowledge of the Fathers. In the *Epistle to King Francis*, Calvin explicitly refers to patristic testimonies no less than eighteen times, and in the four books of the *Institutes* there are over eight hundred direct citations or allusions, some of these undoubtedly taken from the patristic collections of the *Decree of Gratian*, Lombard, and the writings of other Reformers.[36] For instance, Calvin presents a strongly pro-Nicene position in his scriptural defense of the God as Trinity. Numerous Fathers from the fourth century are cited in support, as well as in criticism of pre-Nicene writers (anachronistically) like Tertullian, for their subordinationist views.

34. Calvin, *Institutes*, praef. 4.
35. *Ibid.*
36. Johannes van Oort, "John Calvin and the Church Fathers," in *The Reception of the Church Fathers in the West*, vol. 2, 671. There are many more hidden references to the Fathers that are not explicitly made in the text.

Despite Calvin's defense of Scripture's integrity on all matter of doctrine and practice, he defends the patristic position that nonscriptural terms must be used to define the scriptural understanding of God.[37] By the end of his discussion it is said that all the major Fathers of the church confirm the orthodox doctrine of the Trinity upon which Calvin has obviously depended for his own discussion, such as the eternal nature of God or the human inability to speak definitively about God's substance.[38] Not surprisingly, the majority of quotations or allusions made throughout the *Institutes* are from Augustine's corpus.[39]

Calvin rarely spoke about tradition (small "t") in a positive context. For him, tradition was *de facto* the custom and practices of the Roman church, what he called "this tyranny of human tradition."[40] In this case, tradition consisted of extrascriptural decrees and canons that had been justified by the arbitrary power of the clerical offices with little or no regard to the authority of Scripture.

This tradition was not to be confused, however, with the ancient credal teaching that could be found in the first five centuries of the church. For Calvin, the Nicene Creed and its language of consubstantiality was "simply expounding the real meaning of Scripture," being the work of the Holy Spirit.[41] He freely admits that he venerates the ancient councils "from my heart and desire that they be honored by all." They should have a determining authority for the faith so that it cannot be said that everyone has the right to accept or reject what these councils decided. At the same time, we are called to discernment. Not all councils are on the same par, and not all are authoritative simply because they are called by the official name, "councils." Calvin lays down some guidelines for assessing the validity of councils:

37. Calvin, *Institutes* I.xiii.3.

38. Cf. A. M. Harman, "Speech about the Trinity: With Special Reference to Novatian, Hilary and Calvin," *Scottish Journal of Theology* 26 (1973): 390. Calvin comments regarding Hilary, "He is wholly concerned with the defense of the very faith to which we adhere." *Institutes* I.xiii.29.

39. Calvin interjects passages from Augustine both with an apologetic aim, viz., protecting himself against the charge of innovation, and for theological purposes, such as in his important assertion that humanity's salvation consists in God's mercy alone, or his views on the doctrine of the sacraments. His specific use of Augustine's works would indicate a personal reading of them. See van Oort, "John Calvin and the Church Fathers," 667.

40. Calvin, *Institutes* IV.x.18, 23.

41. Calvin, *Institutes* IV.viii.16.

> But whenever a decree of any council is brought forward, I should like men first of all diligently to ponder at what time it was held, on what issue, and with what intention, what sort of men were present; then to examine by the standard of Scripture what it dealt with. . . .[42]

Calvin willingly embraces Nicaea, Constantinople, Ephesus and Chalcedon as closely fulfilling these requirements of validity, since their creeds contain nothing but "the pure and genuine exposition of Scripture" which the holy Fathers applied with spiritual prudence against the enemies of the faith. At the same time, these councils should not be deemed as infallible guides, for their human foibles were just as apparent as their benefits. Only Scripture stands in the higher place with all else subject to its standard.

In his commentary on the Gospel of John, Calvin uses 4:20 ("Our fathers worshiped on this mountain") to lash out at the papists who "steal the deeds of the Fathers as a cloak for their own errors." That is, they claim to follow the Fathers in the most uncritical fashion by sanctioning any religious activity according to some precedent of the ancients. Calvin may have had in mind the principle articulated by canon 17 of the Lateran Council of 649: anyone is condemned who does "not confess, in accordance with the holy fathers, by word and from the heart, really and in truth, to the last word. . . ." With no regard to Scripture, the Fathers are employed as the sole legitimating authorities. The problem for Calvin is one of balance. On the one hand, contemporary practices or doctrines are attributed to the Fathers, though these cannot be legitimated in their writings, and on the other hand, it is faulty to attach great weight to the ancients with no discrimination of their varying opinions. Just because an early church Father said something, it is not automatically correct or worth emulating.

Typical of the critical attitudes prevailing among Renaissance humanists, Calvin partly rejected the medieval tendency to venerate the testimonies of the ancients simply because of their antiquity. We must remember that the Fathers, as the *auctoritates* (authorities) during the Middle Ages, included much more than patristic writings. Papal decretals and conciliar canons established after the fifth century also circulated in various collections. And while the *Decree of Gratian* exalted the ancient Fathers as the primary expositors of Scripture, it claimed that in all matters of church polity and legislature, papal decrees and decisions from councils

---

42. Calvin, *Institutes* IV.ix.8.

were given greater authority.[43] Confronted with these mass configurations of texts, Calvin could be quite critical of the patchwork approach and found that a more discerning scheme for interpreting the *auctoritates* was necessary.

In sum, Calvin's use of the Fathers is very often for polemical reasons, particularly in the *Institutes*. He will resort to the Fathers as ammunition against current Roman Catholic and Scholastic opinion as a means of justifying Reformed theology. Nonetheless, the patristic writers had a subsidiary authority to that of Scripture. As the *Institutes* reveal, it is the Scriptures which are his principal source and norm, but second to them are the supporting writings of the Fathers, which are usually in agreement with the right meaning of Scripture. This is not to insinuate that "second fiddle" is of little consequence or could be dispensed with, if need be. With each edition of the *Institutes,* including the final one in 1559, Calvin included considerably more testimonies from the Fathers. The 1559 version was divided into four sections purposely corresponding to the topics outlined in the Apostles' Creed: the Father, the Son, the Holy Spirit and the holy catholic church. Like Luther, Calvin emphasized the unique authority of the Apostles' Creed and the first four general councils for defining Christian doctrine. That was the golden age of "the primitive and purer Church."

Overall, it was clear to the magisterial Reformers that the ancient Tradition in the hands of the Roman church had become secondary to the traditions of medieval Catholicism, which asserted its ecclesiastical authority not solely on the basis of its derivation from Scripture and the Tradition, but by virtue of the church's claim to the office of authority. Herein was the conflict with Scripture. As the ancient Tradition became increasingly interpreted by tradition, regulated as it was by the office of the papacy, Scripture alone was the bulwark affording the grounds to reject the Roman claim as the only interpreter of Tradition. In no way did Luther or Calvin reject the authority of the church's Tradition, although it had to be regulated by Scripture. Their knowledge of the early Fathers was the inspiration for their convictions. One must see, Luther argued, how the Fathers always subjugated themselves to Scripture and cannot be utilized, therefore, as a source conflicting with Scripture or with the Tradition.

---

43. J. Werckmeister, "The Church Fathers in Canon Law," in *The Reception of the Church Fathers in the West*, vol. 1, ed. I. Backus (Leiden: Brill, 1997), 74-75. As a result of this "relativization" of authorities in the *Decree of Gratian,* papal rule came to take precedence over the patristic writers (80).

It might reasonably be objected at this point that a book foiling with the theological ancestry of the Free Church should include an analysis of Lutheran or Reformed movements of the Reformation. In reponse let me say that we have reviewed enough history in the previous chapters to realize that the Protestant Reformation was anything but homogenous. Despite a basic core of similar affirmations and objections, the sixteenth-century evangelical movement was polycentric and its message pluriform. Religious communities that would become part of the Free Church movement strongly opposed some of the ecclesiological and civil affiliations which so-called magisterial Reformers maintained. There are important historical distinctions to be made, of course. Nevertheless, it is difficult to separate all the hermeneutical strands that make up the theological inheritance of what we received from the sixteenth century. The "borders" between the magisterial and Free Church sides of the Reformation are in reality more ambiguous than the analytical distinctions would suggest.[44] "Protestantism" has generally been indicative of a cluster of beliefs and convictions with which Free Church and evangelicals associate themselves, even if such association lacks a direct historical descendancy. For there are indeed many blurry areas of doctrine and practice between Protestant churches, such as Calvinist Baptists, the Lutheran piety of the Brethren, and the persistence of the (Anglican) episcopal model within Methodism. The phenomenon of the Free Church is itself a cacophony of strains, historical and theological, that come from Anabaptism, Puritanism and Pietism, all having intersected with other Protestant churches. It is therefore quite relevant for our survey to include an understanding of the attitudes and usage of the patristic Tradition in the magisterial Reformation's most prolific writers, who not only continue to be heard among Free Church congregations, but who are quoted more often in sermons and articles than the more historically direct ancestors.

The "Radical" Reformers

Given the historic Free Church mistrust of councils and creeds in light of its ecclesiology of a "fallen" patristic era, one would think that there would

---

44. T. Campbell, *Christian Confessions: A Historical Introduction* (Louisville: Westminster John Knox Press, 1996), 186. The author provides several illustrations of this point.

be no positive recognition of early church writings. This is not altogether true, since some of the earliest and best educated figures of the various Anabaptist sects utilized the writings of the Fathers in a context of approval. Exploring all the relevant texts and their ramifications goes beyond what we can do here, so the following observations should be taken in a preliminary way.

Just as there were numerous groups that fall under the rubric of Anabaptist or radical Reformers, so was there variation of perspectives on post-apostolic Christianity. There was no question that the authority and traditions of the papacy had to be rejected, along with the teaching of those — Luther is foremost — whose reforming efforts to purify the church had not gone far enough. For Sebastian Franck and some of the Spiritualist Reformers, departure from the institutional church meant a radical separation from all its classical authorities, including the patristic. For other Anabaptist groups, the reformation of the church meant a restoration of the apostolic age — via the New Testament and the Spirit — and thus cutting back to that root, freeing the church from the suffocating growth of ecclesiastical tradition. However, among the surviving literature of the "Radical Reformation," one encounters citations from Augustine, Chrysostom and others for reasons similar to Calvin's: polemical validation of their theology. In these instances the Fathers are seen to be bringing assistance to a proper understanding of Christian faith or practice, even though not all their guidance was acceptable. Let me very briefly cite three instances.

In Conrad Grebel's letter to Thomas Müntzer (dated 5 September 1524), one finds signs of Grebel's former humanist training. Whereas he is prepared to speak of the "rule" only that appears in the words of Christ in Scripture, Grebel also cites Augustine, Tertullian, Cyprian and Theophylact (a bishop from the eleventh century) in confirmation of the view that baptism does not save. In addition, the baptism of infants is contrary to Scripture and to the evidence of Augustine and Cyprian.[45] For Grebel, at least, the teaching of the Fathers served as a useful support for scriptural exegesis.

Although the Spiritualist Reformers tended to reject the witness of the patristic church out of hand, Caspar Schwenckfeld found his reading of Augustine and the Greek Fathers useful for informing his understanding of the mystical experience of the Lord's Supper. In a letter of remon-

45. L. Harder, ed., *The Sources of Swiss Anabaptism* (Scottsdale, Penn.: Herald Press, 1985), 290-91.

stration to Luther's views on the subject, Schwenckfeld shows familiarity with patristic texts from the *Decree of Gratian* and certain scriptural commentaries of Augustine. Concerning the latter, he declares, "[I stand] with Augustine, to whom, next to the Bible, I appeal; and since he has been accepted by the Christian church, I hope to remain unmolested therein with all Christians."[46] It is a utilitarian statement. To what degree Augustine is being revered as an authority here is unclear, but he is acknowledged as a pillar of doctrinal theology that Schwenckfeld can use to bolster his case. The implication is that Augustine and Scripture share sufficient theological harmony for Schwenckfeld's appeal to Christian truth.

Balthasar Hubmaier also resorts to Augustine, quite selectively, in his discussion of human free will. Various arguments from Augustine's anti-Pelagian treatises are cited, as are those from Fulgentius of Ruspe, as reinforcement for the orthodoxy of his views before the duke of Brandenburg (1527). The sources for Hubmaier's knowledge of the Fathers seems to be from existing versions of edited works, at least of Augustine, and his knowledge is fairly extensive. Certainly his use of Augustinian texts demonstrates more than an illustrative reading. Hubmaier's reference to medieval Scholastic categories and patristic literature sets his work apart from the biblicism of many other Anabaptist treatises.[47]

Any generalization we might draw about the attitude of Anabaptists toward the early Fathers from these few texts must be superficial. Nevertheless, we can say without hesitation that Scripture, through the inner working of the Spirit in the life of the believer, was the norm for faith. That the writings of the Fathers are used at all is perhaps the most striking feature, given the violence with which they were used as witnesses against the Reformers, based on the prevailing medieval view of the indissoluble unity that existed between Roman Christianity and the early church Fathers. To a lesser extent than Luther or even Calvin, select passages from the Fathers were incorporated by some Anabaptist writers as a means of confirming their interpretation of the teaching of Scripture. From this we can infer that many among the Free Church knew and read the Fathers, whether through collections of excerpts or full text editions.

It is probably an exaggeration to say that Anabaptist leaders per-

---

46. G. H. Williams, ed., *Spiritual and Anabaptist Writers* (Philadelphia: Westminster Press, 1957), 177.

47. See G. H. Williams, "*On Free Will* by Balthasar Hubmaier," *Spiritual and Anabaptist Writers*, 113.

ceived the message of the ancient Fathers as an extension of the Bible. However, for a few writers, the Fathers represented the historical mind of the church in opposition to Romanists and magisterial Reformers. Patristic commentaries and sermons could lend secondary support for defending New Testament Christianity. Scriptural exegesis was easier to appropriate than doctrinal theology. Yet the prevalence of primitivistic or restorationist ideals of church history, along with those hostile perspectives toward the Fathers on certain issues of Christian practice,[48] prevented a more general embrace of the post-apostolic church.

Creeds or Confessions?

It has been wrongly asserted that Free Church Christianity is an anticredal Christianity. Certainly this was not the case with historic Anabaptism, except perhaps that its statements of faith were concerned with ethical rather than doctrinal issues. As one finds in the Schleitheim Confession of Faith (1527), the notion of a ban, like excommunication, was enforced among many groups, but it pertained to moral conduct, not intellectual conformity. There was no lack of confessions or articles of faith promulgated by Anabaptists: Pilgram Marpeck's Confession, Peter Riedman's Account of Our Religion, Doctrine and Faith (1524), Hubmaier's Twelve Articles (1526); Bernhard Rothmann's Confession of Faith (1533), and the Bern Colloquy (1538), to name only a few. Some of these are obviously modeled on patristic creeds and stand on the same grounds of orthodoxy as fourth-century theology concerning the doctrines of God and Christology. Even those writers who eschewed the Fathers and ancient creeds confess a Chalcedonian-like theology, except of course for the Spiritualists and anti-trinitarians.

Other communions within the Free Church likewise have had to recognize that their noncredal position flies in the face of the great many creeds called "confessions" that they have produced in the last three and a half centuries or so. Baptist history is a good example of this anomaly. On the whole, the general patristic creeds have been perceived by Baptists as a norm competing with the Bible and have therefore been rejected in princi-

48. For Menno Simons, the Fathers endorsed the practice of infant baptism, though he cites contradictory views among them in "Foundations of Christian Doctrine," vii. The value of patristic creeds is ambiguous, sometimes quoted with approval as vindicating the apostolic truth. *The Complete Writings of Menno Simons*, ed. John C. Wenger, trans. Leonard Verduin (Scottsdale, Penn.: Herald Press, 1956), 137, 734.

ple. Only the Word of God contained in the canonical Scriptures, as the First London Confession states, is said to be the "Rule" of "Knowledge, Faith and Obedience."[49] In practice, however, the doctrine taught in the major creeds is usually accepted as Christian orthodoxy,[50] despite the fact that any dogmatic pronouncements, usually associated with creeds, conflict with the Baptist emphasis on the liberty of the individual conscience and voluntary association of believers.

Some English Baptists of the seventeenth century show evidence of familiarity with and use of the ancient Fathers, especially as their writings could be utilized to defend the practice of believers' baptism or against religious persecution by the state. On the whole, early church documents were used simply as a means of combating Anglican charges of religious innovation, a common accusation lodged against Nonconformist groups. Very few Baptists, such as Thomas Grantham (d. 1692), argued that Baptists accepted the best of the ancient Christian tradition as housed in the contents of the Apostles' and Nicene Creeds.[51] Whatever ambivalence Baptist communions had toward creeds, this did not stop Baptist associations (General and Particular) from producing nearly a dozen confessions in their first one hundred years. Almost the same story can be told about most of the communions within the Free Church, as a glance through any handbook of Protestant confessions and creeds will demonstrate.[52]

E. Glenn Hinson suggests that the antipathy of Baptists and other Free Church groups toward the concept of creeds in general and toward the ancient creeds in particular could be ameliorated by viewing creeds as covenants of faith which serve to establish the identity of the people of God: "Considering them in relation to covenant highlights their personal and relational character rather than in their dogmatic character that has domi-

49. *The First London Confession* (1644), VII.

50. The Baptist confession of 1678, known as the Orthodox Creed, includes in its body the Apostles', Nicene, and "Athanasian" Creeds.

51. Michael A. Smith, "The Early English Baptists and the Church Fathers" (Ph.D. dissertation, Southern Baptist Theological Seminary, 1982), 104-29. Smith observes that after the Toleration Act of 1689, which legalized nonconformity, was passed and religious persecution ceased, Baptists turned inward and increasingly used only the language of Scripture for defining their communion. There was, in effect, no longer a need to claim the authority of the ancient Fathers.

52. For a selection of texts from Congregationalism, Methodism, Society of Friends (Quakers), and the doctrinal bases of the Evangelical Alliance of 1846, see "The Evangelical and Protestant Creeds," in *The Creeds of Christendom*, vol. 3, ed. P. Schaff, rev. ed. (Grand Rapids: Baker Book House, 1983).

nated historical accounts in the past."[53] We have already seen the validity of Hinson's proposal in the way in which early baptismal confessions and catechetical guides laid the foundation for the fourth- and fifth-century creeds. These creeds were not constructed apart from the life of the church as it preached, instructed converts, baptized, and prayed. The faith formulated in these creeds was based on how Christians had lived their "personal and relational" faith, a faith in the living God who is Father, Son and Holy Spirit. Stressing the difference between a creed and a confession is a matter of semantics. The ancient creeds were truly confessions of faith based on the experience of believers, and not merely statements of dogmatic propositions. To recontextualize the very notion of creeds in this way lays open the possibility of understanding them in a new light, as important voices of the church which came from within the activity of the worshiping church and its internalization of the message of Scripture.

Scripture and the Ancient Tradition

In stressing the preaching of the Word and importance of doctrine, the Reformers believed themselves to be obedient to Scripture, but also to be following the practice of the patristic church. Illustrative of this attitude is the method of preaching on a book of the Bible, chapter by chapter or verse by verse, which became standard exegetical practice of Reformers like Huldrich Zwingli, who derived it from the practice of Chrysostom and Augustine.[54] Forms of discipline, liturgy and church government used in Reformation churches were also consciously following patristic models. Our evidence shows that the Reformers considered the patristic tradition as second only to biblical authority, and used it as a critical source in vindication of their views. The Tradition of the church was not the same as the traditions which they opposed; in fact the former helped to expose the nature of the latter. To this end, ancient Christian writings were deemed important enough that provision was made in some Protestant church ordinances for patristic literature to be available to the congregation. Such a

53. E. Glenn Hinson, "The Nicene Creed Viewed from the Standpoint of the Evangelization of the Roman Empire," in *Faith to Creed: Ecumenical Perspectives on the Affirmation of the Apostolic Faith in the Fourth Century,* ed. M. Heim (Grand Rapids: Eerdmans Publishing Company, 1991), 120.

54. Backus, "The Early Church in the Renaissance," 302.

move takes seriously the idea that the task of theological renewal is for the engagement of the whole congregation!

We can readily agree that "Scripture is indeed the central legitimating resource of Christian faith and theology, the clearest window through which the face of Christ may be seen."[55] The point of the Protestant insistence on the sufficiency of Scripture reflects a historical tendency not to permit anything outside the Christian gospel to set norms for what is truly "Christian." Whereas Scripture does indeed define the center of gravity of the true faith, it does not set the limits of its reading or knowledge. The Reformers' appeal to scriptural sufficiency was crafted on the assumption that the Bible was the book of the church's faith. That faith of the church, New Testament and patristic, was seen as contiguous with the biblical narrative, so that the only proper way to read the Bible was within the framework of the church's teaching and practice.

The Search for Reformation Today

A new campaign has begun among various groups of evangelicals who are attempting to respond to the general problem of theological illiteracy afflicting contemporary evangelicalism. Their response consists of revitalizing and reasserting Reformation principles as a means of grounding evangelical identity and emphasizing the differences between Protestants and Roman Catholics against those who are seeking some common ground.[56] Groups such as Christians United for Reformation (CURE), The Alliance of Confessing Evangelicals (ACE),[57] and other similar organizations are busy sponsoring conferences and publishing books with the aim of reinvesting evangelical Christianity with a new awareness of its Protestant heritage. The current theological crisis facing evangelical Protestantism, however, I contend, requires more than repackaging theological mandates and arguments from the Reformation and asserting them with new vigor.

By all means, Protestant Christians should be versed in the critical reforms which sixteenth- and seventeenth-century Christians strove with their lives to obtain. As a Protestant with a Puritan heritage, I celebrate the

55. McGrath, *Evangelicalism and the Future of Christianity*, 61.
56. See Appendix II.
57. ACE, which advocates a return to the five "solas" of the Reformation, is made up of members from the Missouri Synod Lutheranism and conservative sectors of the Reformed church.

Reformation as a much-needed restoration in Christian thought and life, as well as a historical renewal that highlighted important elements of biblical teaching that needed to be heard again. No one can read the accounts of believers suffering for their Protestant convictions in *The Martyrs' Mirror* or John Foxe's *Book of Martyrs* without being deeply moved. They willingly confronted the high price of a nonconformist faith. And yet for all its theological and historical importance, the Protestant Reformation should not be the sole means of identity for any Christian. It was (is) not the primary basis on which the Christian faith is founded — something the Reformers themselves knew quite well. Here I am referring to how one "reads" the history of Christianity. As I have been arguing since the first chapter, the Protestant mind has been shaped in specific ways to think about itself as the Christian faith, not as a reform movement of Catholicism, but as a restoration of the apostolic church and therefore a dismissal of everything that followed the New Testament church and was prior to the "Reformation." In the name of rejecting ecclesiastical authority as "hierarchy" or "tradition" as theological manipulation and bondage, we have instead created a hermeneutic of suspicion and have invested every biblically informed conscience (instead of a pope) to speak *ex cathedra*. It is a Pyrrhic victory for Free church Protestantism when the net effect of its teaching results in the replacing of the tyranny of the magisterium with the tyranny of individualism.

As reform is meant to alter the course or path of a movement, so the Protestant Reformation realized alternative constructions of how one thinks and expresses fidelity to Christ, though not to replace utterly that faith, much less introduce a new one. When Luther argued that the faithful need to believe in the "holy catholic church," exemplified in his discussion of the four "ecumenical" creeds, he meant not Protestantism, and certainly not Lutheranism, but a non-Roman Catholic Church — one which is renewed after the orthodox teaching of historic catholicity. How one should think and believe in accordance with Scripture and the historical hermeneutic of interpreting the faith (that is, Tradition) is based upon a notion of evangelical catholicity — a term which has appeared again in the last decade to define a kind of centrist mentality toward the historic faith, regardless of the competing claims of Roman Catholicism, Protestantism, or Eastern Orthodoxy. If the Protestant Reformation tried to do anything, it tried to restore the ancient catholicity of the church — which arguably ought to be the goal of today's evangelical Protestants. As an important phase of redefining the true church, the sixteenth-century Reformation needs to be integrated within the larger picture of what it means to be catholic. The very ideal of the Reformation pointed beyond itself to a more foundational past.

Evangelicals and Free Church believers need to hear again the great Protestant historian, Philip Schaff, who warned us 150 years ago of the "poisonous plant of sectarianism" which has grown ponderously upon the ground of Protestantism. Inherent within Reformational piety and puritanism there is always the impulse to retreat into a subjective spiritualism and ahistoricism, seeking a personal experience of God at the expense of centuries of ecclesial authority. Like a centrifugal force, to use another metaphor, the sectarian mentality has tended to fling out the very structures of history that gave rise to it, declaring that the Scriptures are the only source and norm of saving truth. Yet the Bible-only principle, in its abstract separation from tradition, or church development, furnishes no security against sects.[58] All too often the Protestant appeal to Scripture as the final authority in practice is tantamount to the view "that any institutional or corporate expression of it becomes unthinkable . . . and that anyone with a Bible in his hands can hear God speaking directly."[59] This was the very outcome that the sixteenth-century Reformers were anxious to avoid, being aware that the *sola scriptura* principle, however useful against Romanists, could also act as the opening of a hermeneutical Pandora's box.

Because Free Church polity stresses the autonomous nature of every congregation, it is particularly susceptible to the increase of sectarianism, as the last four hundred years or so have shown. Countless times has some individual, who has an inward religious experience and a ready tongue, persuaded himself that he is called to be a reformer, and proceeded to break with the historical life of the church to which he counts his spiritual sensitivity superior. Overnight a congregation is formed, upholding an untainted faith, governed solely by the model of the apostolic age and the Spirit.

Certainly personal experience and an emphasis on life-changing conversion must continue to have a critical place in the Christian faith, but such elements are perceived as self-authenticating often in isolation from ascertaining the larger picture of Christian truth. They have functioned as

58. Philip Schaff, *The Principle of Protestantism*, trans. John Nevin (Chambersburg, Penn.: Publication Office of the German Reformed Church, 1845), 115.
59. B. A. Gerrish, *The Old Protestantism and the New: Essays on the Reformation Heritage* (Chicago: University of Chicago Press, 1982), 90-91.

substitutes for the role that the consensual voices of our faith were meant to play in shaping the Christian understanding. Bluntly put, the principle of an experiential and voluntary foundation of any congregation, detached from the Tradition of the historic church, makes Free Churches rife for division. This is what I mean by "sectarianism" (as opposed to "counterculturalism," a common meaning of "sectarianism" in sociological circles). The individual person or group more or less set the terms of the faith, often along the lines of their experience and goals, indifferent or even hostile to the deposit of faith laid down within the institution of the church in history. Small wonder that there exist thousands of evangelical and Free Church denominations or congregations.[60] Despite the efforts of faith-affirming ecumenism[61] and cooperative platforms such as the National Association of Evangelicals, Free Church Protestantism and evangelicalism are more fragmented than ever. So Schaff concludes,

> The most dangerous foe with which we are called to contend, is again not the church of Rome but the sect-plague in our own midst; not the single pope of the city of the seven hills, but the numberless popes, German, English, and American, who would fain enslave Protestants once more to human authority, not as embodied in the Church indeed, but as holding in the form of mere private judgement and private will. What we need to oppose these, is not our formal principle; for they all appeal themselves to the Bible, though without right; but the power of history, and the idea of the church, as the pillar and ground of the truth, the mother of all believers, with due subordination always to the written word.[62]

The point here is that the Reformation needs to be seen in continuity with how the church developed after the apostles and the New Testament. This church is no less a real and valued part of the history of our faith, providing the critical basis for how one should read the Bible, understand the Trinity, or ponder the meaning of the incarnation. When a local church makes a theological statement, it needs to see itself standing under the au-

---

60. Campbell, *Christian Confessions*, 189.

61. Such as the "Faith and Order" conferences of the WCC, especially at Lund, Sweden (1952), Montreal (1963), and Lima, Peru (1982), from which came publication of the statement, *Baptism, Eucharist and Ministry* (1982). The doctrinal orthodoxy and scriptural integrity of these collaborative efforts have taken many evangelicals by surprise.

62. Schaff, *Principle of Protestantism*, 121.

thority of the confessional and doctrinal umbrella of the early church, which assumes the primacy of Scripture and the apostolic faith.

No amount of singing or preaching about "spiritual unity" will successfully combat the sectarian approach which regards its own interpretation of the gospel as the only correct one. It cannot be overstated how much this attitude has helped to polarize evangelicals from other evangelicals and church communions from other communions of like faith. To check the tide of "sectarianism," a more comprehensivist understanding of our faith — catholicity — will have to characterize our churches.

My emphasis ought not to be confused with the plea for a return to denominationalism, nor is it to undermine the Free Church spirit. In any case, such a plea would be futile in light of the juggernaut of independent church growth movements in the Western Hemisphere. And yet, the sectarian mentality so prevalent among Free Churches is but a crude caricature of true Protestantism. When rigorously applied, the autonomy of the local church (however much it has served as a buttress against the interference of outside authorities) provides a false security for maintaining Christian truth. Without the external "check" of the church's theological history and ancient standards of doctrinal identity, the sectarian approach will eclipse the congregation's ability to know its place within the larger Christian story, much less retrieve it for self-understanding and worship. This is already happening to many churches whose goals for renewal and growth have completely marginalized any real apprehension about their communion with the church of ages past. If Free Church Christians and evangelical churches are going to insist on their status as "Protestant," no matter what denominational affiliation is declared or denied, they had better begin making the same pilgrimage back to the roots of their faith, just as the Reformers did.

The Way of Defining
Christian Faithfulness

Every time a Christian renewal has blossomed in our West,
whether in thought or in life (and the two are always linked), it
has blossomed under the sign of the Fathers.

Henri de Lubac

In the year A.D. 165, a Christian philosopher by the name of Justin and six of his disciples were arrested in the city of Rome on suspicion of treason, that is, for confessing Christianity. The brief official court proceedings survive wherein the prefect Rusticus questioned each of the defendants, adjuring them to sacrifice to the gods or else face capital punishment. In response Justin declared that he held the "true doctrine," to which the prefect inquired in a manner reminiscent of Pilate's question of Jesus, "What is the [true] doctrine?"

Throughout this book I have been working on the assumption that there is a positive answer to this question about determining Christian truth and that the early Tradition of the church provides the grounds for ascertaining its foundation. This Tradition is older than any one denominational appropriation of it, and therefore offers itself as a fundamental source for all who seek the "rule" of the church's historic teaching. Neither

Roman Catholic, Eastern Orthodox, nor Protestant can stake a claim upon this source as peculiarly its own, though each has preserved important elements of the Tradition in unique ways.

Before he was led away for execution, Justin (a layman) professed his faith in terms that sound as if he were drawing on a credal-like framework that he knew well and was probably teaching to his students. His words are not a betrayal of soul liberty or spontaneousness of the Spirit so dear to the hearts of Free Church Christians. Elsewhere Justin had written that both Scripture (Old Testament) and the church's teaching were indebted to the inspirational activity of the "Holy prophetic Spirit." He was rather handing over *(traditor)* to these new Christians, and to Rusticus, a definable content to the meaning of "I believe."

It cannot be denied that "tradition" in church history has been an elusive and divisive theological concept. Various meanings have been attributed to it and very different approaches have been taken toward its authority. Beyond a very broad agreement with Vincent of Lérins about the function of tradition, there is no general consensus about the degree of correspondence between Scripture and the Tradition, or about the exact parameters of tradition, or about the manner in which tradition is conveyed. And yet it is just as true that no Christian can escape its influence, because Christianity is foundationally a historical religion, and "tradition" is therefore built into its very fabric, whether written or interpretive. From a historical perspective, the contours of the faith were first determined by the Jesus tradition as it crystallized through the apostolic preaching and as portions of it were later written down. Ever since that time there has been an interplay between Scripture, the Tradition, and Christian experience — the latter two subject to mutability — each providing balance for the others. Without the maintenance of this balance, the faith falls prey to religious authoritarianism of one kind or another.

Thus, the Tradition is not merely a set of commonly held practices or ideas; for the believer it represents a bond which defines the way of faithfulness throughout the passing ages of the world. This is an important perspective for Free Church and evangelical Christians to adopt, as I have tried to argue in the previous chapters — namely, that the church's history and its Tradition are two converging realities. K. E. Skydsgaard usefully observes that the gospel is not a manifesto settled once and for all in the sense that no written text can successfully circumscribe, much less, confine it. Rather, the gospel of the living Christ is a living proclamation, a handing over in space and time of a *kerygma*, that was and will

have to be delivered, received, preserved and understood in each generation.[1]

Focus upon the consensual Tradition of the ancient church demands
that we as Christians do not become so enthralled with the promises of the
future, especially with the growing hype about the next millennium, that
we forget to look also to the past as the baseline for our identity. Apart
from the New Testament, the patristic age was the most formative period
for determining this identity; both of these share in the continuum of how
the apostolic faith developed and was articulated. The risk, however, of
seeing the church's Tradition as something "past" is that it may deceive us
into thinking the Tradition is equivalent to the historical past, leading to a
perception that begets rigidity or obduracy. If the Christian Tradition
functions in any normative way at all, it is not simply because it lies in the
past or because it is an accepted way of doing things. It has a normative
role because it represents the corporate voice of the faithful, very often in
moments when the faith was being tested by some controversy, proclaiming what it has received in light of what it must confront. The Tradition of
the church is just that, the outcome of a testing and sharpening process by
which the Spirit moved through the worshiping, praying, baptizing and
confessing community of believers, or what can be aptly called a consensus
of faith through time.

This is the pattern established in the aftermath of Peter's sermon in
Acts 2: the embryonic church teaching, praying, and celebrating their
communion with God and one another as they commenced with the challenge of living out the gospel. Because the Tradition has always functioned
dynamically within the concrete moments of history, its essential character
involves the duality of conservatism and change. In other words, we find
within the operating domain of Christian Tradition the joint imperatives
of preservation (or conservatism) and renewal; the former requires that
the Tradition be immune from the attrition of time, whereas the latter declares that its use is subject to abuse and corruption, and recovery and correction.[2] This is not merely a "protestant" way of looking at the Tradition,
but a historical construction of how doctrine and practice were shaped
within the early church.

1. K. E. Skydsgaard, "The Flaming Center or the Core of Tradition," in *Our Common History as Christians*, ed. J. Deschner, L. Howe, and K. Penzel (New York: Oxford
University Press, 1975), 4.

2. K. Morrison, *Tradition and Authority in the Western Church 300-1140* (Princeton: Princeton University Press, 1969), 7.

Tradition or Technique?

As the prime informant of a uniquely Christian use of Scripture, the deep roots of the ancient Tradition can provide a faithful commonality for Protestant Christians, especially for those who do not identify with a particular denomination or who consider such affiliation to be irrelevant to their faith. What one encounters in a retrieval of the Tradition is the recognition that Christianity is far richer than one's own personal and ecclesiastical experiences. Finding such a common ground is essential if Free church and evangelical Protestantism is going to avoid a loss of its identity through its own internal splintering and accommodation to Western culture.

My concern with the continuing direction of Free Church Christianity is that its usual (alleged) traditionless and noncredal approach to the Tradition lacks the centripedal force necessary to keep its tendency toward fragmentation and detachment at bay. This is not a new problem, of course. Nearly fifty years ago, Protestantism was said to have proliferated into over 250 separate bodies in America, though approximately eighty-five percent of those who are comprised in these bodies belong to twelve major denominations.[3] This is nowhere near an accurate appraisal anymore, as the number of community and independent churches have been steadily on the rise. To be sure, nondenominational churches are the fastest growing segment of American religion.[4] For good reason, therefore, has Stanley Hauerwas stated we are swiftly coming to the end of (what Tillich called) "the Protestant era."[5] The theological differences created by the Reformation are no longer the central defining points for Christian adherence or essential in the selection of a worshiping community. Since the 1970s, denominationalism has been a decreasing factor in the maintenance of Christian identity. According to the survey studies of Robert Wuthnow, religion in America has seen a dramatic decline in observing the organizational lines of religious institutions, both Protestant and Roman Catholic: "People switched denominations with ease, married across

3. J. Dillenberger and Claude Welch, *Protestant Christianity Interpreted through Its Development* (New York: Scribner's, 1954), 3.

4. Donald Miller, "Postdenominational Christianity in the Twenty-First Century," *The Annals (of the American Academy of Political and Social Science)* 558 (1998): 198.

5. Stanley Hauerwas, *In Good Company: The Church as Polis* (Notre Dame: University of Notre Dame Press, 1995), 92.

faith boundaries and generally saw little reason to revere the distinctive traditions of their own faith."[6] Marketplace strategies have been substituted for the denominational loyalties that once governed where and how families worshiped. The majority of believers attend a local church not because of its theological position or ecclesial heritage, but because they want a vibrant youth program, or a strong Sunday school, or because the singing is good.

Moreover, the dramatic rise in small groups has been a critical part of church growth, since these groups bring both community and the very concept of God to the believer in a personalized way often lacking in large congregations.[7] The relational bonds created by small groups is another way of redefining church commitment without the use of denominational tenets or a doctrinal platform. Regard for the hermeneutics of theological standards or ethical values based on a shared religious history have almost no role to play in the structures that govern a small group. Norms of individualism and privatization of faith still function as governing principles of Christian piety, even if they are extended to include the few chosen group members. Interpretation of the Bible and issues of morality are mostly determined by the shared life experience and opinion of the group. As useful as the "community" which the small group provides, it can offer no certainty that Christian orthodox teaching will likewise be transmitted in its midst.

My comments are not meant to promote an avoidance mentality toward small groups, but I do want to offer a warning that fostering deep personal experiences and the building of community, important as they may be, are not a replacement for preserving theologically coherent and historically faithful Christianity. Dynamic can never be a substitute for content. One quick look at the exchange and interplay of faith between the "house churches" of the first century will bear out this observation. The epistles of Paul or of John show that the substantial role of doctrinal understanding and fidelity was never traded away for enterprising schemes of "outreach" or methods for making Christianity seem more attractive to outsiders.

But even more significantly, the differences between Protestants and Roman Catholics and Eastern Orthodoxy are shrinking in comparison to the threat that Christianity is confronting in the effects of (post-) moder-

---

6. Robert Wuthnow, *The Struggle for America's Soul* (Grand Rapids: Eerdmans Publishing Company, 1989), 15.

7. Robert Wuthnow, *Sharing the Journey* (New York: Macmillan, 1994), 23.

nity on our post-Christian culture. Enough has been written on the nature of this threat not to require elaboration here. Let me say only that this threat is not an opposition to the value of the religious organization or benefits of spirituality; it is rather a rejection of the historical distinctives of Christianity as something that restricts the exploration of genuine self-expression and discovery. This is essentially the argument of systematic theologian Daphne Hampson, to take one example, who claims that once we acknowledge that Christianity is "a masculinist religion, one which legitimizes patriarchy," we will realize that Christianity cannot possibly be true and will naturally leave it behind. And although Christian doctrine is deemed incredible, this does not preclude the practice of personal piety: "The importance of there being a spiritual dimension to our lives seems more evident than ever. It is simply that Christianity can no longer be the vehicle for that spirituality."[8] For radical feminist thought, historic Christianity amounts to a kind of conspiracy that has effectively duped most of the world about its male-dominated projection of God, and only in this post-Enlightenment age are we sufficiently able to comprehend alternative forms of religious reality that will usher in a new era of liberation. Of course, this approach is part of an ongoing movement of "re-imaging" Christianity that began in the early 1990s which, despite its connections with various Protestant mainline denominations, exhibits the rise of a gnostic-type of spiritualism that perceives the classical Christian understanding of doctrine and ethics as an obstruction to accessing the divine prerogative within oneself. From such perspectives, theological structures of Christian orthodoxy about the nature of God, the relation of creation to God, the incarnation, and so forth need to be either allegorized as universal symbols or rejected altogether.[9]

Contrary to the death of God prophets in the 1960s who predicted that religion was on the road to becoming extinct in a secularized American culture, interest in matters of faith, the supernatural, angels, spirituality and the like has shown no abatement. The claims of (post-) modernity have become more accommodating to religion as long as the latter is will-

---

8. Daphne Hampson, *After Christianity* (Valley Forge, Penn.: Trinity Press International, 1996), vi-vii. For Hampson, Christianity is not only masculinist, but is also what she calls necessarily heteronomous in that it understands God as distinguished from the self and known through revelation. Because the classical understanding about God is internally problematic, "Feminists must stand for human autonomy."

9. As does Laurel Schneider in *Re-imagining the Divine* (Cleveland: Pilgrim Press, 1998), who rejects Christian trinitarianism in favor of a monistic type of theism.

ing to be philosophically pluralistic and completely tolerant of all forms of sacred experience as equally genuine. Postmodern spirituality, like the *daemones* of ancient Roman paganism, is an eclectic system that ascribes to itself a morality focused on the self-realization of the individual in the world. A good example is found in the books of Walter Wink, who opposes a materialistic view of the universe, especially as it concerns the existence of evil. Using Christian terminology and biblical references, Wink claims that we must confront the spirituality of all corporate institutions or social systems around us by identifying what he calls the Powers, which are impersonal spiritual realities intrinsic to the fabric of the world, at once good and evil, though capable of moral improvement.

> As the soul of systems, the Powers in their spiritual aspect are every-
> where around us. Their presence is inescapable. The issue is not whether
> we "believe" in them but whether we can learn to identify them in our
> actual, everyday encounters. The apostle Paul called this the gift of dis-
> cerning spirits.[10]

In gnostic fashion, the spiritually aware person is urged to acquire a more integral worldview which affirms spirit at the core of every created thing. Soul permeates the universe, and God is not only within persons, but within everything, since the universe is diffused with the divine. There is an indissoluble link, therefore, between the knowing self and the universe. Unapologetically does Wink admit that this "worldview" is panentheistic ("God" or, more precisely, divinity is in everything like a world spirit), declaring that it makes the Bible more intelligible and offers us the key to identifying the Powers which affect us in our every action. These Powers become "demonic" when spirituality becomes diseased through corporate or governmental systems of domination and oppression, but this is not to say that these are metaphysical entities such as demons. The reader is encouraged to embrace the new integral worldview as an interpretive opening for perceiving true spiritual realities, a means of our reuniting science and religion, spirit and matter, and the inner and outer. Wink's work has been well received, with one of his books having won three religious-book-of-the-year awards.[11]

10. *The Powers That Be: Theology for a New Millennium* (New York: Doubleday, 1998), 29.
11. *Engaging the Powers: Discernment and Resistance in a World of Domination* (Minneapolis: Fortress Press, 1992).

To argue that spirituality must be informed by doctrinal canons of truth only introduces unnecessary encumbrances of the past that invite potential discord and loss of personal satisfaction. Finding faith, as a recent book dictates,[12] is through experience, not institutions. Nor are evangelicals immune to these forces; they are so immersed in Western culture that self-interest is replacing or overwhelming their sense of moral indignation and commitment to theological truth.

Related to the demands of pluralism and the erosion of denominational identity is how religious belief has become one more consumer item. In his book *Selling God: American Religion in the Marketplace of Culture* (1994), Lawrence Moore argues that religion has remained a potent force in American life but has done so through its "commodification." This is how Moore believes we are to understand the effects of secularization. Christianity has not disappeared, but it has been affected to the point of transmutation by the commercialization of our market-driven culture. The result has been the commodification of religion; religious leaders have engaged in commercial practices to promote their product. The credit given American religious leaders for keeping religious faith in the American cultural mainstream must be balanced with the observation that religion, in responding to market forces in our culture, has compromised its prophetic power to speak to the culture.

One of the more disturbing features of this market-type of orientation is its relative acceptance among churches. That George Barna's bestseller *Marketing the Church* (1988) has gained a widespread hearing among evangelicals can only be attributed to the fact that he and his audience share certain assumptions about the nature of the church and its place within our culture. Because Western culture is so thoroughly shaped and governed by management and market relationships, it tends to transform everything (and everyone) into manageable objects and marketable commodities, including the church.[13] The standards of measuring success in the business world, quality and quantity, are now regularly applied as a means of determining the effectiveness of church ministry. State-of-the-art ministry, we are told, should be about the business of assessing the needs of potential religious consumers and meeting those needs. The

12. D. Lattin and R. Cimino, *Shopping for Faith: American Religion in the New Millennium* (San Francisco: Jossey-Bass, 1998).

13. Philip Kenneson, "Selling (Out) the Church in the Marketplace of Desire," *Modern Theology* 9 (1993): 319.

church is thus viewed as "a service agency" which exists to satisfy people's needs, and its success is measured by how well it is fulfilling this goal.

It is wholly naive to think that such a model for church growth leaves the self-understanding of the church unaffected. Management strategies and marketing tactics are in fact value laden, as Philip Kenneson succinctly states it: "Once a church allows its identity to be transformed into one more forum for mutually beneficial exchanges between producers and consumers, an entirely new set of questions arise that frame ecclesial thought and practice."[14] We therefore foster congregations and new generations of church leaders who understand that the primary task of the gospel within the community of faith is not costly transformation and sacrifice, which would challenge the very ethos of our consumer-driven culture, but fulfilling the needs of religious consumers with a smorgasbord of programs and services.

If anything is certain about the business management approach to the church, however, it is that it cannot address the real problems facing the church in our society — in particular, a prevailing confusion about its own identity and purpose. What is worse, some church growth strategies believe that they *are* confronting, if not solving, important identity issues when congregational attendance exhibits growth. Despite its apparent successes, the vogue of marketing technique and its methods for determining "successful" churches cannot measure the crucial calling for the church: faithfulness. The very notion of remaining faithful requires that the church must exercise theological judgment, which may well be at odds with the notion that the church ought to perpetuate itself by attracting new customers and make itself more appealing for the sake of the gospel. Whatever emphasis evangelicalism has placed on the importance of doctrine is in danger of becoming so diluted that the kind of preaching that will guide the future of the church will be dictated by strategies driven by popular appeal, disseminating the most infantile forms of Christian knowledge. The "meat" of theological reflection and spirituality which the aostle Paul claimed should characterize Christian maturity (1 Cor. 3:2) will have become permanently replaced with "milk" in order that everyone can most easily drink it.

In some respects this phenomenon should not surprise us. So long has the role of the Tradition been marginalized within Free Churches as a means of informing contemporary ecclesiology that it is easily susceptible to being

14. *Ibid.*, 326.

replaced by the new priorities and promises of marketing methods as the preferred hermeneutic for translating the goals of the Christian calling.

This loss of the Christian *memoria* afflicting contemporary Protestant Christianity is exacerbated by the fact that there is little homogeneity between the multitude of ecclesiastical communions and independent churches that think of themselves as evangelical. If anything has characterized the literature produced by evangelical intellectuals over the last twenty years, it has been the repeated attempts to articulate just what the shared distinctions of an evangelical theology are.[15] It is nearly impossible to think of evangelicals as speaking with a united voice, much less the broad religious expanse that makes up the Free Church. For all the religious fervor and biblical emphasis that evangelicals have wrought over the years, the fragmentation of the Christian faith in Western society has not been abated by the presence of the collectivity called "evangelicalism."

In some contexts there is a greater openness on the part of evangelicals to interchurch activity, and as a result, a sympathetic awareness that the Christian faith transcends any one expression of that faith. As new generations of believers abide in today's postdenominational landscape, there is a growing preoccupation with what it means to be a faithful Christian in the larger sense of the word "Christian." But it is not yet apparent whether this emerging openness will assist in the reclamation of catholicity or produce such vague forms of Christianity that they have little redeeming effect on the surrounding culture.

Retrieving the Tradition

It is time to correct the excesses of the former correction that Free Church Protestantism has spawned within Christianity. Too much has been thrown out in the name of Reformation at the cost of our impoverishment. To begin, we must discard our paranoia of the church's Tradition as a derivation of human invention and so necessarily antithetical to inspired Scripture, or as something that bridles the dynamism of the Spirit in the life of the believer and the local church. This perspective of Scripture versus Tradition poses a false dichotomy and is not at all commensurate with

---

15. See D. Wells and J. Woodbridge, eds., *The Evangelicals: What They Believe, Why They Are and Where They Are Changing* (Nashville: Abingdon, 1975); John Stott, *What Is an Evangelical?* (London, 1977).

how the notion of "tradition" began and functioned among the first churches. When instructing new converts, Augustine taught, "For whatever you hear in the Creed is contained in the inspired books of Holy Scripture." Its content was to be written on their hearts once regenerated by grace so that "you may love what you believe and that, through love, faith may work in you and that you may be pleasing to the Lord God, the Giver of all good gifts."[16]

The sixteenth-century Reformers could have written the same thing. Only afterwards, in the theological developments of the later seventeenth and eighteenth centuries, did the authority and sufficiency of Scripture become calcified into an antitraditionalism that Luther never imagined. Under the pens of certain Puritan and Free church proponents, the principle of *sola scriptura* functioned as a blanket condemnation of any practices — clergy wearing robes, features of the liturgy, creeds — that lacked clear scriptural warrant. All notions of tradition became marked as "Romanish" and contrary to the self-perfection of Scripture, whose use was perceived as independent of any need for Tradition. The decisions of the Roman Catholic Council of Trent (1645), which seemed to address Tradition and Scripture as two independent sources of authority, helped promote such reactionary biblicism. Unfortunately, the Protestant evangelical reaction to Roman Catholicism's own loss of balance created an increasingly distorted view of the way in which Scripture, Tradition and the church operate in a triadic structure of authority. In order to preserve biblical authority, divine revelation was disconnected from the Tradition and from its formative context, the church. In effect, the Bible was separated from history. It became possible to use the Bible with little or no recognition that its canonization and interpretation had an extensive history in the church.

From our investigation, however, we have seen that Scripture was not (and could not be) separated from the essential Tradition. Scripture is an integral part of the Tradition, which possesses a unique authority. A recent paper by Richard John Neuhaus rightly observes, "As the Tradition is grounded in Scripture, so also the determination of what is Scripture and the requirement that the Tradition be grounded in Scripture are themselves grounded in Tradition."[17] Like Scripture, the consensual Tra-

---

16. Augustine, *Sermon* 212.2.

17. Richard John Neuhaus, "A New Thing: Ecumenism at the Threshold of the Third Millennium," in *Reclaiming the Great Tradition: Evangelicals, Catholics and Orthodox in Dialogue,* ed. James S. Cutsinger (Downers Grove, Ill.: InterVarsity Press, 1997), 55.

dition of the church has its source in the triune God himself, coming to us from the Father, through the Son in the Spirit. Scripture and the Tradition are not two different sources of authority and truth. It is time to stop throwing our reproach of Trent's unfortunate expressions of paring "written books" and "unwritten traditions" in Roman faces and move on with the task of reappropriating the ancient resources available to evangelicals. The great creeds, sermons, hymns, poetry and prose of patristic writings which partly enshrine this Tradition need to be heard again in sanctuaries, worship assemblies, corporate prayer, and through preaching and conferences that promote theological training and spiritual formation.

Herein is the kind of hermeneutical guidance necessary for reading the Bible and being able to understand words like "God" and his creative and redemptive relation to the world. The great confessions and early theology of the church help define the God whose story the Bible tells. Precisely because the Bible is a composite work, multi-authored and edited over a period of fifteen hundred years or more, it is possible to read it and miss the central ideas. More than one reader of the Bible has come away asking, "What's the point?" Specifically, what is the "center" of the entire biblical story from which the Christian interpretation should be generated? The early creeds enable believers to know that Israel's history in the books of Chronicles are to be read in light of Paul's preaching in the letters to the Corinthians, or that the prophetic announcements of Jonah and Jeremiah are to be understood in light of Jesus' Good News. In this way, the consensual statements of faith are not supposed to displace Bible reading, but to prepare us for it.[18]

This patristic Tradition is what has bequeathed to Free Church and evangelical Christians their essential identity and a faith that endures. Instead of perpetuating a kind of religion that is so infatuated with contemporization and self-fulfillment — tantamount to spiritual idolatry — the early Fathers assist us in taking our eyes off of ourselves and focusing upon what throughout the ages is truly important. They require us to think; and to think about the Christian faith, not as another consumable item, but as Spirit-directed, holy, and living, by which we are molded. A contemporary chorus by Rich Mullins which puts to music a portion of the Apostles' Creed drives home the point with its opening words:

18. Donald Juel, "The Trinity and the New Testament," *Theology Today* 54 (1997): 323.

I believe what I believe is what makes me what I am.
I did not make it, no, it is making me.
It is the very truth of God and not the invention of any man.[19]

The church's Tradition and the traditioning process is indeed the work of God in the world. This means that we are related to Christ in a twofold way, in communion vertically through the Spirit and horizontally across the centuries through the consensual memory of the church.[20] Both are necessary for the achievement of Christian orthodoxy, despite the fact that Christians have had a tendency to dwell on either one to the point of extreme. Putting the focus of one's faith on the mechanics of sacred rituals can have a deadening effect and quench the vitality of the Spirit, whereas an overemphasis on the spiritual response of the individual as the primary means of authenticating the faith can lead to historical isolationism and religious subjectivism, which lies at the basis of most cultic movements. Christian orthodox teaching has always taken the path of intersection between the horizontal and the vertical, following the pattern found in the incarnation of our Lord.

For evangelicals to ignore or to be in ignorance of the great Tradition of the church is to have lost their foundational heritage. With its passing, the faithful will have less and less of a place to stand when challenged by pseudo-Christian spiritualities and the confused perambulations of contemporary theology. An absence of the church's theological past will produce believers who are not sure how to interpret their Bibles, apart from relative or fashionable opinion, or who are not able to position their interpretations within the wider framework of competing claims of new theologies. Despite the information boom affecting biblical study over the last twenty years, it is apparent that mere knowledge of the Bible does not assist in the critical task of understanding and integration. Scripture, without the Tradition to guide its interpretation, can too easily devolve into an insipid spiritualism. Even worse, believers become highly susceptible to repeating old heresies, and unknowingly undermining the Christian identity and mission.

The Tradition as found in the ancient confessions, the rule of faith, and the doctrinal theology of the Fathers provides truth about God, in fact, primal truth about God. These sources point us beyond ourselves and ask us to peer out from the confines of the Protestant "ghettos" we have created into the main street of catholic Christianity.

19. Rich Mullins, "Creed," BMG Songs, Inc., 1993.
20. J. B. Torrance, "Authority, Scripture and Tradition," *Evangelical Quarterly* 87 (1987): 249.

To be "catholic" is indeed a confession of faith; it is a confession of our *wholeness* as believers scattered throughout the world, placed upon the bedrock of the consensual truth as expressed in the New Testament and the Fathers. We might agree with Nathan Söderblom, who thought it was wrong to reserve the honor of this name for the Roman church, suggesting that what he described as "the three principal divisions" of Christianity should be called Greek Catholic, Roman Catholic and Evangelical Catholic.[21] The emphasis on the church's catholicity is not merely on its universality and encompassing character, but on its authenticity, that is, its continuity with the apostolic truth which throws into relief what is right and wrong Christian teaching. Or, to use an analogy, the catholic church is not a melting pot, but a stew. Every ingredient is preserved in the mix of many differences, not melted down.[22]

It should be apparent by now that an emphasis on catholicity is not an attempt to dilute the distinctives of evangelical faith or to seek an overthrow of the Protestant identity in the name of an over-zealous but myopic ecumenism. On the contrary, our search has been for what originally generated our various church or denominational confessions, that which provided a central core of faith around which our different Christian traditions have grown, and which can better enable us to reassume the task of theology as the rightful role of the church. Only as this occurs can fruitful (viz., having doctrinal integrity) ecumenical discussion take place between Protestant, Roman Catholic and Eastern Orthodox brethren.

De Lubac was right in his words quoted above. Whenever there has been an emphasis on reformation within church history, broad or small in scope, believers have inevitably returned to the "map" of ancient Christian thought and practice. By means of its well-worn roads and clearly marked streets, they have rediscovered stability in an unstable world and a sense of the parameters for the risky business of theology. This is not to imply that the reclamation of the early church should involve its idealization or promote its infallibility. There was nothing abstract about Christian living and thinking within the patristic churches themselves, and we are not helped by depicting them in an ideal form. The retrieving of early Christianity is not an "end" but a "means" of offering us a place to stand as we seek to ad-

---

21. Cited in Gustaf Aulén, *Reformation and Catholicity*, trans. E. Wahlstrom (Philadelphia: Muhlenberg Press, 1961), 177.

22. Peter Kreeft, *Fundamentals of the Faith: Essays in Christian Apologetics* (San Francisco: Ignatius Press, 1988), 257.

dress the current challenges facing Christian integrity. To the degree that we admit the church's fallenness, we must also bear in mind that the ancient confessions of faith in "the holy catholic church" were statements of trust in God's provision, present and future, and in his sanctification of the church despite its weaknesses and fraility. No one was more aware of the church's precarious existence and utter dependency on the grace of God than the Fathers.

Here, at the very end of the twentieth century, we are in the midst of a crisis within contemporary theology that could lead to further fissiparousness and dissimulation or to a new reformation among the descendents of the sixteenth-century Reformation. If there is to be another reformation of the church out of the chaos of our present cultural climate, then it will undoubtedly come through new and unexpected works of the Spirit, but it will come no less in a manner that connects us to the way of theological faithfulness, moral righteousness, and suffering that formed the Tradition of the early church.

Why All Christians Are Catholics

For almost two millennia, Christians in all parts of the world (Protestant, Roman Catholic and Eastern Orthodox) have professed the great confessions of the Apostles', Nicene, Chalcedonian and "Athanasian" Creeds, which state with some variation that the essence of true faith includes belief in "one holy catholic church." For many Protestants, however, the word "catholic" presents a serious problem because it sounds like affirming belief in the Roman Catholic Church. A confession of catholicity seems to entail a commitment to the authority of the papacy, the Roman magisterium, and its conciliar decrees. They wonder why Bible-believing Christians should express faith in the "catholic church."

In light of these and related concerns, some evangelical churches have altogether rejected using the creeds, while others substitute the word "Christian" or "universal" for the offensive term "catholic" as if to maintain a critical distance between the two. The point here is not a trivial one about religious language. Behind it all lurk the enduring hostilities that evangelical Protestants have toward Roman Catholics (and vice versa), so that whatever is "catholic" is something not to be embraced. Witness, for example, the stiff resistance which Christian musicians Michael Card, an evangelical, and John Michael Talbot, a Roman Catholic monk, faced from evangelical churches and radio stations in 1997 when the two artists joined forces in an album recording and concert tour. Some evangelical radio stations and bookstores refused to air or sell their songs. A similiar sort of resistance at the theological level was registered against those evangelicals who signed the two concords of "Evangelicals and Catholics Together."[1] The very title sounded like a contradiction in terms to many conservative Protestant leaders, who continue to oppose the dialogue as the work of the devil.

Nevertheless, there is no avoiding the fact that catholicity is an indispensable mark of the church and must be factored into our contemporary perspective, inviting further exploration of its meaning. The most important question is, Why did the early Christians regularly declare their belief in the "holy catholic church"? What were they trying to affirm, and how should it be recovered as a means of ensuring a faithful ecclesiology?

No one can deny the significant theological differences that exist between evangelicals and Roman Catholics, but to dwell on these differences is to miss the point. Let us not forget that the first use of the term "catholic" predates the establishment of Roman Catholicism by hundreds of years and that it is the source upon which Roman Catholicism draws for its own religious validation. In other words, "catholicism" is not a shorthand way of saying Roman Catholicism or acknowledging the office of the papacy. It is much older than both and more expansive in meaning.

Modern Roman Catholic theology is itself in need of reappropriating the catholicity of the ancient church to which its name makes claim. It is no secret that Roman Catholic universities, for example, are in the midst of a serious crisis as they ask how they can preserve their Roman Catholic identity while having embraced Western pluralist philosophy with its dizzying array of moral and religious orientations. Some commentators within Roman Catholicism are expressing deep concern that Catholic universities are traveling the same road many Protestant colleges journeyed in the eighteenth and early nineteenth centuries, repeating the same history of secularization and thus leading to the eclipse of the uniqueness of the Catholic character within the academy.[2] It is becoming increasingly difficult to point specifically and concretely to the affective role of catholicity within Roman Catholic academia.

1. "Evangelicals and Catholics Together: The Christian Mission in the Third Millennium" was published in *First Things* 43 (May 1994): 15-22, as the result of a consultation begun in September 1992 which included Richard John Neuhaus, Charles Colson, George Weigel, and Kent Hill. Since that time, a second statement has been published by "Evangelicals and Catholics Together" in *Christianity Today,* 8 December 1997, entitled "The Gift of Salvation."

2. David Carlin, Jr., "From Ghetto to Hilltop: Our Colleges, Our Selves," *Commonweal* 120.3 (12 February 1993): 7f.; Charles Curran, "The Catholic Identity of Catholic Institutions," *Theological Studies* 58 (1997): 103-7.

I have taught at a Roman Catholic university long enough to know that the inner complexity of Catholicism cannot be reduced to a certain set of principles or a single philosophy of faith. Its very elasticity is an element of strength in the face of the innumerable cultures, ideas, and language groups which it embraces. Many Roman Catholic intellectuals are so deeply concerned that any definition of catholicity not revert to the older dogmatic and parochial perspectives that they are prepared to be much more latitudinarian when it comes to the theological response to contemporary culture. The question is whether such a religious and ideological latitudinarianism, which persistently worries about being shaped by the theological agendas of fundamentalism and sectarianism, will result in the eventual loss of its catholic substance.

One of the basic lessons of church history, the Roman Catholic bishop and historical scholar Jacques-Bénigne Bossuet once declared, is that the Roman church has at different times been saved by the catholic church.[3] Not only is catholicity not the private domain of Roman Catholicism, but it is no less necessary for sustaining the future integrity of Roman Catholic thought as it is for grounding the Protestant identity. Whatever ongoing tension exists between evangelical Protestants and Catholics is a tension between evangelical Protestants and *Roman* Catholics, not with Protestants and catholicism.

Although the term is not mentioned in the Bible, "catholic" first appears in writings that immediately followed the New Testament and that are therefore closely linked with the apostolic mind and influence. One of these documents comes from the pen of Ignatius, the pastor of Antioch and younger contemporary of John the apostle, who, in his letter to the Christians in Smyrna (c. 115), speaks of that congregation as "the catholic church" which is maintained through the mutual presence of the bishop (pastor), the congregation and Jesus Christ.[4] His concern is not organizational, that is, a particular style of church polity, as much as it is structural beyond the local level. Within the context of the succession of truth which is shared among churches of like faith and order, one can be certain of orthodoxy. This places an emphasis on the corporate nature of the church's faith as the primary work of the Spirit. An individual may be said to be catholic only because he or she is a worshiping, serving participant of a catholic church. Patristic

3. Richard Costigan, "Bossuet and the Consensus of the Church," *Theological Studies* 56 (1995): 658.
4. Ignatius, *To the Smyrneans* 8.2.

Christians would not have understood how someone could be an orthodox believer apart from the structure (wholeness) of the church.

We can deduce, then, that the use of the term "catholic" was not unknown prior to Ignatius, since his mention of it to the Smyrneans is unqualified and assumes his readers' familarity. This interpretation is borne out by Polycarp, a reputed disciple of John the apostle and pastor of the church at Smyrna, who is said to have prayed for "all the catholic church throughout the world" on the day of his martydom (A.D. 156).[5] Whereas there is an emphasis on the universal character of the church as "catholic," Polycarp likewise refers to the single church at Smyrna as "the catholic church" (16.2), just as Ignatius did in his descriptions of the local church as "catholic." One can find the language of catholicity in a later confession of faith that comes down to us in fragmented form and appears to have been used strictly at the local level: "I believe in God the Father Almighty, and in his only-begotten Son our Lord Jesus Christ, and in the Holy Spirit, and in the resurrection of the flesh, and the holy catholic church."[6]

Historical reinforcement for this language comes from a simple overview of those early church creeds which include a statement of belief in the "holy, catholic church." They appear almost solely within the confessional contexts of baptismal formulas of local churches. In other words, profession of the church's catholicity grew out of the worship life of the local congregation and not out of statements framed by councils who were attempting to represent the mind of the whole church. Throughout the third and fourth centuries, the church's catholicity finds its voice in confessions which were already celebrated in individual churches throughout the Christian world. The fact that there exists an emphasis on the church as catholic in the Nicene-Constantinopolitan and Apostles' Creeds — neither of which originated from conciliar pronouncements[7] — demonstrates (1) that confes-

5. *Mart. Poly.* VIII.1.

6. From the Dêr Balyzeh Papyrus in *A New Eusebius: Documents Illustrating the History of the Church to AD 337*, ed. J. Stevenson, 2nd ed. (London: SPCK, 1987), 122. The date of the document is unknown, perhaps late third or fourth century, though the confession is surely from an earlier time.

7. The Apostles' Creed has a long history of congregational development and is never associated with the activity of a council (just as the "Athanasian creed"), whereas the so-called Nicene-Constantinopolitan Creed, which has been commonly linked to the council of Constantiople (381), was almost certainly in use before 381. While there is still much debate over its actual origins, the council probably took over a preexisting baptismal creed for its own purposes.

sional authority stemmed first, not from the councils, but from the warrant of congregational practice, and (2) that an understanding of catholicity confessed in these creeds is derived from the local churches.

It is clear from the early Fathers that "catholic" meant much more than "universal" or "general." The word is a Latinized version of the Greek *katholicos*, which can be translated as "whole" (or as an adverb, *katholou*, "entirely," "completely"). Expounding on the confession of faith used in the church of Jerusalem in A.D. 350, its pastor, Cyril, explains the meaning of the phrase "and in one holy catholic church" near the end of the confession. For Cyril, the church as catholic had multiple levels of meaning that functioned as characteristic of its "wholeness." On the one hand, catholic defines the church in space and time as that which is spread as a harmonious body throughout the world. This is reminiscent of Irenaeus's late second-century definition of the church as "scattered in the entire world, carefully preserving [the apostolic preaching and faith], as if in one house."[8] But just as important is Cyril's emphasis that the catholic church is comprehensive in its message in the sense that there is no saving doctrine that it fails to teach. Genuine catholicity is that which pertains to everything necessary for the justification and sanctification of the believer. It is a wholeness of faith that offers the complete counsel of God to all peoples in all times and places.

> It is called catholic because it brings into religious obedience every sort of men, rulers and ruled, learned and simple, and because of it is a universal treatment and cure for every kind of sin whether perpetrated by soul or body, and possesses within it every form of virtue that is named, whether it expresses itself in deeds or words or in spiritual graces of every description.[9]

Without making any pretense at supplying a comprehensive definition here,[10] I wish to emphasize that the wholeness of catholicity also implies parameters of what constitutes truly Christian beliefs. Ancient catholicity has to do with the substance of our faith, as Augustine once cited in a ser-

---

8. Irenaeus, *Against Heresies* I.10, 2.

9. Cyril, *The Catechetical Lectures* XVIII.23.

10. Insightful presentations on the catholicity of the church by Protestant theologians can be found in Gustaf Aulén, *Reformation and Catholicity*, trans. E. Wahlstrom (Philadelphia: Muhlenberg Press, 1961), 183-88, and more recently, the third volume of Thomas Oden's *Systematic Theology: Life in the Spirit* (San Francisco: Harper, 1992), 323f.

mon on the Trinity, "the true faith, the right faith, the catholic faith, which is not a bundle of opinions and prejudices . . . but founded on apostolic truth."[11] For too long members of both Roman Catholic and Protestant communions have danced around the meaning of *catholic,* celebrating its plurality and symbolic observances without squarely confronting the inner pillars of its historic identity, namely, its doctrinal character.

The catholic faith had a definable content that could be articulated and transmitted within worship or preaching. It was not merely an organizational framework by which Christians practised their faith. A catholic Christian was an *orthodox* Christian. Because there were (and are) many groups who identified themselves as Christian, it was (and is) necessary to have normative guidelines which establishes what is meant by Christian. Hence, replacing the ancient term "catholic" with "Christian" suffers from the disjunction of trying to replace a distinctive term of identity with one of generality that has been easily co-opted for a host of theologies and practices.

This means, *ipso facto,* that there is a certain quality of exclusivity within catholicity. To stress catholicity as a principle of universality and wholeness which breaks down walls of division[12] is useful only to the degree that we understand that it contains inherent limitations. As we have seen, the inclusive character of catholicity is based, not on a kind of all-incorporation of diversity that invites theological syncretism or dilution, but on the reception from God of a unique message and gift that transcends any one history or location. Practicing catholicism should not be confused with contemporary notions of inclusivity and tolerance that are grounded on the assumption that all moral and religious boundaries are derived from personal taste, genes, or cultural background, and cannot be generally applied without violating another's boundaries. For something to be just or true, however, means that its contraries cannot equally be just or true. This emphasis on doctrine may sound insufferably narrow to some of my Roman Catholic friends or perhaps to a few Protestant confrères. Nevertheless, to have a substantive validity, I contend, catholicity operates on the understanding that there exist true doctrines and practices, an understanding which is meant to distinguish the Christian church from theological or moral corruption. That there is not perfect agreement on these

11. Augustine, *Sermon* 52.2.
12. As does Frank Griswold, "Experiencing Catholicity," *America,* 27 September 1997, 8-11.

essentials does not entail that the opposite is true, namely, that there are no essentials and all is left to the standards of each generation or cultural context. In effect, a mark of catholicity always entails the reality of heresy.

To claim that catholicity has to do with an attitude of embracing the world as all part of God's creative and redemptive activity may well be true.[13] But surely there is more to it than that. The third paragraph of the so-called "Athanasian Creed" (fifth century) is very specific: "Fides autem catholica haec est" (And the catholic faith is this). It then proceeds to delineate a series of central and non-negotiable points about the Trinity, Christology, salvation and judgment. Does this mean that Christianity is reducible to a rigid set of propositions? Certainly not, but nor can the Christian faith maintain its essential integrity without appealing to those elementary truths that have defined it throughout the ages.

Likewise, there is an element of continuity within the meaning of catholicity. In sermon 213.2 Augustine spoke of his baptismal creed as that which he shares with all believers of his time, as something by which "Christians can recognize each other." For the patristic writers, the mark of catholicity was that faith which had been received — the *receptum*. This idea assumes there was and is a doctrinal link which ties us to the church of the past ages. It helps to ensure fidelity to the gospel, namely, that the Christian faith is not something any individual or congregation establishes. Thomas Oden refers to this aspect of catholicity as "centered orthodoxy." While there is flexibility, diversity and openness to cultural variety, the catholicity of the church does not substantially change from culture to culture or from age to age without maintaining its own distinct identity and norms.

Of course, catholicity cannot be divorced from two other marks of the true church, holiness and apostolicity. The distinction theologians make between these terms is really an artificial classification. John Hus opened his treatise, *The Church* (1413), with the words, "Every pilgrim ought faithfully to believe the holy, catholic church." This admonition was not an endorsement of the Roman church whose head was the pope, but

---

13. The "Protestant impulse" has been described as a quest for purity and separation which is always on its guard against alloys and compromises. Roman Catholicism, on the other hand, strives for purity while accepting the provisional combination of the pure and the impure. Whereas Protestantism stresses the fallen nature of creation, Roman Catholicism insists "on the immanence of eternity in time, and on the impregnation of nature by grace." Avery Dulles, *The Catholicity of the Church* (Oxford: Clarendon, 1985), 8.

the church of which Christ alone was the head. True to the Reformers' viewpoint, any consideration of what makes the church catholic is the continuity of its holy and apostolic character. Catholicity without its apostolic character and separation from the kingdom of this world becomes an insipid pattern of inclusivism that leads to a loss of integrity like a hollow shell. Conversely, elevating the importance of apostolicity without catholicity leads to a kind of doctrinal parochialism or even elitism that renders the older and broader continuum of the Tradition irrelevant for an understanding of the faith. It is this latter problem — apostolicity without catholicity — which most affects evangelical communions in practice.

It is ironic that as the catholicity of the church is meant to embody Jesus' prayer in John 17, "may they be one," the church is more fragmented than ever. Admittedly, the catholic principle is both a present reality and an eschatological hope. Its full realization will be on that day when we will drink anew with Christ the cup of communion in the Father's kingdom (Matt. 26:29). With this hope we *confess* our belief in the "holy catholic church," just as we confess our belief in one God who is Father, Son and Spirit whom we love but do not see, or in the resurrection of the body which will not occur until that body has died. Our confession is in that which we possess only in part, but what we possess is sufficient to bring stability to our experience and fidelity to our calling in Christ Jesus.

APPENDIX II

Sola Scriptura *in the Early Church*

As a result of increased attention to evangelical, Roman Catholic and Greek Orthodox relations,[1] there is reviving interest on the part of evangelicals to investigate the early sources of Christian doctrine and exegetical practices. This is certainly to be welcomed, albeit with cautious enthusiasm, since the current reconsideration of the patristic era is often not along the lines of a *ressourcement,* a return to the ancient sources of the faith for their own sake. Several publications by evangelicals have argued that the doctrine of *sola scriptura* was practiced, though implicitly, in the hermeneutical thinking of the early church.[2] Such an argument is using a very specific agenda for the reappropriation of the early church: reading the ancient Fathers through the lens of post-Reformational Protestantism and looking for criteria, such as *sola scriptura,* embedded within the religious consciousness of the patristic church. The point is, presumably, that an ancient vindication of such religious ideas would further the Protestant claim as the upholders of true faith *contra* Roman Catholicism and its traditions, which claim the authority of the early Fathers and councils.

Witness the recent attempts to find a "patristic principle of *sola scriptura*" in Irenaeus[3] or in Athanasius, from which the conclusion is

1. See, for example, *Reclaiming the Great Tradition: Evangelicals, Catholics and Orthodox in Dialogue* (Downers Grove, Ill.: InterVarsity Press, 1997).

2. For a fuller treatment of this issue, see my "The Search for *Sola Scriptura* in the Early Church," *Interpretation* (Fall 1998): 338-50.

3. J. Armstrong, ed., *Roman Catholicism: Evangelical Protestants Analyze What Divides and Unites Us* (Chicago: Moody, 1995), 40. In his essay, Tom Nettles seems

reached, "Sola scriptura has long been the rule of believing Christian people, even before it became necessary to use the specific terminology against later innovators who would usurp the Scriptures' supremacy in the church."[4] The concern is a polemical one. Since the sufficiency of Scripture is regarded to mean that the Bible is the only normative source for establishing Christian faith and practice, a sharp distinction is made between the authority of Scripture and that of the church's claims to authority expressed in its tradition and office.

There are at least three difficulties with making such assertions as they concern the early church. First, we have already seen in chapter 2 that the apostolic Tradition had chronological and logical precedence over the texts which would eventually become the New Testament. It is a historical reality that the church and its Tradition were primordial. The church received its Scripture in light of what had been handed down *(tradere)* by and about Jesus Christ. As I attempt to convey to my first-year theology students, the gospel was not originally a text, but an oral message focused on the incarnation of the Living God. The Word of God preached had a precedence long before the testimonies to that Word were preserved in writing.

This is not a datum that is damaging to the sufficiency and normativity of Scripture as if to say that Scripture is subject to the authority of the church and is only authenticated by that authority. Protestants would reply that it is Scripture that creates the church. One thinks of Karl Barth's insistence that we must never "reverse the sequence whereby *event*

---

oblivious to the crucial distinction between written and oral authority in Irenaeus when he says, "The Scripture is that which is 'handed down', that is, tradition." W. Robert Godfrey also poses the problem of the "divide" between Roman Catholics and Protestants as "the Word of God" versus "church traditions."

4. In *Sola Scriptura! The Protestant Position on the Bible,*, ed. D. Kistler (Morgan, Penn.: Soli Deo Gloria, 1996), 53. The essay entitled "Sola Scriptura and the Early Church" exhibits an extremely limited familiarity with patristic doctrinal history such that it claims Athanasius stood against Liberius, bishop of Rome (p. 42), whereas in fact, Athanasius sought the protection of Liberius's successor Julius during his western exile, and he, of all the Greek fathers, remained the most intimate with Rome after Julius's death in 352. There is hardly a case here for a proto-opposition between Protestants and Roman Catholics. Moreover, it is quite striking that the writer of this essay argues how Athanasius makes no appeal to unwritten tradition, and yet in the very citation offered as proof of this point (*Oratio Arianos* III.29) we are introduced to Athanasius's mention of Mary as Theotokos, bearer of God, an Alexandrian tradition which few Protestants would espouse!

[of God's revelation] precedes *institution,* which is also established by the entire Bible."[5] It is true that the Word called the church, which is built on the foundation of the prophets and apostles (Eph. 2:20), into being, but it is, as Harold O. J. Brown admits, a historical anachronism to say that the Bible created the church.[6] The first and second generations of Christians received the written texts of Scripture into their churches for the reason that they enshrined the canon of faith or Tradition.

The second problem with inculcating a theory of *sola scriptura* into early Christian thinking is that it introduces a dichotomy between Tradition and Scripture which did not exist. To treat the Bible in isolation from the Tradition of the church as located in the ancient rule of faith, its baptismal confessions, and its conciliar creeds would have been incomprehensible to the Christian pastors and thinkers of the patristic era. As Jaroslav Pelikan writes, "There was simply no way of imagining possible conflict between the Christian Scripture and the Christian Tradition — and, therefore, no necessity to choose between them."[7] This is precisely how Irenaeus understood the relation between Scripture and the church's "rule of truth," both of which manifested the source (revelation): "we draw up our faith, the foundation of the building, and the consolidation of a way of life."[8] To claim, as many evangelicals do, that the primordial Tradition was a human corruption of the gospel that came later is patently false.

Such a view also calls for a reassessment of the perspective of Tradition in the sixteenth-century Reformation, the position evangelicals claim to be espousing. The dichotomy of Tradition versus Scripture is partly fueled by a stereotyped historical paradigm in which Luther (as a representative of the Reformation) is perceived as one who rediscovered New Testament Christianity, which had become obfuscated and distorted due to the encrustations of Roman Catholic "traditions." David Yeago observes that "Luther is read as saying something radically incompatible with anything said in the Church since the death of Paul (except for a few glimmers in Augustine). The Catholic tradition figures in the story [of the early Lu-

5. Karl Barth, "The Humanity of God," in *The Humanity of God* (Atlanta: John Knox Press, 1982), 63.

6. Harold O. J. Brown, "Proclamation and Preservation: The Necessity and Temptations of Church Tradition," in *Reclaiming the Great Tradition*, 78.

7. Jaroslav Pelikan, "Overcoming History by History," in *The Old and the New in the Church*, WCC Commission on Faith and Order (Minneapolis: Augsburg Publishing, 1961), 39.

8. Irenaeus, *The Apostolic Preaching*, 6.

ther] only as what Luther had to overcome to rediscover the Gospel."[9] But it is hardly feasible to polarize the Scripture principle of Protestantism versus the "tradition" of Roman Catholics à la David versus Goliath for the reason that many of the stones in David's slingshot came from Goliath's own.[10] Nor is it at all clear that the sixteenth-century Reformers espoused the kind of views regarding Scripture and Tradition that evangelicals have attributed to them, foremost being their concept of church and its Tradition. Magisterial Reformers, like Luther or Calvin, did not think of *sola scriptura* as something that could be properly understood apart from the foundational Tradition of the church, even while they were opposing some of the institutions of the church.

Third, any view approximating a view of *sola scriptura* as defined above would have been deemed doctrinally hazardous to one's orthodox health. Even if one can detect a strict biblicism within the patristic age that approximates *sola scriptura*, it in no way guarantees a Christian doctrine of God or of salvation. Let me offer a poignant but little-known example. In a public debate with Augustine in A.D. 427, an "Arian"[11] Christian named Maximinus was most insistent that his doctrine was derived solely from the Bible: "We ought to accept all the things that are brought forth from the holy scriptures with full veneration. . . . How I wish that we may prove to be worthy disciples of the Scriptures!"[12] Not only does Maximinus advocate the full authority of the Scripture, but he refuses to accept "under any circumstances" theological language which is not drawn directly from the Scripture.[13] If John 17:3 speaks of "the only true God and Jesus Christ whom you have sent," then the Father alone is true God, as he is alone good (Mark 10:18) or alone wise (Rom. 16:27), just as he is called by the apostle Paul "the God of our Lord Jesus Christ" (Eph. 1:17). To Maximinus these passages made it clear that God the Father was wholly unique in his divine nature. It follows that the Son could not be "true God" because such

9. David Yeago, "The Catholic Luther," *First Things* 61 (1996): 37.

10. *Ibid.*, 39-40.

11. The epithet "Arian" or "Arianism" was used rather inaccurately of those who rejected the Nicene faith. See the introduction in M. R. Barnes and D. H. Williams, *Arianism After Arius: Essays on the Development of Fourth Century Trinitarian Conflicts* (Edinburgh: T. & T. Clark, 1993).

12. *Debate with Maximinus* 15.20.

13. *Ibid.*, 1. Implied by Maximinus's remark is that the Nicene Creed did employ nonbiblical language in support of its trinitarianism when it asserted that God the Son was *homoousios* (the same substance) as God the Father.

phrases were used only of the Father, and because the Gospels spoke of the Son's nature in starkly human terms as the Word who became flesh. By stringing together "testimonies," i.e., scriptural texts, sound theology is produced that ought to be self-evident and inherently perspicuous. Maximinus speaks of this type of literalist approach to biblical language as a "rule" for the proper construction of doctrine. The upshot of his argument is that the Bible was completely sufficient not only for all matters of faith and practice, but also for how one should articulate that faith and practice.

Maximinus's tendency during the debate to recite an abundance of scriptural testimonies in praise of the Holy Spirit, or citing that Christ came in the flesh or is seated at the right hand of the Father, was a waste of time, Augustine complained, since it was not the point. Both of them accepted the complete authority of the whole Bible and the sufficient clarity with which Scripture speaks in its fundamental points. However, Augustine rightly insists that orthodox Christians and "Arians" alike understand from the Scriptures more than they read in them. Both agree that the Son is begotten and is sent from the Father, though exactly how the Son is related to the Father is an issue which takes them both beyond what they read in Scripture. The longstanding "Arian" defense that they alone follow the text of the Bible is unfounded since, in fact, neither side can avoid going beyond a literal repetition of the text if its meaning is to be grasped. Augustine was quite correct. Maximinus's use of the Bible was indebted to the interpretative grid of "Arian" theology no less than Augustine was guided by the Nicene faith. Indeed, this was one of the fundamental lessons about biblical exegesis learned as a result of the "Arian" controversies, namely, that one must go outside of the Bible and biblical terms in order to interpret them.

It comes as no surprise that Augustine asserted the necessity of consulting the rule of faith in order to properly interpret Scripture. While the principle is not exactly as Tertullian or Irenaeus understood it in their age, the "rule" for Augustine means the same as the "authority of what is taught in the Church," determined by the true faith. Its significance is not that the Bible is subservient to the dictates of an episcopal hierarchy, as evangelicals would have it, but that Scripture cannot be faithfully understood apart from the way Nicene orthodoxy had come to be received and utilized in the churches. That is, the hermeneutic of the church's "faith" guides the exposition and reception of Scripture.

One might argue that *sola scriptura* underscores the historic Protestant contention that the Tradition and the church cannot be severed from Scripture, which must act as the arbitrating authority. To say that the ancient creeds of the church have "no independent authority and are not to be accepted if contrary to Scripture at any point"[14] is fair enough. However, the reverse is also true. Scripture can never stand completely independent of the ancient consensus of the church's teaching without serious hermeneutical difficulties. To assert that it is self-interpreting may be true for the most immediate aspects of the gospel. Yet only a brief review of the history of biblical interpretation demonstrates that the piling up of biblical data offers no guarantee of a faithful interpretation of Scripture, much less a Christian doctrine of God. The issue, then, is not whether we believe the Bible or whether we will use the Tradition — the real question, as the patristic age discovered, is, Which tradition will we use to interpret the Bible?

In sum, *sola scriptura* cannot be rightly and responsibly handled without reference to the historic Tradition of the church, and when it is, any heretical notion can arise taking sanction under a "back to the Bible" platform. The early church was only too well aware that a Scripture-only principle (no less than biblical inerrancy) is no guarantor of orthodox Christianity. And any search for a doctrine of *sola scriptura* in the writings of the Fathers fails to grasp how the early church understood apostolic authority and the reciprocal relation that necessarily existed between Scripture, Tradition and the church.

---

14. A. N. S. Lane, "Sola Scriptura? Making Sense of a Post-Reformation Slogan," in *A Pathway into the Holy Scripture*, ed. P. Satterthwaite and D. F. Wright (Grand Rapids: Eerdmans Publishing Co., 1994), 324.

Index of Premodern Authors

Amberbach, Johannes, 181
Ambrose (of Milan), 133, 144, 147n.,
    148, 153n., 167-68, 181n., 186, 189
Aquinas, Thomas, 181
Aristides (of Athens), 81
Arnobius, 181n.
Athanasius, 28, 96, 122, 137, 148, 150-
    52, 162-63, 169-70, 229, 230n.
Augustine, 6, 33, 34n., 63n., 71, 74,
    113n., 137, 144-48, 167, 170, 175,
    181, 183-84, 186-87, 189, 191n., 195-
    96, 199, 215, 226-27, 231-33

Baronius, 111
Basil (of Caesarea), 122, 145, 152, 177,
    181
Bellarmine, 111
Bernard (of Clairvaux), 110
Béze, Théodore, 122
Braght, Thieleman J. van, 114n.
Bucer, Martin, 178

Calvin, John, 101, 111, 179, 189, 190-
    93, 195-96, 232
Cassian, John, 166
Chrysostom, 104, 177n., 189, 195, 199
Clement (of Alexandria), 96n., 136
Clement (of Rome), 35, 56, 85-86

Cyprian, 94, 104, 143, 145, 148, 155,
    157, 181n., 186, 189, 195
Cyril (of Jerusalem), 104, 160-61, 164-
    65, 168, 225

Damasus (of Rome), 144
Dante, 110
Dionysius (of Alexandria), 94
Dolcino (of Novara), 113

Epiphanius (of Salamis), 145, 161, 166
Erasmus, 177, 181
Eusebius (of Caesarea), 44n., 86n., 89n.,
    105n., 110n., 113, 137n., 140-41,
    146n., 157n., 159n., 160n., 161

Felix, Minucius, 49n., 69n.
Fortunantianus (of Aquileia), 165
Foxe, John, 71, 121, 201
Francis (of Assisi), 107

Gerson, Jean, 107
Grantham, Thomas, 198
Grebel, Conrad, 195
Gregory (of Nazianzus), 152-54, 168
Gregory (of Nyssa), 77, 152-54

Index of Modern Authors

237

Townsend, Henry, 127n.
Troeltsch, Ernst, 116
Tuck, William P., 21n.
Turner, H. E. W., 82, 83n.

Ullman, W., 109n.

Walter, Victor, 90n.
Weaver, J. Denny, 142, 155
Webber, Robert, 13, 31
Weber, Max, 2
Weigel, George, 222
Welch, Claude, 208n.
Wells, David, 24-25, 214n.
Wenger, John, 104n., 197n.
Werkmeister, J., 193n.
White, Ellen, 118n.
Wiles, Maurice, 29, 163-64

Wilken, Robert, 7n., 18, 30n.
Williams, D. H., 63n., 119n., 150n., 152n., 153n., 164n., 167n., 229n., 232n.
Williams, G. H., 104n., 196n.
Williams, Rowan, 171
Willimon, William, 123n.
Wilson, R. M., 45n.
Wink, Walter, 211
Woodward, Kenneth, 23n.
Woodbridge, John, 3n., 214n.
Wright, D. F., 234n.
Wuthnow, Robert, 208, 209n.

Yeago, David, 183, 231, 232n.
Yoder, John Howard, 124-26, 131
Young, Francis, 29

Index of Subjects

Roman Catholic, 1, 3, 7-8, 18, 29, 42, 75, 102, 107, 117, 119-21, 139, 173-74, 176, 181, 193, 201, 206, 208, 215, 221, 223, 229
Rule of faith, 87-99, 166, 205

Schleitheim Confession, 197
sectarianism, 14, 202-4
Serdica (council), 143n., 165
Seventh Day Adventism, 2, 19
Shepherd of Hermas, 45
sola scriptura, 19, 23, 98-99, 175, 215, 229-34

Sylvester (pope), 108-10, 112

Theodosius (emperor), 123, 152-53
Tradition (defined), 34-39 (in New Testament), 48-58 (related to the Spirit), 56-58, 69, 207, 213-17, 219
Trail of Blood, 116-17
Trajan (emperor), 69
Trinity, 11, 27, 63, 67-68, 76, 79-80, 82, 93, 138, 153, 158-59, 216

Waldensians, 108, 110, 114, 118, 121